ip at ~~19.95~~

1st Am. ed.

60

The Elusive Peace

The Elusive Peace: The Middle East in the Twentieth Century

WILLIAM R. POLK

ST. MARTIN'S PRESS   NEW YORK

Library of Congress Cataloging in Publication Data

Polk, William Roe, 1929-
    The elusive peace.

    Includes index.
    1. Jewish-Arab relations—1917-   2. Near East—
Politics and government.   I. Title.
DS119.7.P65 1979   327.5694'017'4927   79-16393
ISBN 0-312-24383-9

Printed and bound in Great Britain

CONTENTS

For Eliza

deaf to the sounds of hate
reading the signs of understanding

INTRODUCTION

In school most of us were taught to view history as a sort of nomadic experience: the eye roves from one area to another as the pages unfold. First there were the ancient Egyptians and the Mesopotamians, then came the Phoenicians who were replaced by the Greeks who were defeated by the Romans who in turn fell before the Huns and so on. School texts rarely encourage the student to consider what happened to the Egyptians while the Greeks were 'becoming'. They were no longer relevant. Like school texts, the contemporary media focuses our attention on fleeting incidents and fosters our mental migrations. Crises, wars and, rarely, peace negotiations seize our attention and hold it briefly, but it is soon diverted to another area where something more arresting or novel is happening.

Like ancient peoples, current issues rarely disappear. Often they remain just as relevant to those involved and return to seize our attention when they again appear newsworthy or again novel. But even when the issues fade or even be resolved and when the stirring events are forgotten, they form patterns which, unseen, stratify the political geology, shaping the contours of the future.

Working from this visible and contemporary ground downward, so to speak, both the historian and the statesman must constantly re-explore the unseen and older strata of memory since what appears today merely of antiquarian interest may tomorrow acquire the most painful relevance. Like the oil hidden under its sands, the Middle East 'yields' contemporary refinements of history which are the very stuff of its politics. Throughout this story, we shall see example after example.

It is primarily as an historian that I have written this book, but I have also observed and participated in many of the events with which it deals over the last thirty years. I have known a number of the major participants and have been allowed access to the confidential thoughts of several of the governments. More important, I have had the opportunity to talk with, live among and read the literature of the various peoples. These experiences contain their own rewards; they were not means to any end, certainly not to this book. But based upon them, I have been able to make accurate predictions and projections on Middle Eastern events — the war of 1967, the war of 1973, the failure of several peace initiatives — and more importantly to devise ways to work toward peace. Time after time, I have watched an opportunity lost, often through misperceptions of the issues and problems, and I seek here to set out what I think are the essential facts and interpretations to help us seize the peace.

A few words about the structure of the book may help the reader. I begin with the deeper, more distant memories of the Arabs and the Jews, trying to show what I have called the political 'geology' of contemporary events. These, even when not exactly 'remembered', contribute to what I understand Jung to have thought of as the collective unconscious. Put another way, they have helped to make Egyptians, for example, distinctive. Insiders do not need to 'know' them for they acquire the feel of them as they mature; outsiders, lacking the intimate life-long experience, must seek artificially to know them to understand the culture.

Beginning with 'The Coming of Nationalism', the memories become more immediate and more imperative. Every child is taught these events and consequently they form the language, set the style, and give the syllabus of contemporary events. As becomes apparent in the chapter on Begin and Sadat, however much these two gifted and dedicated men may wish otherwise, they see the world and act within this schooling. I have dealt with these issues essentially chronologically but within the sequence I have sought to single out several main themes. The two most important are the struggle for independence — with a clear admission that in our times nationalism is still the strongest and most popular single political idea in the Middle East as it is in Africa and Asia — and the growth of capacity. Capacity is a concept often neglected in political discussion. Economists deal with it more routinely. They often quantify it in terms of Gross National Product (GNP) or, to refine it in human terms, GNP *per capita*. So we can compare Israel and Egypt, for example, as countries with GNPs of roughly $12 thousand million versus roughly $14 thousand million. Or when divided by the populations of each roughly $3,370 versus $350 *per capita*. Other figures crowd forward. Israel has a population of roughly 3½ million and Egypt 40 million; Israel has a land area of 8,000 square miles and Egypt of 386,000 square miles, but to use the geographical equivalent of 'per capita' roughly 40 per cent of Israel's land is urban or waste compared to about 98 per cent of Egypt's. Effectively Egypt is a land of only 10,000 square miles. My question is essentially how to make sense of these and other concepts in analysing both the relative power and capacity of the various countries and their performance today compared with the past. A different aspect of this change, with projections for the future and some discussion of the 'interface' of the Middle East and the world financial community comes in Chapter 10, 'Potential for the Future'. There I also try to show the problems which have arisen within both Israel and the Arab countries as a consequence of rapid development.

Finally, and to me most important, I suggest that the normal avenues of diplomacy are not only limited but also misleading. Misleading in one crucial aspect: diplomacy normally occurs between states. This has been the experience of Western Europe since the Renaissance and that experience has become the world norm. But the final, unresolved issue of Middle Eastern peace is not between the states. It is the fate of a non-state: the now roughly 3 million displaced Palestinian Arabs. In the spectacular events of 1978 they were not present or represented. So, while giving due credit to the statesmen and their states, I lay particular emphasis on this issue. The Palestinian Arabs are the 'Jews' of the modern Middle East. Their exodus and diaspora, although more recent and of shorter duration, is a tragedy comparable to that of the Jews. And without losing any sympathy for the tragic history of the Jews, one can also understand and sympathise with the Palestinians. While certainly not approving of all of their actions, I attempt to show how and why they have come to feel and act as they have and why such issues as Lebanon are today intertwined with their fate. I conclude that no real peace is possible which does not comprehend them.

Books on the Middle East suffer from the passions of both writers and readers. I have written as I see the events. For that I make no apology. But here I end with the observation that all the peoples of the Middle East deserve admiration and sympathy: sympathy for the much that they have suffered and admiration for the ways in which they have accepted the great challenges this century has brought them. In focusing on the tasks of the present, it is easy to forget the much that has been done. From this they and we can draw courage. The history of the Middle East is not just crises and wars, but also the growth and struggle of the human spirit. This also I have tried to include.

William R. Polk
Lagonisi, Greece

PART ONE

1 MEMORIES OF THE PAST

More than most peoples, Middle Easterners look back over their shoulders before taking each step forward. Probably no place in the world is more conducive to persistent and vivid memories. Everywhere symbols and artifacts of the past are to be found. Whether the Egyptian ploughs his field or catches a bus to a factory, he does so under the shadow of the pyramids; many Iraqis live atop what are virtually slow growing pyramids, the mounds formed from thousands of years of urban rubble; and Jews, Christians and Muslims find Jerusalem to be both a city and a living museum. Even where there are no giant monuments, one is constantly reminded of tradition by the clothes, the jewellery, the customs and the mores of neighbours. In language, above all, time and man and experience are distilled into something which seems to transcend the individual and the present and link them with forebearers time out of mind of this generation.

And the area is not discrete: its symbols affect outsiders — as Jerusalem and Mecca particularly do, so that the Middle East becomes a focal point for larger communities. Islam is encoded in Arabic and sprang from an Arabian environment so that today Mecca is the target of prayer of the whole Islamic community of which only a small fraction is Arab. In even more complex ways, Israel affects the scattered Jewish communities of the world who since the migrations nearly 2,000 years ago have dreamed of 'tomorrow in Jerusalem'. Of these things everyone is aware but what is even more important for those who live in the Middle East, outside events and memories have altered their lives. Probably no recent events have been seared into any people more painfully than the European holocaust into the Jewish community, and the memories of European imperialism still haunt the Arab political mind.

Of other peoples, it has been truly said that those who neglect the past are doomed to repeat it; of Middle Easterners it must be said that the past is sought out, sometimes to be repeated indeed, but sought out and used for every contemporary purpose. As a matter of policy each state mines the past so that memories are renewed, reinforced, woven into the present in school texts, cinemas, radio and television programmes, folk drama and dance, in street names, in mass cere-monies and national and religious celebrations. And where the state falters or fails, the people do the job themselves. No statesman can afford to view any issue purely in its contemporary guise or on the basis of its contemporary merits; rather he must approach it within the collective memory of his people. If he is a genuine leader, he can hardly do otherwise. But genuine or not, if he is to lead and stay in office, he must cherish and respect the tender nerve of memory. Let us begin to analyse these memories as Middle Easterners themselves do with religion.

The Islamic Tradition

Most of the people in the Middle East today are Muslims, adherents of the religion of Islam, which was revealed by the Prophet Mohammed in the seventh century. While proclaimed in Arabic for the Arabs, Islam is closely related to Judaism and Christianity in emphasising the unity of God and upholding a similar code of conduct and in revering most of the same prophets. But, in important ways, Islam differs. More than a faith, it is a way of life with exact rules of conduct governing everything from customs of childbirth to circumcision to marriage to funerals to division of inheritance — from before the cradle to after the grave. Indeed, Islam is not only a set of rules for the game of life but a detailed training programme on how to play it. Even among those who do not practise all of its ceremonies or accept all of its tenets (and they are today in the vast majority), the religion, like a dye, has permeated their lives. It colours the minutiae of daily experience, so completely that no conversation, even between illiterate men, occurs without the invocation of more theologically oriented terminology than would be heard in the course of weeks in a western divinity school.

Moreover, Islam even as it is understood today has become confused with the memory of a more glorious past in which Muslim Arabs were in the vanguard of civilisation and ruled an empire stretching from the frontier of China to the Atlantic. For Muslim school children today, the life of the Prophet Mohammed who died in AD 632 is more vivid and more contemporary than that of their grandfathers, living statesmen or even cinema stars. It is really the memory of the stirring times of early Islam that may be said to link the peoples of the Middle East. Even Christians, and until recently also Jews, found in Islamic-Arabic civilisation, if not in the religion itself, a matrix in which their lives took shape.

Islam is today the religion of about 500 million people. Of these only about one in seven or eight lives in the Middle East, but each year upwards of three million make the pilgrimage to Mecca from Africa, South and Southeast Asia, Central Asia and the Balkans. Flowing back to these non-Arab areas are not only books, films and tracts but also teachers. Islam was spread over much of Africa and Asia not by soldiers or administrators but by merchants and teachers. Today, as for centuries, the graduates of the Islamic university of al-Azhar in Cairo, are to be found in villages and towns of Nigeria, Tanzania, Pakistan, India, Malaysia, the Philippines and even parts of China and Russia. Recently, as we shall see, the richer Islamic countries have joined together to create such powerful new institutions as the Islamic Bank which seeks to apply Islamic principles to the new tasks of economic development and domestically each state has attempted to turn the formerly private religious foundations, the *Waqf* (plural *Awqaf*), into departments of government seeking to derive from them enhanced legitimacy and means of effecting social programmes.

While Islam has developed no exact equivalent to the papacy or even to the Orthodox patriarchate, and has no priesthood, it has found its own forms of organisational strength. In part it filled the vacuum left by governments which traditionally restricted themselves to external defence and internal security. Religious institutions performed such social services as were required. Today, of course, the state has taken over education and public health and, for the most part, civil law, thus depriving the religious establishment of much of its original function. Faced with this apparent growing irrelevance to contemporary life, reformers have sought to 'modernise' the religion but Islam has not been, and probably cannot be, 'reformed' piecemeal. In practice it has been pushed aside as the Middle Eastern states have become increasingly secular in the middle years of this century. Thus, outside observers find it easy to overlook religion and to deprecate its hidden strength only to be jarred by occasional violent assertions of its basic tenets by both reform and fundamentalist movements still active and still popular. At the present time, the most obvious example is in a non-Arab Muslim country, Iran, where a disaffected religious establishment formed a revolutionary power from an outraged population to topple what had appeared, to outsiders, to be the most efficient power in the Middle East. There are signs that similar sentiments, if not yet movements, are gaining in popularity and urgency in the Arab countries. The first points of attack are liquor, tobacco and immodest dress — issues now notable even in such 'liberated' countries as Egypt — but these are merely the outward signs: they are symbols of anger over excessive class privilege and the inroads of Western mores. But what is significant is that it is in the idiom of religion that the message is conveyed.

Christianity

Christianity is, similarly, of very antique experience. While the texts focus our attention on the era of Jesus, it was in the second century that its political and administrative structure matured. Then, combining with the majesty of the Roman Empire to create an unprecedented homogenising force, Christianity sought to attack and efface the monuments and legacies of the pagan past. Yet, at the same time, it borrowed both local ideas, such as monasticism from Egypt, and organisational concepts, such as the structure of town organisation from Syria, to create something far different from the relatively simple teachings of the early Christians. Indeed, within its new unity, it found room – and a means – for expressions of diversity which in part derive from older linguistic and 'national' divisions of Middle Eastern society. The great schisms of the Church can hardly be understood apart from the separate histories of the communities which entered Christianity: the Copt and the Orthodox differed not only on points of ritual and dogma but in fundamental matters of outlook and mentality and in the experience which coloured these.

Despite the 'fall' of Rome in the West, the Church-State Empire continued for a thousand years in the east in the form of a Greek revival. Severely challenged by a reconstituted Persian empire in the sixth century, it was nearly overwhelmed by Islam in the seventh and eighth and was sacked, occupied and fatally weakened by a rapacious and barely Christian West in the period of Crusades. Yet it survived and has left its legacy to the present. Less rich today than Islam in adherents, Christianity has been much more deeply and seriously affected by recent inroads of Western European thought and culture. More easily than Islam, Christianity could 'bend' to accommodate change. Born, unlike Islam, in persecution and defeat, it has proved the more flexible. Taught by centuries of tolerant but religiously alien rule to divide church and state and to care for most of its own social and even political needs, the Christian 'national' churches easily identified with the European powers and enabled their adherents to gain new wealth and power from the modernising and Westernising thrusts of the last century. For this, of course, they paid a price: by their Muslim neighbours they were often regarded as quislings of the imperial (read Western Christian) powers. Consequently, as the Western powers lost their hold on the Middle East after World War II, their Christian protegés often suffered. Only in Lebanon were the Christians able to capture a predominant political position. Elsewhere, in Iraq, Syria, Egypt and Israel, their numbers have dwindled. The Christian community of the former British Mandate of Palestine was shattered by the successive wars between the Arabs and the Israelis; most of them fled to Lebanon where they became a refugee community and that community today finds itself locked in bitter hostilities against fellow Christians and allied across religious lines with Muslims.

Over the centuries, Christianity has been a pool from which the politically and militarily more successful Islam has drawn adherents. Almost no Muslims and very few Jews converted to Christianity so that today, despite its antiquity and its historical contributions, only a few million adherents remain in the Middle Eastern Christian community.

The Jewish Community

Judaism is, in a sense, the root of both Christianity and Islam. While largely dispersed after their unsuccessful revolts against the Roman Empire, the Jews survived in various parts of the Middle East. Jewish communities were particularly notable in the cities along the Mediterranean coast but large numbers also planted colonies in the towns and villages of Arabia and even converted some local Arabians. Judaism took particularly firm root in Yemen, which was ruled by a Jewish dynasty before Islam. It is evident from the Koran that the Prophet Mohammed had Jewish contacts, for Islam is formally and theologically closer to Judaism than to Christianity. Indeed Mohammed announced, at least in the early years of his prophecy, that he was merely preaching the religion of Abraham in Arabic to the Arabs. He could not understand why the large orthodox Judaic community in the city today called Medina did not recognise Islam as their religion which he was merely reasserting. (In a curious echo in this century, the early Zionists asserted that the Arabic-speaking Palestinian peasants were 'really' Jews who would rediscover their identity upon contact with Zionism.) In his time, Mohammed accused the Medina Jews of having 'corrupted' pure Judaism and only slowly and reluctantly recognised that his religion was essentially new. But Islam continued, and continues today, to assert its kinship, with both Judaism and Christianity as parts of 'The Book'. Whatever the theological effect, the political effect has been beneficial: only rarely have relations among the religions been marred by the sort of intolerance common in Europe. Islam had no pogroms, no concentration camps and rarely even offensive discrimination.

For their part, Jews entered into Islamic society more readily than into Christian. Jewish merchants were often business partners of Muslims in medieval Cairo and were never forced to live apart in ghettos or to abstain from the practice of the more prestigious professions, as in Europe. Incredibly, they could and did call upon the Islamic state to punish offences to their religion. Their rights were protected under law and they were able to use the courts for redress of grievance. How sharply this contrasted with contemporary Europe was demonstrated when Queen Isabella expelled the Jews from Spain in 1492 — most went to live in Islamic countries.

Of course, one should not be blind to the fact that the religions were rivals, but in an age of general intolerance it was far better to be a Jew or a Christian in a Muslim land than even an unorthodox Christian in a Christian land. Many Jews were among the most highly educated, affluent and respected citizens in the Islamic area — at least one was the equivalent of prime minister of a Muslim state and in our era the first minister of finance of Iraq was Jewish. As we shall note, Jews and a quasi-Muslim Jewish sect played a major part in the Young Turk Revolution and, indirectly, in the events that led to the Balfour Declaration. Until the 1948 Arab-Israeli war most of the cities of the Middle East contained sizable Jewish communities.

But the fundamental historical memory of Judaism for the contemporary Israeli is not Middle Eastern. Rather it is the tragedy of the European experience. The history of the European Jewish community is an epic of cycles of toleration and extortion, protection and massacre, offset by the less dramatic but remarkable tenacity of small groups and isolated individuals in keeping alive the heritage of the religion and the nation. Before the Norman invasion, England had no Jews. While loathing them, the Normans found the Jews useful. While forbidding them from owning land, the Normans tolerated them as pawnbrokers and bankers. Kings as well as peasants became their customers. Indeed, the kings employed them as a sort of sponge to sop up the wealth of the nobles which, at the first opportunity, could be squeezed. The nobles saw the crown and the Jews as joint enemies of their class and, in part, the Magna Carta was a demand by impoverished nobles to escape both royal and Jewish foreclosures and heavy interest on the inheritance of orphans. But however useful the monarchy found the Jews, it wasted no affection on them. Richard the Lion Heart began his reign with a special tax, the 'Saladin tithe' to finance the Third Crusade and forced the Jews to pay two and a half times the rate of Christians. And, since each Crusade began with an anti-Jewish massacre in Europe (and often ended by a massacre of oriental Christians in the Middle East), the monarchy often was able to confiscate the estates of those Jews who were killed. If there was more to be got, Jews were arrested, tortured and ransomed or whole communities expelled so that their property could be taken and bribes collected. When the kings moved too slowly, the towns took the law into their hands as Cambridge did in 1275 when it expelled its resident Jews. What government chose not to do directly, vigilantes or the Church did independently. It was rare that anyone in authority was outraged by any barbarity inflicted on Jews and even where disapproval was registered the motive seems hardly humane. When Isabella expelled her Jews, for example, various European rulers and the Pope welcomed the most prosperous to their lands but hardly questioned Spain's purpose. The fact that the exiled Jews fled mainly to Muslim lands seemed a confirmation of their essential alienness. Even in the most civilised areas, Jews remained pariahs even when rich and cultured; when poor and ignorant, they were often treated as sub-human. This was their fate in eastern Europe and particularly in Russia where they were restricted in residence, employment and travel, denied civil rights, and used as scapegoats for popular discontent. While common over the centuries, this abuse reached a critical point in the nineteenth century when vicious pogroms, always tolerated and often instigated by government, brought on a new wave of migration and new impulses of social and political thought to produce a Jewish nationalist movement.

Different only in scale and intensity, the pogrom was resurrected in Nazi Germany which sought a 'final solution' to the problems of domestic aliens by slaughtering Jews, gypsies and others. The Nazi genocide, the holocaust, is so horrible, so gripping and so recent a memory as all but to overshadow other historical memories for the Western and Israeli Jewish communities. It was the shock of this slaughter that finally pushed the European Jews across the brink of despair and gave them the energy and determination to create their own land. Until the Nazis, Zionism was a minority tendency among European Jews and was all but unknown elsewhere; once Hitler had put the Jews' backs to the walls of Auschwitz, Buchenwald, Dachau, Triblenka and the other camps, many came to feel that the only alternative to the creation of an Israel was death.

Underpinning and shaping this sense of desperation was inherited religious belief and cultural experience. Theoretically, this pool of memory derives from a common history of the Jewish people — earthly kingdom in ancient Israel, expulsion and the diaspora. However, while this is the accepted national myth and, like all national myths, it is only partly true and true only for a part of the nation. The experience of the Oriental Jewish community was obviously very different from that of the Polish or Russian Jews and that of the Sephardic Jews differed in important ways from both of the others. Even racially the community is not one. Those who can 'tell a Jew by the way he looks' have supra-biological insight since a high proportion of today's Jews are not Semitic but derive from an entirely different racial stock. Many could no more trace their ancestry (even if they knew it) to ancient Israel through the exodus, than could Americans to England through *The Mayflower*. Like Americans, many are 'converts' from other peoples. In addition to the various oriental groups from India, Yemen, and Africa, many, perhaps most, Ashkenazi are descendants of Turks from the Khazar kingdom in what is today southern Russia which converted to Judaism in the eighth and ninth centuries. The Khazars, then poised dangerously and uncertainly between the Orthodox Christian Byzan-tine empire, the Islamic Arab Caliphate and Buddhist Central Asia, sought the additional strength of a distinct religion for its empire and only Judaism was unclaimed. The Khazar conversion to Judaism, like others to Islam and Christianity was undoubtedly opportunistic, but it has left a major genetic residue which fused by religion, nationalism and outside pressures forms part of a powerful and cohesive nation.

Other Minorities

Apart from Jews, Christians and Muslims, remnants of other religious or religiously defined groups are still to be found in the Middle East. A few are communities numbering in the hundreds of thousands of which the largest are deviants and variations of the major religions. Thus, in fact, there are no 'Christians' but only Orthodox Christians, Coptic Christians, Catholic Christians, and Protestant Christians, each of which in recent times was legally a separate 'nation', called in the Ottoman Empire a *millet*, which was largely self-governing. In matters of taxes, law, religion and politics each sect was set apart not only from the Muslims and Jews but from one another. The languages they use, the emphases they place on their historical experience and their sense of religion differ significantly and, in their eyes, fundamentally. In Egypt, the Coptic Church looks back to ancient Egypt, through the lens of Hellenism, while there and elsewhere the Orthodox Church is inspired by memories of Byzantium. Weakened and held suspect by its affilia-tion with the modern Greek nationalist movement, the Orthodox community provided such converts as the Protestant missionaries enrolled. Lastly, the Catholics have found their most vigorous local community in the Maronites, the largest of the Lebanese minorities, but are well represented in missionary and educational societies throughout the Arab world.

Like Christianity, Islam is divided into many sects. The 'orthodox' Muslims, the Sunnis, generally have been the rulers in the Arab countries while the 'partisans', the Shiis, formed protest or dissatisfaction groups. In non-Arab lands, notably Iran, the Shiis won political power — as they did briefly in Egypt and for long in Yemen — but like Christian Protestants the Shiis have fragmented into a number of mutually hostile sects. Today, among the more important are the Druzes of Mount Lebanon and Syria and the Alawis of Syria.

The Village Identity

The second major category of memory of the past is embodied in neighbourhood. Most of the people who live in the Middle East live in villages or in what amount to villages within cities. Until recently, if asked what his 'nation' was, a villager would say the name of his village. Indeed, one of the contemporary Arabic words for nation, *watan*, is still commonly used to mean village. In the mountains and desert oases, villages and towns occupy sites whose foundations were laid thousands of years ago. Particularly striking are the northern Iraqi towns built on the debris of ancestors' homes; rising more than 100 feet above the plain, these mounds or *tels* give awesome testimony of their antiquity. Even many of the towns and villages of Arabia are documented on their present sites before the coming of Islam while many in Lebanon are known from Biblical times. In Egypt, of course, the antiquity of sites and the continuum of human residence is without parallel.

It is not only the town but also the field to which emotions attach. Among the peasants the identification of man with land is almost mystical. The terrace walls one's father, grandfather or great grandfather built, the fields in which one plays as a child and in which one's ancestors are buried, the localities where saints have been venerated and besought, and finally along the great rivers the tangible contact with life forces beyond the ken of simple folk give rise to emotions virtually impossible for Western industrial man to understand. Yet, for the majority of the people who live in the Middle East today, these are real, immediate, intense, so intense and demanding in fact as to transcend the more abstract ideas of nationhood and to motivate the struggles of both Arabs and Israelis.

Where men have moved to the new cities, they have often recreated their villages in the new settings. Even so sophisticated a city as Beirut contains neighbourhoods which correspond to village communities, mosaics of the countryside without fields and streams. In politics, when real popular participation has been allowed, urban perpetuation has tended to promote a surprising degree of domination by predominant rural families. This is particularly notable in Lebanon where 'feudal' families who have ruled over villages and whole districts for centuries have found their ways naturally and easily into parliaments and political parties introduced from Europe in the 1920s. Sometimes the consequences are bizarre, as when Kamal Junblatt, the leader of the Lebanese traditional Druze district of the Shuf, became the leader of the radical socialist party and welded together, in his person, a reforming social movement and a tradition-bound rural community. More normally, of course, the traditional leaders are conservative and have made of parliaments the instruments of vested interests and so tending to discredit representative democracy before it could be tried. In the eyes of the radical reformers of Egypt, Syria and Iraq, the parliaments and constitutions became a part of the disease rather than a form of cure.

Traditionally, in the cities, something like the village community was the social unit. Each quarter or district (Arabic: *hara*) focused on its own mosque, market, school and public bath. Often the *hara* was walled off from its neighbours so that it resembled a small fort. It is still visible in many of the Lebanese towns, in the remnants of medieval Cairo, in Fez and in the madinas and casbahs of the North African cities. The city proper was the focus of the quarters on a congregational mosque and the common defence manifested by the often massive walls. As late as the 1950s, Sanaa, Jeddah, and Kuwait were enclosed by walls and the remnants of the walls of Jerusalem, Cairo and Rabat form imposing backdrops to the older urban centres. Functional until a generation or so ago, they segregated the secure city from the lawless countryside and gave the men of the city a common cause which in no small part made them into a city. Less imposing although even more common was another feature of urban life, the creation of outlying 'ports of call' for the nomadic visitors, away from the cities, where fairs and bazaars could be safely held, as it were on neutral and less tempting grounds; these also had the effect of isolating the city from the outlying areas.

Identification with a locale was often branded upon an individual by his 'placename' (Arabic: *laqab*). Even after generations spent in distant parts, a person — either an Arab or a Jew — might be known as 'the North African' (al-Maghribi), the 'Yemeni' (al-Yamani) or the 'Aleppan' (al-Halabi). But this placename meant no more than a reference: it was in no sense commensurate with a sense of separate national identity. Until the 1930s, there was little political import to the words 'Syrian', 'Iraqi' or 'Lebanese'. An urban man would not have called himself an 'Arab', for that meant a nomadic bedouin, but he would, probably, call himself a Muslim and further say that he was from Baghdad, but he had little reason to feel alien in any other Arabic speaking area. In the next chapter I will discuss how these national differentiations have arisen and become so potent a factor in the contemporary scene.

Livelihood

Memories of the past are also embodied in forms of livelihood. The Arabs traditionally have differentiated sharply three categories, the city man, the rural peasant and the nomadic bedouin. City people, who have written the histories, viewed the bedouin ambivalently — on the one hand, they saw the bedouin as destructive, unproductive, uncultivated, crude and dangerous. Where possible wise rulers would divert their energies, divide them through force or bribery, and beat them back into the deserts. On the other hand, even the most hostile writers saw the bedouin as the repository of the great tradition of Arabic culture, men who spoke the best of the language and who relished and virtually lived its noble poetry. Reluctantly, the settled peoples viewed the bedouin as a sort of genetic pool from which, periodically, new sources of strength and vigour were deposited into settled communities. Thus, they thought, while the incursions of the nomads were almost always destructive, they left behind, like the yearly floods of the Nile, an invigorating new biological 'silt'. Even today, when the time of the bedouin has passed, there is a grudging admiration of the bedouin *virtu* even though, as yet, there is little nostalgia for what is still too freshly seen as a life of hardship, poverty and danger.

In contrast to the bedouin, whose material life was known to be hungry and threadbare but whose heart and mind were assumed to be brave, noble and free, the villager was seen to live in degrading and enervating poverty. Treated by their Ottoman governors as little more than sheep to be periodically sheared, the villagers lived in close symbiosis with their animals, with which, like the medieval European peasants, they shared their living quarters. They rarely had the leisure to lift their hands or minds from the soil. And, although they produced the wealth essential to urban society and provided needed trading partners for the bedouin, the peasants were unloved, unsung, relegated generation after miserable generation to oblivion. This is particularly ironic because peasants have always comprised the vast majority of the people in the Middle East. The deserts and steppe could not and did not

ever support many nomads and the size of the cities was ultimately set
by the ability of the peasants to feed them. As one of their sympathetic
western observers wrote of them, 'A receptive people, yet unyielding;
patient, yet resistant . . . they remain as tranquil and stable as the
bottom of a deep sea whose surface waves are lashed with storms.'

Both Islam and Judaism have always been urban civilisations. Both
evinced a profound distrust for the nomad, and a contempt for the
peasant. Their supreme cultural achievements have been those possible
only within an urban environment. The medieval city achieved an extraordinary, intricate and complex pattern of industry and commerce.
Universities, schools, mosques, churches and synagogues in the Middle
East perpetuated early learning, disseminated among contemporaries
and, from time to time, contributed new ideas and new formulations of
old. Craft, industrial and religious brotherhoods merged so that the city
had a popular participation which made it more akin to ours than the
merely administrated population centre, the city of the Roman Empire.
And, while the state normally assisted in industry and commerce, it
generally created a permissive, laissez-faire but safe atmosphere in
which Muslim, Jewish and Christian merchants and artisans were able
to seek out and exploit opportunities on a truly cosmopolitan scale. We
know from the accounts of Muslim and Jewish merchants of trading
missions deep into Central Asia, northwards to Scandinavia, south
across the Indian Ocean, deep into Africa, and across from China to
Spain. Hoards of coins have been found showing the extent of this
commerce in astonishingly scattered locations from Norway to Zanzi-
bar. The travels of Marco Polo were doubled many times over in the
regular course of business. Today, the memory of a more glorious,
richer, more powerful, more self-respecting past leaves a residue in the
Arab states and in Israel which marks them off from the mainly non-
historical societies of Africa which, like them, have emerged to statehood in the last generation.

Foundations of National Identity

Lastly, the countries of the Middle East have been marked by the
peculiar ways in which religion, neighbourhood and livelihood have
been fused in recent centuries under foreign domination. Without
putting too fine a point on it, some form of national 'identity' has
survived from very ancient times. Egypt is perhaps the extreme case
while changing his language, his religion, his crops, his markets, his
government and his relationship to the outside world — and some of
these several times — the Egyptian has maintained an essential charac-

ter, which, however one calls it, marks him off from others. In recent centuries, under the domination of the Ottoman Empire, the Egyptians like the other peoples of the Middle East were moved off the centre stage of politics. It was this experience which has so marked the political strivings of this century.

Remarkably tolerant of religious and ethnic diversity, the Ottoman Empire insisted upon a bare minimum of military and financial submission rather than upon active participation or ideological loyalty. The Empire justified itself by keeping internal order and maintaining external defence. It gave no more to its subjects and expected little of them. Economy was its principal objective. So what it could not or would not do, it encouraged or allowed others to do. Like all poor administrations, it could not collect taxes so it farmed these out to fiscal entrepreneurs and religious communities. For our history at this point, the latter, the religious communities, are the most significant for they are the origin of the Middle Eastern notion of nationhood. Each religious community (Turkish: *millet*) was recognised and its appointed or tolerated leadership was made responsible for most of the functions we today associate with sovereignty, taxation, maintenance of law and order within the community, personal status (marriage, divorce, inheritance) and all the relationships with the state. From the point of view of the state the system was cheap and simple — the leader of the Jewish community, for example, was held personally responsible for the payment of a specified tax each year, but how it was assessed within the community was no business of the state. A result, naturally, of this tolerant policy was the strengthening of internal cohesion of each 'nation'. This process was most notable among the Christians who, combining religion with neighbourhood and language, and encouraged by the European powers, were the first to assert what we can recognise as nationalism.

Beginning in the nineteenth century with the Greeks, one minority after another became sensitive to national definitions and aspired to a more satisfying assertion of its individuality than could be afforded within the polyglot empire, particularly under its ruling Muslim-Turkish *élite*. For non-Muslims, the past was best defined when based on the Church; but the last of the minorities to revolt, the Arabs, were divided by religion with a part being Christian and the rest sharing with the Turks in the Islamic community and so had slowly and painfully to define and agree upon a new form of ethnic, linguistically based identity. As common as that was in Europe, it was novel in the Middle East and even today is not fully articulated or accepted. Only by the Jews of

Israel, and even there with considerable strain, is the nation capable of being seen as a unity of language, religion and ethnicity; for the Arabs, still, the problems of the welding of territoriality, religion, ethnic origins and ecology are unresolved. Even to the degree that they are resolved, they are because of outside pressures of a kind that is new to the Middle Eastern experience.

2 THE RISE OF NATIONALISM

By the nineteenth century, Russia had accumulated the largest Jewish population in the world. Widely scattered, the Jews were also diverse in origin. As we have seen, many became Jewish when the Turkish Khazar kingdom converted to Judaism in the eight and ninth centuries, and Russian when conquered by the forces of Ivan the Terrible. Others, of earlier Jewish stock, found their ways as traders with the Vikings along the great Russian rivers from the Black Sea to the Baltic. The history of still others, driven from Western Europe, are lost in the mists of time. Finally, between 1772 and 1795, Empress Catherine the Great incorporated the large numbers who lived in Poland and the Ukraine.

The Russians, like Western Europeans, found the Jews useful but hated them. The Jews performed tasks which others despised but needed. Those tasks made them vulnerable, kept them alien, and caused others to covet the riches they accumulated. Relatively recent converts to Christianity themselves, the Russians regarded the Jews as outside the laws and mores of Christian society. Even more than the Western Europeans, the Russians regulated their residence, forcing them into special provinces, weakening them by reducing their intellectual horizons and setting limits on their wealth by prohibiting them from owning land or practising most of the professions. Periodically, when they were thought to be too rich or when some unexplained outbreak of disease or famine occurred, popular hostility was roused against them and they were looted and massacred.

Remarkably they survived and were more numerous by the nineteenth century than ever before. In that turbulent century, the Jews, like other Russians, began to break out of the older restrictions and were stirred by the waves of thought loosed by the French Revolution. More widely scattered by then, they were more available and more obvious as targets. And the ramshackle empire needed scapegoats. Several times mobs were encouraged to vent their frustrations and anger against this safe — and ofen more immediately attractive — target. It was, however, the assassination of Tsar Alexander II in 1881 that triggered the most widespread and violent of the pogroms. Hundreds of separate riots throughout Russia were stimulated by the government and some were aided by the police. Once again, as in fifteenth-century Spain and thirteenth-century England, the Jews took to the roads. By the end of the century, the migration had turned into a flood.

Coming out of the narrow, restricted life of Russia, the Jews found Western Europe a land of milk and honey. Like medieval peasants they found that city air makes a man free. But the reception they found was often unfriendly. Western Jews who had gradually and painfully won a more secure and prosperous place for themselves in Christian society, many indeed shedding their Jewish past, felt threatened by the new arrivals. Anti-semitism was already well developed in Germany and France by the 1880s and the brashness and alienness of the new arrivals might further encourage it. The new arrivals shared the worry and, in the words of one of them, realised that they seemed to carry anti-semitism on their backs. It would not be until they emancipated themselves, as the Jewish writer Leo Pinsker suggested in his book *Auto Emancipation*, that they would be secure. To Pinsker and others true emancipation required a territorial base. But where? Most of the Jews leaving Russia identified the real promised land as America, to which some 160,000 emigrated in the decade following the murder of Tsar Alexander II. Palestine was then no more than a dream in the minds of the religious and the unworldly. Almost unnoticed even by Jews, the first modest settlement was established in Palestine in 1882 near the Arab city of Jaffa.

Following the assassination of Alexander and the imposition of a relatively efficient tyranny upon Russia under Alexander III and Nicholas II, the tempo of social and political criticism greatly increased among Russian university students and gradually among industrial workers. The same factors which had led to large scale Jewish migration, official persecution and the pogroms, led numbers of young Jewish men and women into Russian movements of social protest. Many joined the new and still small revolutionary parties and terrorist groups, while others in 1887 formed a Jewish socialist party, the Bund.

Throughout these years the idea of a new order was 'in the air' although there was no consensus about what it could or should embody, or whether its criteria should start with class or religion. The first Jewish settlement in Palestine had been not simply nationalistic or religious but also an expression of the desire for a fundamental reordering of Jewish life. With private land ownership seen to be at the root of evil in Russia, and ethnic landlessness at the root of weakness in the Jewish community, a 'return' to the land but in settlements whose property would be owned in common, the *Kibbutz*, offered a programme of visionary power.

But such ideas — social revolution in Europe and Utopia in Palestine —

were disquieting to the more assimilated, better established and more prosperous Jewish communities in the West. The very involvement of Jews in dangerous and suspect social revolutionary movements, the idea that the grand conception of Judaism would be or could be reduced to merely another example of nationalism from which cultured people had already suffered so much and, above all, the notion that Jews were unalterably alien everywhere were equally and profoundly disturbing. In 1897, the Central Conference of American Rabbis resolved that, 'We totally disapprove of any attempt for the establishment of a Jewish State . . . such attempts do not benefit, but infinitely harm our Jewish brethren where they are still persecuted, by confirming the assertion of their enemies that the Jews are foreigners in the countries in which they are at home . . .'

At roughly the same time as the American rabbis passed their resolution, the first Zionist Congress was meeting in the Swiss city of Basle under the presidency of Theodor Herzl.

Theodor Herzl, who is now revered among the Jewish community as the spiritual father of Zionism, emerged from the same wing of the Jewish community as the American rabbis. At home in the most advanced and cultivated European society, he had led a comfortable and protected life since his birth in Budapest in 1860. A lawyer by training, he worked as a journalist in Paris in the 1890s and there found his whole way of life, his philosophy and his hopes for his people shattered by the events surrounding the trial of Captain Alfred Dreyfus, a wealthy Alsatian Jewish member of the General Staff of the French Army. While covering the Dreyfus trial, Herzl was stunned by the occasion it gave for an outpouring of virulent anti-semitism in that most advanced and integrated of European societies. If a serving officer of a national army could be ruined because he was Jewish, on charges which many then felt, and were later proved to be, spurious, so Herzl and others reasoned, what Jew was safe anywhere? Herzl despaired of assimilation and began to feel that only if Jews could acquire for themselves a territory on which to express their own sense of identity, to become a nation-state, was there any hope for them to escape the cycles of poverty to riches to persecutions which seemed to have been the predominant theme of Jewish history in the Diaspora. In his major writing, *Der Judenstaat* (*The Jewish State*) Herzl summed up in one sentence the thrust of his programme, 'Let the sovereignty be granted us over a portion of the globe large enough to satisfy the rightful requirements of a nation and the rest we shall arrange ourselves.'

Hardly noticed outside the Jewish community, *Der Judenstaat*

immediately brought forth a storm from within. Those who had hoped
to promote the settlement, relatively quietly, of Jewish communities in
Palestine, then a province of the Ottoman Empire, feared that the
Ottoman Government would regard their settlements as a Trojan horse,
designed ultimately to carve a separate state out of the empire's body,
and would expel the Jewish settlers. Those who still hoped to assimilate
into Western European or American society feared that Herzl offered
confirmation (as the American rabbis themselves explicitly said) of the
alienness of the Jewish community. Those within Russia who hoped
either to reform the system or to overthrow it saw Jewish nationalism
as a petty bourgeois phenomenon, a heresy destructive to the revolutionary movement or a delusion followed by the naive. Finally, the
orthodox religious establishment saw in this nationalistic interpretation
of Judaism a profound subversion of the entire Judaic idea of the
diaspora and of its end in a Heavenly Kingdom. Still, the congress at
Basle was Herzl's personal triumph. According to contemporary observers, he seemed to embody in some majestic fashion the aims and aspirations of each opposing group. To some he seemed a Messiah, to others a
social revolutionary and to yet another group a statesman who could
negotiate with sultans and kings. As Herzl himself wrote, '. . . at Basle I
founded the Jewish State. If I were to say this today, I would be met
by universal laughter. In five years, perhaps, and certainly in fifty, every
one will see it. The State is already founded in essence, in the will of
the people to the State.'

But despite this great boost to morale, Zionism not only had no
organisation but no clear objective. A Jewish state, well enough. But
where? For whom? Who was to pay? Who would support it? All these
questions were immediately to be faced. Herzl was flexible on the location and merely optimistic on the means. He met with some mild but
evasive encouragement from the Ottoman Government and even more
evasive encouragement from the British. Various alternative schemes
were put forth and passionately debated; the Sinai Peninsula could be
acquired from British-controlled Egypt; Cyprus could be taken over and
used either as the basis of a Jewish state or a swap of territory for a
Jewish state in Palestine; Uganda could be colonised by Jews. Various
attempts were made to set up Jewish settlements in Argentina, Angola,
Cyrenaica and Australia. None caught the attention of a critical mass of
people. Gradually it became clear that in order for the disparate and
often distinct ideas and ambitions of Zionism to come into focus, some
tangible, immediately agreeable objective must be constantly in the forefront. This could only be a return to 'Palestine' and by the eve of World

War I, the Jewish individuals and groups which made up the Zionist organisation had reached unanimity on this point.

But how to get there?

As it did for so many national groups, World War I showed the way.

As despised as they usually were in Christian Europe, the Jews once more became attractive to the embattled governments: each credited them with great power and influence in the others' territories. The British Government believed that the Jews had great influence in America upon whose financial resources it came to depend; in Russia, where leaders of the various revolutionary parties were Jewish, and whose armies Britain desperately wanted to keep in the war; and in the Ottoman Empire whose ruling junta contained both Jews and those Muslim converts from Judaism known as *Donmeh*. Germany, likewise, was alert to Jewish influence in neutral America, where it wished to cultivate the then strong anti-British sentiment, and in Russia whose revolutionaries (including Lenin) it helped to take Russia out of the war. For their part, the Zionists wished to remain neutral and to use their influence on both sides to achieve their aims in Palestine. To put all this in perspective, we must go back a few years.

Shortly after the Zionist Congress of 1897, Theodor Herzl began negotiations with the Ottoman Sultan, with the German Government and with Britain. The Sultan was aloof and, while the Kaiser was sympathetic, Germany refused to give the Zionists effective support. Britain, in 1902 and 1903, discussed various schemes in territories it then controlled, notably what is today Uganda, but the 1903 Zionist Congress rejected them. Following Herzl's death in 1904, the Zionists lost their effective 'foreign minister' and most of their efforts lapsed. The tide seemed to be running against them. The Young Turks, despite their Jewish and *Donmeh* members, feared the nationalism of minorities and wished to assert their own; to them, the Zionists were little better than Armenians or Greeks. Indeed, their one virtue over Armenians and Greeks was that they were resident in other lands; prudence argued that they should be kept there. Moreover, while the Turks were increasingly dependent upon Germany, they feared German ambitions for the Ottoman Empire and saw the Zionists as an arm of German foreign policy. This estimate seemed confirmed when the Zionists established a school in Haifa to be taught in German rather than in Hebrew. A controversy between the school and the Zionist organisation caused Jewish riots in Jerusalem in which the German consul and the Turkish police became involved.

The records of the German Government reveal, however, that after

Herzl's death, the Germans had lost contact with the Zionists until the events of the Haifa school brought about a cautious rediscovery in late 1913 by the German Embassy in Constantinople. By the eve of the war, Germany was again in close contact with the Zionists. When the war broke out, the Zionist Executive Council met in Berlin and decided upon a neutralist policy: to suspend publication of its newspaper but to keep the headquarters in Berlin. Zionist anti-Russian feeling was strong and the Germans were seen to be in a better position to influence their Turkish ally than the hostile British. Moreover, many Zionists, particularly those resident in Germany and Austria, assumed that Germany would win the war.

In Britain, meanwhile, the Zionists had been active. The negotiations of 1902-3 had not been successful but through them the British Government had learned about Zionism, and in 1906 the Zionist leader in England, Chaim Weizmann, first made contact with Arthur Balfour whose name would come to figure so prominently in Zionist affairs a decade later.

When the war broke out, neither Great Power coalition was prepared to fight a protracted conflict. No one assumed that modern war could last long. All recent military experience bore out that estimate. But, as the months wore on, Britain's search for money to buy equipment and sustain the war effort overcame almost every other consideration. America was soon the only available source as England mortgaged or sold its overseas assets. The then secret British Government papers indicate that their statesmen decided that the anti-Allied American Jewish community was the key to their success in winning loans from the American financial community. The other key to staying in the war was to keep the Russian armies in the field: if Russia withdrew, the full weight of the German army could be thrown against the Western front with fatal results. One part of the Allied task was to keep Russia supplied with food and arms — that is what made so crucial the opening of the Turkish Straits to Western shipping. But Turkey was firmly on the German side and its troops were holding the British and the Russians on their scattered fronts. Desperately, Britain decided to thrust at Gallipoli in the spring and summer of 1915. Gallipoli was a failure. The Strait remained sealed and Russia suffered famine and shortage of arms until it finally collapsed in revolution in October 1917.

That Russia could even stay in the way so long seemed unlikely after its first massive defeats in 1914. Piece by piece the army fell apart. Food riots paralysed the home front and politicised the soldiers, workers and even the peasants. Agitators of all the revolutionary groups flocked into Russia to take up the cause they had lost in 1905. The government's fate hung by a thread. Then came the first revolution with its moderate socialist government. Russia stayed in the war, but the enemies of that government made the issue of war itself the point of attack. The personalities of a handful of people thus came to assume critical importance, for they articulated the voiceless discontent of Russia's masses and channelled their energies against the war effort. Of the few who were then known, several were thought to be and others known to be Jewish. Still others were known to be socialists with whom the Bund shared fundamental ambitions. Consequently, the British Government sought to convince the Jews that they had a reason to continue the war effort. Britain and the British cause, they argued, were not of a piece with the old Russian autocracy but would help, indeed even then were helping, to realise the new aspirations of Jewish nationalism.

To appeal to Jews in both Russia and America, the British Government discreetly urged the English Jews (who until then had not been particularly involved in the Zionist movement) to request a pro-Zionist declaration. This was to result, in 1917, in the Balfour Declaration, the best known of the several efforts of the Zionists because Britain won the war and could effect its declaration, but at this time the Germans were also at work on their bid for Jewish support. They were late because the Turkish officers and governors advised their government, Germany's ally, that a pro-Zionist declaration of policy would cause an insurrection in the Arab areas of the Empire. Nevertheless, after the Balfour Declaration was issued, under German pressure, the Turkish Government announced that it favoured Jewish colonisation of Palestine. This was not quite a Balfour Declaration but the German and Austrian Governments seized upon it and immediately announced (particularly on the Russian front) their approval and support. Under German prodding, negotiations were opened to establish a new, quasi-government corporation to facilitate Jewish land acquisition and settlement in parts of Palestine. It was altogether too little and too late for, during the course of the negotiations, Palestine was overrun by British troops and shortly thereafter Turkey collapsed. It was to be the British, not the Turks or the Germans, whose writ would run in the East.

What was that writ and how did it emerge?

Like all questions about government plans and programmes the answer is not simple. As has been truly remarked, successful government programmes have many fathers but those that fail are orphans.

Yet much has been written about the Balfour Declaration and we are
fortunate in having a remarkably full collection of papers on the
months of negotiations and discussions which gave it birth. For our
present purposes, most of that discussion is irrelevant since it illumin-
ates European rather than Middle Eastern history, but it is important to
note that the Declaration was the result of the most careful and search-
ing debate in the War Cabinet and is one of the most carefully phrased
of all diplomatic documents. As delivered to Lord Rothschild on 2
November 1917, it ranks as one of the most remarkable statements
ever issued by a government. Just 68 words long, its two contradictory
clauses are precariously balanced on a comma with studied ambiguity.
A reproduction of the original is on page 37.

When the text was being debated in the Cabinet, Lord Kitchener
remarked that he was sure that the half a million Arab inhabitants of
Palestine 'will not be content as hewers of wood and drawers of water
for the latter' [the incoming Jewish settlers]. Lord Balfour in reply
stressed that 'If we could make a declaration favourable to such an
ideal, we should be able to carry on extremely useful propaganda both
in Russia and America.' It was this 'purely diplomatic and political
point of view', he felt, which had to govern at that stage of the war
when the Western front was just reaching a crescendo of violence and
Russia was about to sign a separate peace.

Other Diplomatic Moves

The British needed all the help they could get immediately and they
sought it everywhere. To give heart to their European allies, they were
involved in complex negotiations designed to whet appetites for the
spoil of victory. Worked out during 1916, the agreements, known by
the names of their British and French drafters as the Sykes-Picot Agreements, divided the Ottoman Empire into zones of British, French,
Italian and Russian domination or, more euphemistically, 'influence'. In
the central area with which we are here concerned, five zones were to be
created: (1) the Levant coast (to be French); (2) the Syrian hinterland
(under French influence); (3) Baghdad and Basra provinces, about half
of the modern state of Iraq (British); (4) the steppe and desert of what
is now Jordan and Iraq (British influence); and (5) 'Palestine' (which
was to be international, except for the port of Acre which was to be
British). These understandings were kept secret from both the Zionists
and the Arabs until the Bolshevik revolutionaries published them late in
1917. The British then explained to the Arabs that Messrs Sykes and
Picot had merely had an 'exchange of views' which were no longer rele-

Foreign Office,
November 2nd, 1917.

Dear Lord Rothschild,

I have much pleasure in conveying to you, on
behalf of His Majesty's Government, the following
declaration of sympathy with Jewish Zionist aspirations
which has been submitted to, and approved by, the Cabinet.

'His Majesty's Government view with favour the
establishment in Palestine of a national home for the
Jewish people, and will use their best endeavours to
facilitate the achievement of this object, it being
clearly understood that nothing shall be done which
may prejudice the civil and religious rights of
existing non-Jewish communities in Palestine, or the
rights and political status enjoyed by Jews in any
other country".

I should be grateful if you would bring this
declaration to the knowledge of the Zionist Federation.

vant since Russia had dropped out of the war. France, although non-committal at the time, did not agree and subsequently at the Peace Conference was to insist upon its due. How and at what price comprises much of the history of the next generation.

It was also in the middle of the war that the forces of Arab nationalism, neither so well articulated as Zionism nor so clear as French ambition, entered world history. Let us now see what they were, who held them, and how they arrived on the stage.

Arabism

The word 'Arab' does not figure in the Balfour Declaration. The 'existing non-Jewish communities in Palestine', a circumlocution that does not spring readily to mind, is what the document calls the Arabic-speaking inhabitants. Since that group was at least 80 per cent and perhaps even 90 per cent of the population and thought of itself as Arab, how and why was the simple word 'Arab' avoided? Two answers appear possible and each tells us something crucial about the events to follow.

First, as we have seen, it was religion not language or ethnicity which defined group identity in the Ottoman Empire. Legally, 'Arabs' were not a *millet* or nation but were divided into Muslims (who were theoretically at one with the Muslim Turks, Kurds and others) and various sects of Christians. Regardless of his language or his 'race', a Christian was not a full citizen of the empire nor a member of the nation of Islam. Moreover, the Christians were not unified. Legally there was no such thing as a 'Christian'. A Christian was either a Greek Orthodox, a Catholic or a Copt and as such a member of a different 'nation' with his separate community government, taxes, privileges and duties. Each, moreover, associated with a different foreign power from whom he drew protection, schooling and inspiration. Only in popular usage, not in law, were all these Arab. As we shall see, this sense of ultimate separation was then, and was to remain, a major obstacle to the formulation and development of Arab nationalism.

Second, even among the public and in popular usage, the sense of 'Arabness' was still weak. It was being formed, partly in rediscovery of linguistic and literary roots and partly in opposition to the assertion of *Turkizm* in the generation before the war — and it would grow thereafter in opposition to British and French rule and to Zionist aspirations — but during World War I more Arabs fought on the side of the Ottoman Empire than participated in what was later called the Arab Revolt.

These two factors were to play such a crucial role in the history of our times that we must now examine them more closely beginning with the formulation of ideas of Arab nationhood in the early years of this century.

Partly as a result of Western missionary activity in the nineteenth century, more, perhaps, as a result of growing economic linkages of the Middle East with the world markets, the Middle East was 'awakened' from what was a relatively torpid and tranquil four centuries of Ottoman rule. Gradually what had been merely lethargic became oppressive in the minds of increasingly restless young men and from the generation of the 1880s — ironically the same generation as produced Zionism — these feelings began to find a vague expression in literary revivalism, in a rediscovery of the Arab classics and in a fascination with the publications of European orientalists. Others, particularly in Egypt, sought to 'purify' and restore Islamic fundamentalism or to render it more relevant to the contemporary world. Their road was to be a rocky one for, on the one hand, they accentuated the division of the Arabs by religion and, on the other, they split the Islamic community among traditionalists and modernists and among those who saw the Ottoman Empire as the best hope of Islam and those who thought of it only as a burdensome anachronism. The ideas of the French and American revolutions, insofar as they were then known, seemed hardly relevant; even the nationalisms of the Balkans, the nearest exemplars, were exotic and alien. However, the assertion of nationalism by the Balkan peoples painfully affected the rulers of the Ottoman Empire and forced Turkish thinkers and statesmen to re-examine *their* assumptions of their empire. If Greeks, Bulgars, Armenians, and others underlined by revolution that they were not 'Ottoman', then who were the rulers themselves? In the urbane, cosmopolitan society of the Ottoman *élite*, the word 'Turk' — like the word 'Arab' among their Arabic-speaking counterparts — meant something like 'rustic' or 'hick'. The 'Turk', like the 'Arab', was a nomadic warrior, probably an ancestor, a heroic figure indeed, but hardly a model for citizenship. As the ruling *élite* began to mull over this problem of identity, some of its members realised how completely they had forgotten their past: some of their writings appear *jejune* today and many of their avowed policies amount to little more than affecting what they thought was folk costume and using antique — 'pure' — words. From these meagre ideas, however, evolved an appetite for *Turkculuk*, Turkishness, and by the early years of this century, many Turks had become ethnically and linguistically as nationalist as the Greeks. Particularly after the 1908 Young Turk Revolution, when the Committee of Union and Progress seized power, the conception of the state underwent a significant change: it was no longer to be supranational Ottoman but Turkish. Even in the Arab provinces Turkish replaced Arabic as the language of education in public schools. In their turn, the Arabs began to wonder: they might be 'Ottoman' but Turkish they were not. The Turks agreed so they suppressed the new 'Arab Ottoman' movement. Ironically, but logically, those with the most developed answer to the dilemma of national identity were those who had found the old religious answer least appealing — the Christians. They had already to face the task of overcoming the permanent and complete minority status that their religious attachment had imposed upon them. Like almost everyone else in the nineteenth century, they found the answer in language. It was partly for this reason that the American University of Beirut, a Protestant missionary institution dedicated to 'good works' (as the road to conversion) played such a significant role in the first phase of Arab nationalist thought. Indeed it was there that the later Arab historian and champion of nationalism, George Antonius, placed its origin.

Of course, Egypt had long since set itself apart culturally and economically, even to a large extent politically, from the rest of the Ottoman Empire. But it had not become in any recognisable sense a 'nation'. From the expulsion of the French invaders in 1801, Egypt had supported a local dynasty, founded by a Turkish-speaking Macedonian soldier-of-fortune and staffed by a Turkish-speaking bureaucracy and military *élite*. For the rulers, Egypt was an available and reasonably suitable base of operations. Its people were assets, like the land, to be exploited to gain wealth and security. The dynasty was separatist because that was the best way to keep one's head on one's shoulders, and it was often in conflict with the Ottoman Empire because until nearly the end of the century, that was the only really dangerous enemy. But in no effective sense was the dynasty 'Egyptian', and it certainly was not 'Arab'. For writers in Egypt, the very word 'nation'was unfamiliar and wherever used required elaborate explanation. Modern Egyptians have tried to portray it as a national state, but it was not.

Nationalist origins are often unimpressive but with antiquity or success or both, we allow myth to magnify and ennoble. Just as the early Zionists derive from a mere 20 or so Russian Jewish university students — or the Christians and the Bolsheviks from similar 'mass' movements — so the Arabs must garner their leaders from tiny literary clubs in the universities. To our ears, their arguments sound naive and unworldly: grand philosophical issues were assumed to turn on minute linguistic distinctions, most of which were questionable anyway, and served merely to obscure what the writers could not face, or, more debilitatingly, faced in divisive ways. The contemporary fact was that they faced different enemies and identified with different allies. Those in the Levant, living under the Empire, saw the Turks and their *Turkizm* as the immediate threat and the Christian West as the missionary teacher while those in Egypt, ruled from 1882 by the British, feared Western imperialism and at a safe distance romanticised the Islamic Empire. Other Arabs were as yet little affected by these currents or affected in ways which made them perceive the contemporary world in different terms. Yet in those years a quest, still today unfulfilled, for national identification, was begun; events beyond the Arab neighbourhood were to bring them into focus.

Imperial Need

Like the Zionists and the French, the Arabs were beneficiaries of British need. In the Middle East, the stake was different — it was not to give heart to an ally as with France or to secure loans or keep a faltering ally in the war as with the Zionists — but imperial. And it hinged not on nationalism or aspiration but on religion.

Britain, France and Russia each dominated an empire in which scores of millions of Muslims lived. Each government feared the possibility that its colonial population would identify with the leader of the Ottoman Empire, the senior Muslim leader of the world, and would respond when he declared a *jihad* or holy war against the Europeans. Britain and the British Government of India were still haunted by the memory of the Sepoy Mutiny of 1857-8 which had convulsed India. The French conquest of North Africa was even more recent and, being combined with colonialism on a scale not even attempted by the British in India, generated more bitter hatreds. Russia, having pushed right across Central Asia, had conquered, but not yet digested millions of Turks and other Muslims. Consequently, the Allies and the British, particularly feared a giant 'Pan Islamic' movement which might destroy them in the East. While now known to have been largely a figment of British imagination, Pan Islamism then seemed very real. The British came to believe that only a split in the Islamic world could forestall massive civil war just when the British, French and Russians needed every man and rifle in Europe. The problem was not so much recruiting men or armies as winning over leaders and spokesmen: this was the need that shaped British policy toward the Arabs.

But who could do the job? Certainly not the young firebrands of the Levant schools or the Cairo law courts. The Asian and African Muslims would not identify with them. Nor was it likely that a Berber from Morocco, even if a venerable figure, would carry much weight in Samarqand or Lahore. Reasonably, the British sought a figure all would know and identify with the mainstream of Islam, an Arab. With their long experience in the Persian Gulf, the British in India were familiar with the more nomadic, less urban folk in eastern Arabia and southern Iraq. Amongst them, the outstanding leader was the young but magnetic Abdul Aziz Ibn Saud, later to be sultan and then king of Saudi Arabia (and father of the present king). He then had a modest but important role in Arabian affairs and was the lay leader of the Islamic revival movement of the Wahhabis. To him, the British (in India) sent a colourful political agent, Captain William Shakespear, but when Shakespear was killed in a tribal battle in January 1915, hopes for a Saudi initiative died with him.

Meanwhile the British (in Cairo) decided to exploit an opening given them in 1913 when Sharif (later King) Abdullah guardedly indicated that his father, Hussein the Sharif of Mecca, might be willing to assist the British in return for help in securing his independence from the Turks. At the time the British had not been interested, but with the outbreak of war, the Sharif seemed an ideal candidate to be the pro-Allied Muslim religious leader: a descendant of the prophet Mohammed, he was the acknowledged (and Ottoman-appointed) guardian of the holy city of Mecca. As such, he was the most widely known and most senior non-Turkish religious figure in the Islamic world. Unlike Ibn Saud, Sharif Hussein had no secure independent power base and so, presumably, would be easier to deal with. Like Ibn Saud, he was conservative and relatively isolated. It was doubtful that he had even heard of the thoughts of the Egyptian and Levantine nationalists. If he had, he did not identify with them. And so, carefully and tentatively, the British sought him out.

The War

More or less independently of these developments, the outbreak of the war in November 1914 brought into focus a surge of popular discontent in Syria. The young men had come out of the universities and entered the army, law offices, the press and businesses. Their dislike for the empire had grown as the young Turks asserted their Turkishness and cracked down hard on domestic political dissent. The efficient and harsh Ottoman military governor in Syria, helped by a reading of the curiously available intelligence files of the French consulate in Damascus, in May 1915 arrested and hanged a number of Arab nationalists. Martial law combined with Allied blockade effectively to starve both the nationalist movement and the population. Syria would do little but suffer during the war.

Meanwhile, in Egypt, under effective but disguised British rule since 1882, the war brought less dramatic change. The British Cabinet considered annexing the country, and so regularising the British position, as it had done in Cyprus, but, as a compromise, on 18 December 1914 proclaimed a protectorate instead. For the rest of the war, Egyptians under a military régime grew fatter but more quiet. Such frustrations as they felt were at first sublimated and suppressed only to erupt explosively after the war.

To the East, just after declaring war on the Ottoman Empire in November 1914, Britain proclaimed the independence, under its protection, of Kuwait and began to invade what is today Iraq. On 6 November an Anglo-Indian expeditionary force seized the little port of Fao and set out for Baghdad.

Although begun with great advantages, the war did not go easily for the British in the East. The Turks were proud and dour soldiers, accustomed to hardship and born to war. In their first actions, they briefly cut the Suez Canal and interrupted the flow of Persian petroleum on which the British navy had come to depend. In their long march on Baghdad, the British lost about 20,000 men and were reduced to a 'dishonourable' and humiliating attempt to bribe the Turks to let go a whole division at the Iraqi town of Kut. The Turks refused and the division surrendered. The 'sick man of Europe' had roused himself and seemed capable of inflicting great damage on the Allied cause.

Here was yet another reason for the British to attempt to conjure an Arab diversion. For this, a special kind of military tactic was needed, which could tie down Turkish units, disrupt communications, and neutralise the modern railroads which enabled the Turks to move their few well equipped units from one front to another. To accomplish this, the British encouraged bedouin tribesmen to become guerrillas.

To get the Arabs into the war, the British began an exchange of letters, the so-called Hussein-McMahon correspondence, with the Grand Sharif Hussein of Mecca. In the eight letters exchanged between 14 July 1915 and 30 January 1916, the British set out the terms on which they hoped to entice the Arabs into the war and the Sharif responded with his demands. The Arabs prepared for war and on 5 June 1916 proclaimed their independence and attacked the Turkish forces in Arabia.

All was seemingly agreed. However, the terms remained secret for over a generation after they were written; they were not officially published until 1939, when they were the subject of British government and Arab states inquiry, and even today their exact meaning remains the subject of controversy. At the heart of the controversy is the question of whether or not 'Palestine' was excluded or included in the area promised the Arabs.

The Hussein-McMahon correspondence was not the only body of commitment to the Arabs, but other proclamations seemed to confirm the most generous interpretation. The most widely circulated was the June 1918 'Declaration to the Seven' (after the Sykes-Picot Agreements had become known and Britain was charged with double dealing) in which British policy was affirmed to 'recognize the complete and sovereign independence of the Arabs'. This was reaffirmed by a statement from Field-Marshal Lord Allenby, the commander of the Allied Forces in the Middle East, that 'the Allies were in honour bound to endeavour to reach a settlement in accordance to the wishes of the peoples'.

More general, but also affecting the Middle East, was President Wilson's ringing declaration on 8 January 1918 of Fourteen Points which included that clarion cry to the world's oppressed nationalities, the right of self-determination of peoples. Wilson's call seemed just that spark to ignite the vague, inchoate yearnings of the Arabs and the by then more resolute desires of the Zionists along with those of dozens of national groups throughout the world. Whatever their private doubts and disagreements, the Allies made the most of the Fourteen Points and all the other statements. For example, a leaflet, printed in Yiddish, was spread among German and Austrian troops in Europe announcing that

> Jerusalem has fallen! The hour of Jewish redemption has arrived . . . Palestine must be the national home for the Jewish people once more . . . the Allies are giving the land of Israel to the people of Israel. Every local Jewish heart is now filled with joy for this great History. Will you join them and help to build a Jewish homeland in Palestine? Stop fighting the Allies, who are fighting for you, for all Jews, for the freedom of all the small nations. Remember! An Allied victory means the Jewish peoples return to Zion . . .

And, with a fine sense of balance the British proclaimed in the Middle East on the occasion of the capture of Baghdad that 'the Arab race may rise once more to greatness and renown amongst the peoples of the earth . . . that you may unite with your kinsmen in the North,

East, South and West in realizing the aspirations of your race.'

Vague? Yes, of course, but as propaganda, all the better since every man could fill in his interpretation.

The Impact of World War I

At this point, another thread must be woven into our pattern. Not only were Jews and Arabs pushed by worsening relations with their erstwhile masters in Russia and the Ottoman Empire and encouraged by their self-proclaimed protector but both began to taste the seductive apple of success and fame. However few they were, the Zionists were courted by kings and however weak their armies or dubious their religious mission, the Arabs were proclaimed allies of the great nations. Even small victories by partisan forces became great military triumphs and a hero, admittedly an English one, was brought forward in the person of T.E. Lawrence ('Lawrence of Arabia') to give that flicker of romance to war as it ought to be — far from the mud and stench of the trenches of France.

While the Zionists formed military units which gained experience and confidence of great use in the years to come, it was the Arabs who reaped the favour and publicity: British officers were attached to their forces; flags were hung; arms and treasure were handed over to them; and various small victories lent them an air of gravity and legitimacy. These factors brought into being a new political reality on which a seal was placed when the British Government decided to allow the Arab forces under the Sharif (later King) Faisal, (brother of Abdullah) the military leader of the Revolt, the honour of being the first troops to enter the city of Damascus and there to proclaim an Arab government.

The capture of Damascus was of double importance: on the one hand it convinced the Arabs that they could rule themselves and gave them a national myth — of having achieved their own independence. On the other hand, the fact that the less developed, culturally more backward Arabs of the Arabian peninsula and the Syrian hinterland were accorded so much attention, so much assistance and then finally the accolade of political legitimacy stimulated in the more advanced and naturally envious Egyptians an even greater desire for independence and for a voice in world affairs commensurate with their evaluation of themselves. Thus, as the war ended, the Egyptian population, fattened by years of prosperity and frustrated by the restrictions of martial law and censorship, exploded in demands for British withdrawal, full membership in the family of nations and a voice at the great peace conference announced for Paris. A delegation of Egyptians gathered under the leadership of the foremost Egyptian nationalist, Saad Zaghlul, to go to Paris. But no longer in need of help to win a war, the British found the Egyptians merely annoying and from long years of ruling them deprecated both their courage and their ability. Whether called a protectorate or something else, they really thought of Egypt as a colony and meant to keep it one. Already embarrassed by their several conflicting commitments in the Asian parts of the Middle East, the British had no wish to be further embarrassed. And so far they had promised nothing: for the Egyptians there were no Balfour Declarations or Hussein-McMahon letters. So the British simply arrested and deported the members of the delegation. But the Egyptians this time did not slink away to sulk. Cairo and Alexandria streets filled with rioting students. Nationalism was still a movement of the educated few and the majority of the rioters were members of the privileged classes, so the government turned upon them the canes of the native riot police in whose eyes the self-proclaimed nationalists were merely spoiled young dandies talking nonsense as they broke windows and burned street-cars.

Only in Libya, where the issues were both more simple and opposite, did the war continue: there, distant and now defeated Turkey was seen as a champion of freedom while Italy, an Allied Power, was the hated invader. But, to the Libyans, nationalism had a special meaning, fading from the memory of other Arabs, it was centred on religion and personified by the bedouin tribes. This was something almost un-understandable to the Egyptian or the Syrian by 1919, and this fact alone puts Libya outside the mainstream of the politics of the Middle East.

Thus it was that, at the end of World War I, the Middle East entered a new stage in which the beginnings of national identification and independence had been shaped by Zionists, tribesmen and villagers from Arabia, former army officers in Iraq, lawyers and civil servants in Egypt, bedouin and religious men in Libya and by army officers and lawyers in the Levant. Contrary to all these forces, however, were the interests of the major powers, particularly Britain and France. For the one, already in 1919, petroleum loomed large and for the other, as ever, national glory was the grail at the end of the middle sea.

THE STRUGGLE FOR INDEPENDENCE

The 30 years from the end of World War I until approximately 1950 was for both Jews and Arabs the time of struggle for national independence. It was the time in which the nation states as we now know them took form and most contemporary issues were brought in focus. While details of many of the events have receded from our memories, in issue after issue these years can be seen to be critical to contemporary understanding.

When the war ended, each of the major allies and each of the Middle Eastern groups had documents or a proclamation upon which to base its claim: in the ensuing years these documents became virtually theological texts upon which a generation of learned men wrote commentaries and glosses and argued over the meanings of obscure phrases. The documents were treated as though Revelation. Never, curiously, did the Zionists or the Arabs seriously challenge the right of the British (although the Arabs violently challenged the right of the French) to give or withhold national independence of the Zionist homeland in Palestine. Even the most violent of politicians adopted the guise of theologian, analysing and dissecting the Writ to derive from it the Truth (or at least that part of the truth of value to him) upon which to judge the actions of the British and French. In their time, the British appeared to both Jews and Arabs as wise, strong and right-minded and both Zionists and Arab nationalists looked to them as guides to lead the way to the promised land. Tragically, the British were to lead both to the same land.

Conflicting Theologies

As the Paris Peace Conference began, the British privately sought to mesh their already conflicting commitments to the Jews and Arabs with those made to the French. The French, as theologically minded as the Zionists and the Arabs, were unwilling, of course, to give up their Holy Writ and accused the British of deception. The Foreign Office text of a confrontation between Prime Minister Lloyd George and Premier Georges Clemenceau on 15 September 1919, now published, is an astonishing diplomatic document. Not that Clemenceau said much. He did not need to debate the morality of the French position since he held a trump card: the British had acquired an area in what became northern Iraq, by military force, after having concluded an armistice with Turkey. Although their title was dubious, to say the least, the British did not want to surrender it because they thought it highly promising for oil exploration (and they were right). To secure their title, the British subsequently bought off the Turks by granting them a portion of the oil revenues but the French price was higher − the French insisted that Britain honour the Sykes-Picot accord by placing Lebanon and Syria under French control.

Lebanon was not a major problem since it could be argued that most of what became Lebanon was excluded. The Balfour Declaration was vague in its key phrase (a national home . . . *in Palestine*) even if parts of what the Zionists then claimed were to be included in French-ruled Lebanon. To the Arabs, the British had made more explicit commitments, including the right of self-determination and promises of Arab self-rule, but the key documents, the Hussain-McMahon correspondence, excluded the area 'west of Damascus' and while one might quibble over the imprecision, presumably the Ottoman provinces of Mount Lebanon and Beirut were intended.

Syria was a different matter. Not only was it clearly promised to the Arabs, it already had a functioning Arab government to which the British paid a subsidy and had seconded and attached military and civil personnel. Moreover, Syria had been captured partly by Arab forces in battle in the Allied cause and much had been made of the Arab seizure of Damascus from the Turks. Commitments were both too public and too current merely to brush aside. But the French demands were too insistent and too important to deny. In the event, the British in biblical fashion stood aside. They cut the subsidy they were paying Faisal, whose government had not had the time or administration to collect taxes for the money it needed to survive, and withdrew their personnel and military units in the full knowledge that the French had been massing troops in Beirut to invade Syria. They urged Faisal, regardless of old promises, to face reality and compromise with the French before it was too late − Britain, Faisal was pointedly told in November 1918, would not confront France over Syria.

Faisal vacillated. He was trapped between the reality of the weakness of his state and the image which he and the British had conjured. His followers at the critical moment chose to believe the myth and allowed him no room for compromise. Faisal was further disadvantaged by his inexperience and isolation − even his aides were British officers. Where could he turn for advice or support untainted by French or British high policy considerations? Where indeed? As ironic as it now seems to Arabs *and* Israelis, he was courted by and in turn sought the help of

Zionists.

When Faisal went to London in December 1918, he consulted with Chaim Weizmann, whom he had met the previous June in what is now Jordan and who had then assured him that a Jewish Palestine would be of the greatest help to an Arab kingdom and that the Zionists did not aim at setting up a separate government in London. Faisal signed an agreement for co-operation the main basis of which was a Jewish offer to help him against the French. Cautiously, Faisal made his agreement conditional on the success of the Zionist effort to stop the French.

One of the beguiling 'ifs' of history is how different the Middle East might have been had this agreement come to fruition! But it was not to be. The French could not be deterred by the Jews and the British would not stop them. Britain and France concluded their deal — which was subsequently to be ratified at the San Remo Conference in April 1920. Faisal might twist and turn but the noose hung. He had nowhere to go but into exile. A French invasion took care of the Syrian problem (at least for the British) but the episode poisoned Franco-Arab and Franco-British relations throughout the 1920s and 1930s.

Britain's relationship with the Zionists was not susceptible to such an easy if morally dubious resolution. There were no oil fields to be swapped for territorial recognition and the British Government felt uneasy about its agreements. Even if they were still largely secret, the conflicting commitments worried the statesmen. The Cabinet minutes are filled with notes which sound surprisingly naive, such as Lord Balfour's 'I do not believe that Dr. Weizmann has ever *publicly* asked.' 'As far as I know Weizmann has never put forward a claim for the Jewish Government of Palestine. Such a claim is in my opinion certainly inadmissible.' These were not public statements but highly confidential and so presumably frank notes among those who had devised British policy, a policy as Weizmann once remarked which was secured after he personally had conducted at least 2,000 interviews with British officials. On 11 August 1919, in an attempt to face the dilemmas created by wartime urgencies, Lord Balfour wrote one of the most candid and remarkable documents in any government archive. In part it read:

France, England, and America have got themselves into a position over the Syrian problem so inextricably confused that no really neat and satisfactory issue is now possible for any of them.

The situation is affected by five documents . . . Each can be quoted by Frenchmen and Englishmen, Americans and Arabs when it happens to suit their purpose. Doubtless each will be so quoted

before we come to a final arrangement about the Middle East.
. . . The four Great Powers are committed to Zionism. And
Zionism, be it right or wrong, good or bad, is rooted in age-long
traditions, in present needs, in future hopes, of far profounder import than the desires and prejudices of the 700,000 Arabs who now
inhabit that ancient land . . . Whatever deference should be paid to
the views of those who live there, the Powers in their selection of a
mandatory do not propose, as I understand the matter, to consult
them. In short, so far as Palestine is concerned, the Powers have
made no statement of fact which is not admittedly wrong, and no
declaration of policy which, at least in letter, they have not always
intended to violate.

So what to do? As Lord Balfour realised, one thing was clear: do not
consult the natives. When President Wilson sought to do this, France
opposed and Britain did not co-operate. Unilaterally, the United States
sent the King-Crane Commission to the Middle East to ask what the
people there wanted. There was no really effective means to ascertain
local opinion, but the answer the Commission received was so loud that
it should have been clear: under no circumstances did anyone want the
French in the Middle East. Independence was the preference and an
American mandate the compromise. America had considered accepting
a mandate over the Armenians, but already popular weariness with the
great issues was undercutting Wilson's political position and his health
was deteriorating. He probably never read the report of his Commis-
sioners. An American mandate was never even considered and the
British and French got on with the job. The former had already established a military administration of conquered territories which performed most of the functions government traditionally undertook. But
administration is quite different from government in the profound
sense of achievement of policy through politics. There, the British
found themselves caught by the very ambiguities of the pronouncements and the divisions among their officials. The famous comma of
the Balfour Declaration manifested itself from the beginning, and
throughout their thirty years in Palestine.

Large numbers of the British officers on the spot were disturbed by
Zionism. Jewish settlers felt, then and later, that British officers, accustomed to 'natives', found it psychologically almost impossible to deal
with European, sophisticated Jews, who as 'natives' had to be administered but who spoke their language, knew their mores, often were culturally superior. One could neither bully them nor develop the sort of

rough camaraderie one could with 'old Ahmad . . . A bloody fine chap and a crack shot . . .'. Generally, no matter how harshly the British dealt with the Arabs — which was harshly indeed in times of disturbance — they enjoyed a hearty familiarity which they were never to achieve with the Jews. But at the same time, the British Government chose to implement a policy which the Arabs saw as completely pro-Zionist: already under the military administration, some 5,000 Jewish immigrants were admitted into Palestine and sale was permitted, by absentee landlords, some of whom were not even in the British area, of several villages of Arabs to individual Jews and Zionist organisations. Symbolically, and perhaps to set a tone with the English officers, the Government appointed as first High Commissioner Sir Herbert Samuel, a prominent English Jewish supporter of Zionism. With the transfer to civil administration, the Jewish National Fund and the Palestine Land Development Co. Ltd were allowed immediately to purchase seven Arab villages in Galilea, from which the resident Arabs were evicted, and an immigrant quota of 16,500 for the coming year was announced. Within the year, Arab attacks on Jews and Jewish settlements began and, in May 1921, the government suspended further immigration. A tremendously important precedent had been set: violence could temporarily change policy.

Equally important, however, the events of 1921 showed that even when the reasons for violence had been officially determined, the long-term policy would not change. A clash between the Jewish and Arab communities, along lines perceived by Lord Kitchener, was inevitable and would continue. Neither the Arabs nor the Zionists could, or would, back off: each had its sacred text, as Balfour had realised, and each was fired by a vision and sustained by a transcendent moral justification. The Jewish settlers, as the Israeli writer Amos Elon deftly describes and quotes them, were marching not only to a different drummer but marching almost in a trance. The ideal of the Third Aliya or wave of immigrants, who arrived at this time, was set by the *Kibbutz* movement and by the labour brigades: the immigrants threw themselves into Zionism like secular worker monks. They thought of themselves, in the words of Joseph Trumpeldor, as

men prepared to do everything . . . men who have no interests and no habits . . . Bars of iron, elastic but iron. Metal that can be forged to whatever is needed for the national machine. A wheel? I am the wheel. If a nail, a screw or a flying wheel are needed — take me! Is there a need to dig the earth? I dig. Is there need to shoot, to be a soldier? I am a soldier . . .

Judged by the moral imperative such men felt, the Arabs were irrelevant or, if relevant, misguided. The Arab *élite* was seen to be thoughtless, selfish, a recreation of that very way of life and class which, in Russia, had been the essence of repression, anti-semitism, exploitation. Trumpeldor the ancestor of the 'hawks' was himself killed in a clash with Arab villagers. The philosophically 'liberal', whom I.F. Stone has called 'the other Zionists', mused that 'perhaps if the Arabs were also liberated, perhaps if their poor could see what they might achieve too, perhaps if they experienced the thrill of working shoulder to shoulder with the Zionists, perhaps . . .' And, as for the British, thought the Zionists of all persuasion: they were of faint heart, finding the Jews useful, as so many others had in the past, but not truly at one with the new cause. Their lives were thin, official, bloodless. One must work around rather than with them. This assessment as the early Zionist leader Max Nordeau had once remarked was the reason for the choice of the curious phase 'national home' rather than state or nation in the Balfour Declaration. But Jewish hard work and investment was beginning to show results. Some pride was justified.

Precisely at this point, the British began to pull back. Winston Churchill, then Colonial Secretary decided to attempt to clarify the limits of policy, discipline the Jews, bring order to the Arabs, and consolidate the British position throughout the Middle East. In 1922 he moved to separate Transjordan from the Palestine Mandate and to create a new government in Iraq; regarding the Palestine issue, he said

> Unauthorized statements have been made to the effect that the purpose [of the Balfour Declaration] . . . is to create a wholly Jewish Palestine. Phrases have been used [by Dr Weizmann among other Zionist leaders] such as that Palestine is to become 'as Jewish as England is English.' His Majesty's Government regard any such expectation as impracticable and have no such aim in view . . . They would draw attention to the fact that the terms of the Declaration referred to do not contemplate that Palestine as a whole should be converted into a Jewish National Home, but that such a Home should be founded in Palestine.

That continued to be the British dilemma: it could satisfy neither the Arabs nor the Zionists. Perhaps if the British had come down clearly on one side or the other, the problem might have subsided or even been resolved. It is tempting to add, from hindsight, that fewer people would then have been hurt; but, of course, from a contemporary point of view, already too many people would have been hurt for the damage to be then acceptable on either side. It seemed to the British that the best they could do was to hang on to that comma while trying to help with both ends of the Balfour Declaration.

In part, Transjordan was created in this spirit: the area was clearly 'Arab' both in terms of the Hussein-McMahon correspondence and in reality. A bothersome situation had arisen when the brother of the Sharif Faisal, Sharif (later King) Abdullah, gathered a small force and set out for Syria, reportedly to avenge his brother's humiliation. Their relations with the French already strained, the British sought to stop him and to show British good faith by tying Abdullah to an anchor, the rulership of Transjordan. But, as the British on the spot knew — which neither the early Zionists nor the British Government at home apparently appreciated — there was almost no connection between the nomadic and the semi-nomadic bedouin of the Transjordan steppe and the settled, agricultural villages of the Palestinian hills. The relationship of the two sides of the Jordan was an issue which would arise again, with tragic consequences in the Jordanian civil war of 1970, but, in 1922, the recognition of Transjordan made a greater impact upon the Jewish community of Palestine (which had some territorial claims across the Jordan) than upon the Arab community.

The British turned back to Palestine with a new proposal. Having failed in 1921 to promulgate a constitution to create a bi-national state, they offered each of the two communities an 'agency'. The Jewish community immediately seized the opportunity and skilfully made of its agency a shadow government which helped to focus community efforts and to give its leaders valuable experience in statecraft. The Arabs set a precedent for what became a major theme of their politics on Palestine: they rejected the British offer. Not a useful political stance in the long run, rejection deprived them of the experience of manning a shadow government and training responsible leaders, losses for which they paid a heavy price in the following years and for which, indeed, they are still suffering.

The French in Syria and the Lebanon

Meanwhile, as we have seen, events in Syria came rapidly to a violent conclusion. The French army, some 90,000 strong, moved into Syria and brushed aside the comparatively tiny Arab force. Faisal was exiled and the French, unhindered by the doubts and conflicts of the British in Palestine, set out to restructure what they had seized. On 1 September 1920, the French established 'Grande Liban' (Greater Lebanon), a state about four times the size of the Ottoman province of Mount Lebanon. The French aim, as everyone realised, was to build a secure, pro-French, Christian state on the coast. In a double sense, this inflicted Lebanon with scars which have become infected over the years and resulted, in part, in the 1976-9 civil war: on the one hand, Lebanon was made, in Arab-Muslim eyes, a quisling state, fattened off Syria, because pro-imperalist and Christian; on the other hand, the relatively stable, predominantly Christian nucleus, Mount Lebanon, was diluted and weakened by the addition of Muslim areas so that what had been a 10:1 Christian majority faded, in a short time, to more like 10:8 or even 10:9. When account is taken of the fact that each of the Muslim and Christian communities is divided internally amongst various mutually hostile, quasi-national sects, the country can be seen to have been deprived of a significant majority. This was to have profound internal political repercussions.

In Syrian (and Lebanese Muslim) eyes, France had conquered an independent state, a wartime ally, in contravention of its own public commitments and in flagrant violation of the spirit of the peace. Then, immediately, it 'balakanised' its conquest: not only was Lebanon, long a semi-autonomous province, set apart and enlarged at the expense of the rest of Syria, but Syria proper was carved into four states — Aleppo, Damascus, Latakia (where the Alawite peoples live) and Jabal Duruz (where many of the Druze people live). In 1923, another area was split off and later given to Turkey. The Syrians predictably reacted bitterly, and the French showed almost no sensitivity to their pride or patriotism.

In Lebanon, as might be expected, the situation was almost the mirror image: many Christians hailed the establishment of Grande Liban as an achievement of national aspiration. The French were thus able to identify the country with them and their policy. Building on a century of Catholic and French education, they cultivated a class from which they could draw administrators and political leaders. French became the second language and, in cultural and intellectual affairs, even surplanted Arabic. The Lebanese were told (and told themselves) that their equivalent of 'the existing non-Jewish communities' was not Arab at all, like the Syrians, but Phoenician. After all Sidon, Tyre, Beirut, Junieh were historic Phoenician ports and many of the villages and towns of Lebanon had names of non-Arab origin; and the Lebanese had never lost the Mediterranean, commercial outlook of their Phoenician ancestors. The Maronite Church came as close as any institution to being 'national'. (All this was true — and true not only for Lebanon: if one applied similar standards, neither Iraq nor Egypt nor even Syria was 'Arab'. Just as the 'existing non-Jewish communities' of Palestine could be regarded as descendants of the Aramaic-speaking peasantry who were its oldest inhabitants, so both Iraq and Egypt were Arabised rather than Arab. Obviously, these thoughts cut to the root of the incipient Arab nationalism and were regarded by nationalists as profoundly subversive and sinister.)

In Lebanon, at least, opposition to the French subsided and the French, with all the cards in their hands, could afford a generosity beyond their means in Syria. In 1926, they proclaimed the establishment of the Lebanese Republic. Lebanon was the success story of the French mandate system.

The precedent of Lebanon set a standard for Syria, and two years after the adoption of the Lebanese constitution, Syria was granted the right to hold a constituent assembly. Dominated by the nationalists, however, the Assembly drafted a constitution which gave no recognition to the French mandate. In anger the French prorogued the Assembly and put forward their own draft of a constitution. As a sop to the nationalists, they reunified the areas of Damascus and Aleppo but established the Alawite area as a separate republic and left the Druze state under a separate administration. The French then summoned another parliament, this time elected with considerable 'guidance', to ratify a Franco-Syrian treaty. Even this hand-picked assembly refused to act as the French wished. To garner votes, the French unified the Alawite and Druze areas. At that point, in 1936, the Syrian popular assembly ratified the treaty, but, ironically after all these efforts, France itself never ratified it.

Looking back, one can trace the origin and growth of the Syrian paranoia toward external interventions in their affairs and of the fear they have exhibited when they perceive attempts to stress their internal differences. However much Syrians have clashed over matters of ideology, their fears of divisiveness form the bedrock of their nationalism, encouraging strong identification with the Arab cause and feelings of envy and disdain for small but wealthy Lebanon. These attitudes and memories were profoundly to affect the Syrian attitude during the Lebanese Civil War in 1976-8.

Perhaps even more crucial for the long term in Syrian affairs was the violence and impermanence of the French rule. Unable to secure an acquiescence to their presence the French punished and intimidated the Syrians with artillery bombardments of Damascus in 1925, 1926 and 1945. Martial law was the norm. Force was flaunted. During most of the 1920s the French kept over 50,000 troops in the mandate.

It is perhaps on these points that the contrast with British administration in Iraq and Transjordan becomes most noticeable.

Both the British and the French brought to the Middle East experience from other colonial areas. The British, in a century of trial and error in India, where they had inherited the Muslim Moghul empire, trained not only a remarkable collection of individuals of great personal charisma and skill but also created an administration which must rank among the most economical and benign examples of foreign rule Since the Sepoy Rebellion in the middle of the nineteenth century, the British had taken so direct a hand in all aspects of administration that there was no field in which they did not have a cadre of highly skilled personnel.

At the lower reaches of the government, they supplemented their own people with Indian clerks. Thus they were able to cope with the supply and administrative problems of their army during the war and subsequently to embark upon civil administration fully staffed. In contrast, the French brought with them a largely African experience Many of the troops in Syria were from Senegal and, although Muslim by background, were regarded with disdain and fear by the Syrian population. The senior officers of the French administration, most of whom were graduates of a Black African experience, tended to treat the 'natives' in a high-handed and insulting way. It is said, for example, that the Druze Revolt in 1925 could have been prevented if, at the right moment, the senior French officer had offered a cup of coffee to the man who became its leader. Both the British and the French administrations, like the previous Ottoman administration, were remarkably *laissez-faire* by the standards of our own times; but where the French differed from the British was in their lack of finesse and attention to the little elements of local etiquette. The British lacked the great strength of the French overseas cultural push, combined as it often was with the religious mission of Roman Catholicism, but the British profited by paying attention to, indeed being genuinely interested in, local customs, language and history. Several of the senior officers of the British administration in India were outstanding scholars and their knowledge of Arabic, regardless of rank or post or political purpose was a passport to local popular esteem. Even so arrogant a figure as the chief of the British military administration in Iraq, Sir Arnold Wilson was an accomplished linguist who, as a result of many years of Indian Government service in the Persian Gulf, had written substantial scholarly works on the Middle East.

But Iraq and Syria were then, as they remain today, profoundly different countries. Syria was caught up in the Arab nationalist rebellion during World War I and had ample reason to dislike the Ottoman Government. Exposed to issues of nationalism, French intervention and the challenge of Zionism, the Syrians were much more politicised. Iraq looked more to the east — a substantial portion of the Iraqi population identified with Persia in religion (both being Shii Muslim); Basra was effectively an Indian Ocean port; and the northern part of Iraq, economically, culturally and socially, was more Turkish than Arab. The tribal element in Iraq was much more numerous and politically important than in Syria. Lastly, although the Iraqis were not so aware of it, at least in the early stages of the British administration, Iraq had a separate and deep tradition going back to the earliest recorded urban civilisation in Sumer. The Iraqis, like the Egyptians, would ultimately find in their neighbourhood rather than — or as well as — in Arabdom a source of national pride and identification.

The British in Iraq

The British came to Iraq earlier and under different circumstances than the French to Syria and this, also, was greatly to influence the nature of the régimes. While the French were to stifle and oust an essentially popular, or at least native, government, Britain's intention in Iraq was to liberate the country, to oust the Ottoman Empire and to help the local population find a new national identification. The war in Iraq was not easy for the British. It cost them four years and nearly 50,000 casualties. As they inched toward Baghdad, the British troops had to live largely off the land. Because shipping was in short supply, they had to buy as much as possible locally and thus the war created for the first time a national market. Intelligent Iraqis found that they could profit from this new opportunity. Those who co-operated were naturally assisted and encouraged to take a larger part in public affairs.

From their Indian experience, the British hit upon a device for keeping public order — to make the head of a tribe responsible for his fellows. But Iraqi tribal society was profoundly different from the Pathans of the Northwest Frontier: politically and economically Iraq had no 'tribes' in the Indian sense and no tribal chiefs. The effect of the British policy was to *create* tribal leaders in whom they vested ownership of tribal lands and to whom they gave money, authority and, from time to time, military force to control the tribesmen. Without realising it, the administrators set in motion what was tantamount to a social revolution like the enclosures of sixteenth-century England. In the few years of British rule, previously free tribesmen found their political and social positions sinking toward serfdom. Indeed, at the end of the British period, the Iraqi government promulgated a law which, perhaps uniquely in the twentieth century, actually created a government-enforced serfdom.

At first almost everyone co-operated with enthusiasm in the war-generated prosperity, but as the war drew to a close the army market contracted. A minor economic slump followed and all of the pent-up anxieties, hostilities and ambitions erupted. On 30 June 1920, a vast tribal uprising broke out all over Iraq. It was a sort of Iraqi version of the Sepoy Rebellion: railroad lines were cut, trains derailed and tele-graph lines ripped down. The army, caught off guard and depleted by peacetime reductions, took four months to crush the rebellion. As T.E. Lawrence bitterly remarked at the time, suppression of the Iraqi revolt cost more than six times as much as was spent during the war to stimulate the Revolt in the Desert. Nearly 10,000 tribesmen were killed before the tribes gave up.

No British Government in those weary and impoverished times could sustain a policy in far-off Iraq which was so expensive. Wisely, the British recognised that the best way to succeed in Iraq was by encouraging the *form* of popular independence while preserving the substance of a discreet British control. A shrewd new High Commis-sioner, Sir Percy Cox was installed and he immediately and remarkably sought a new source of strength for the government by encouraging some 250 young Iraqis who had served with the wartime guerrilla army to return to Iraq. From this unlikely source Cox and his successors skilfully created a pro-British new ruling *élite*. Those who would not compromise were exiled and an election was engineered to bring to Iraq as king Sharif Faisal, the leader of the Arab Revolt and recent king of Syria. So remarkable was the success of this policy that in almost un believable contrast to the French in Syria, the British were able to rule Iraq for twelve years with only a few score Englishmen. On those occas ions when force was required, a combination of the Royal Air Force and trucks armed with machine guns, highly mobile, cheap and incon spicuous, was invincible against the bedouin tribes and the Kurdish hillsmen.

To the south, the vast plains, steppes and desert of the Arabian Pen insula stretched almost beyond the imagination of settled men. Com munications were primitive and much of the peninsula was inaccessibl to wheeled transport. Central Arabia was a month camel ride away from Baghdad or Damascus. Along their line of demarcation, the British pre ferred to rely upon the modern equivalent of the frontier guards used by the Persian and Roman empires two millennia before: local bedouin recruited, subsidised and armed to hold back the raging torrents of the Arabian peninsula. It hardly seemed worth more effort. Not until petroleum was found, many years later, was the wealth of the Arabian Peninsula appreciated. At the time, Arabia was merely a vast waterless wilderness and, so long as no one else tried to intervene, the British and the French were delighted to leave it alone. Poverty gave Arabia its freedom.

Egypt, the Sudan and Libya

The Sudan and Libya were quite different matters. The Sudan had been effectively ruled by Britain since 1898, when it crushed the Islamic reformist rebellion of the Mahdi and his 'fuzzy-wuzzies'. Technically a 'condominium' of Egypt and England, the Sudan was practically a colony of Great Britain. There the British promoted a giant agricultural scheme, the Gezira Project, which created a reasonably prosperous native middle class, but in general they were content to administer the vast areas of desert, plain and swamp rather than attempt to modernise it.

The Italian approach to Libya was more extreme than the French to Syria. In classical times, Libya had been a reasonably prosperous province of the Roman Empire, but long years of overgrazing, neglect and possibly some climatic change had reduced the fertile fringe of the Mediterranean to a mere strip. Most of Libya, like the Arabian Peninsula, was usable only by nomadic bedouin and was regarded as of so little value that it was not even involved in the European powers' scramble for empire. Only the Italians found this scrap of offal appetising. On 3 October 1911 their fleet bombarded Tripoli and put ashore a landing party. The local Turks immediately retreated and the jubilant Italians celebrated their easy victory. They were nearly 20 years premature. Despite landing three divisions and using, for the first time, air power (when an Italian pilot tossed a hand grenade out of his cockpit at a tribesman on 1 November 1911), the Italians became bogged down in a remorseless guerrilla war. It was not until the 1930s when the Italian General Graziani virtually starved the country into submission and 'regrouped' the population into concentration camps that the war faltered to a halt. The Italians were never able to utilise Libya because they were never able to lure very many of their own people to settle in it. The climate was harsh, the soil was thin and the crops were essentially the same as those known in Italy. As a venture in colonialism, Libya was a disaster.

Egypt was an ancient and culturally sophisticated country and its then roughly five million acres of agricultural land were some of the richest in the world. The population, at the end of World War I about 13 million (one third of today's), could easily be supported with a substantial excess for export. The war had invigorated the economy, the population was docile, and the politicians, although noisy and obstreperous, could be managed. At least that is what the British thought until they were caught by the uprisings of 1919. Once that storm had been ridden, however, life continued much as it had before. The British, after all, had been in Egypt since 1882 and all of the key positions in the Egyptian Government were either staffed by or supervised by European, mainly British, 'advisers'. Moreover, there was a large native *élite* who, while culturally and linguistically attached to France, were willing to co-operate. Nation building seemed largely achieved or could be left until 'tomorrow'. Thus, provided the British were willing to play the game of the city-based politicians and the Turkish-speaking royal family, it was possible, without a great expenditure of money or men, to control the country satisfactorily.

As a largely cosmetic device, the British, on 28 February 1922 unilaterally announced the independence of Egypt but left 'absolutely reserved' matters concerning British imperial communications, defence, protection of minorities and foreign interests, and the Sudan. In all other matters Britain appeared ready to allow the Egyptians a large degree of freedom. In the Egyptian view, however, these five issues were central while the fringe freedoms were meaningless. Thus, when the national leader Zaghlul Pasha, Egypt's choice as the representative to the 1919 Peace Conference and the leader of the Wafd party, was allowed to return from a second exile in September 1922, he won an overwhelming electoral victory for the new parliament with 190 of its 214 seats. Zaghlul was named Prime Minister and his first task was to negotiate a new treaty with the British. He refused to do so within the limits of the 'absolutely reserved' points. Withdrawn from the negotiation and, thinking he was on the threshold of victory, he ordered his party into the streets again. In the anger and panic, the British officer who was commander of the Egyptian army and Governor-General of the Sudan, Sir Lee Stack, was assassinated in Cairo on 19 November 1923. Using this event as a pretext, and no doubt also disturbed and enraged, the British presented an ultimatum to the Egyptian Government in the most insulting possible terms demanding 'ample apology' and 'condign punishment' for the guilty, suppression of all 'popular political demonstrations', a fine of £500,000, withdrawal of all Egyptian officers from the Sudan within 24 hours *and* Egyptian agreement that Sudanese farmers could draw an unlimited amount of water from the Nile. The earlier points were serious but the latter appeared to strike at the very spinal column of Egypt's economy. In the face of this un-expectedly violent reaction, the Egyptian Government immediately agreed to apologise, to punish the criminals, and to pay the fine but refused Britain's other demands. Undeterred, the British moved ahead, ejected the Egyptian officers from the Sudan, seized the Alexandria customs as a bond for compliance with its demands and threatened to shoot hostages in the event of any other popular reaction. Powerless but still proud, the Egyptian Prime Minister resigned and was replaced by a puppet government. Immediately thereafter the Wafd-dominated parliament was dissolved and a new, carefully chosen slate was put up for election. Even then, the Wafd party won almost half of the seats. Undeterred, the British dissolved parliament and called yet another election. Thoroughly angry the Egyptians gave the Wafd almost three-quarters of the seats. The British threatened further reprisals and the 67-year-old Zaghlul, undoubtedly fearful of yet another period of exile which would probably be his last, gave up and settled down to enjoy, as well as he could, the power, prestige and wealth of his position. He was not the last nationalist leader in the Middle East to take this sen-sible course. Indeed, the entire Wafd party quickly became tarnished with scandal. In a sense, the failure of Egypt was exactly the opposite of the failure of Syria; whereas Syria found no way of accommodating even to the degree of getting valuable experience in self rule, the Egyptian Government co-operated so far as to lose any semblance of self-respect. These factors were to yield a bitter harvest in the years to come.

The Palestine Mandate

In the Palestine Mandate, the British were forced to rule, being unable to implement the constitution they had promulgated in 1921, since the Arabs and Zionists would not co-operate in a bi-national state.

There is a fairly close correlation between the rise of Jewish immi-gration and that of Arab hostility. Until about 1925 both had steadily increased, but from 1926 Jewish immigrants declined in number and since there was a steady exodus — with often more than half of the new settlers leaving after a short period — in 1927 the total number of Jewish residents in Palestine actually declined. The Palestinian Arabs relaxed in the belief that the Zionist movement was melting away before their eyes. However, from 1929, the economic situation in Europe brought about a sharp reversal of these trends and the number of Jewish immigrants suddenly increased. With it increased the tempo and the degree of Arab hostility. A demonstration in Jerusalem in the old city was followed by large-scale Arab attacks on Jews throughout the Mandate. Alarmed, the British government set up a commission of inquiry, the first of many in that much studied decade. This so-called Shaw Commission set a precedent for subsequent commissions by reporting that the conflict between the Arab and Jewish communities was a direct result of the disappointment of Palestine Arab hopes for independence. It went on to say that Jewish expansion had created a 'landless and discontented' Arab group and urged that restrictions be imposed on the Jewish land acquisition programme which in effect extraterritorialised all land it purchased (since the land was no longer available for resale on the local market). While the results of the study could hardly have surprised the experienced senior British official in Palestine, the government was sufficiently concerned to appoint another commission to study the whole scope of the mandate and recommend a solution to the conflict. This commission essentially repeated the findings of the Shaw Commission, particularly emphasising the Arab fears of losing their country and urged an immediate halt to immigration. When the government accepted the recommendations and issued a White Paper reversing its Palestine policy, it met a storm of criticism from the Jewish community in Palestine and Zionists in Europe. The government at first equivocated and then ignominiously withdrew its policy paper — not even by announcing a new policy paper but merely by a letter from the Prime Minister to the London *Times*.

Meanwhile the Nazis had taken over power in Germany. Their already evident vicious anti-semitism began to cause the exodus of immigrants, mainly to the United States, but also increasingly to the Middle East. As a consequence, the Palestine Jewish community, frightened by the rise of Nazism and chaffing under what it regarded as an essentially unfriendly mandatory administration, protested and rioted; the Arabs, ill-informed about events in Europe and in any event unaffected by what Europeans did to each other, feeling justified in defending what they regarded as their homeland, and in the final analysis buoyed up by the findings of the various British commissions, also began to grow restive and sullen. In April 1936, apparently with little co-ordination, numbers of Arab villages appointed committees to organise their defence. These organisations coalesced into the Arab Higher Committee and all over the Palestine Mandate attacks took place on Jewish settlements. By the summer, Palestine was embroiled in a civil war which was to last for three years.

British policy came down on three points: first, to intervene militarily and exercise drum-head justice. Numbers of mayors of Palestinian villages were hanged and large numbers of houses containing or alleged to have contained Arab terrorists or nationalists or arms were razed. (Parenthetically, the law under which these draconian measures were undertaken forms a precedent for actions which the Israelis have undertaken in similar circumstances and for which they have recently been criticised by civil rights organisations, the Press and the US Department of State.) Second, the British assisted the Jewish community in forming a paramilitary organisation for the defence of their communities. It was this organisation, assisted in the first instance by the brilliant British tactician of guerrilla warfare, Orde Wingate, from which grew, subsequently, the *Haganah*, the Jewish underground army in the last days of the mandate, and finally the Israeli army. Third, the British appointed yet two more commissions to resolve their dilemma. The first, a Royal Commission under Lord Peel, arrived in November 1936 in the midst of the civil war, and rapidly concluded that co-operation between the Arabs and Jews in a Palestinian state was impossible. To the dismay of the Arabs, it recommended the partition of the Mandate. But partition, with the numbers and distribution of the population then in the Mandate, proved almost impossible. If the Jewish state were restricted to areas with a Jewish majority, it would be too small. If it were not restricted, the Arabs would rapidly become a majority even in the Jewish areas. The dilemma appeared almost inescapable so the British appointed another commission to try to find some better means of partitioning. Finally, on the eve of World War II, the British gave up on the idea of partition and announced that they would attempt to hold the balance, as uneasy and uncomfortable as it appeared, for ten years, after which time they would establish an independent Palestine state.

Just as World War I had started the whole process in the Middle East and gave it its initial formulation, so World War II was to provide opportunities that were to bring the process to a head and conclusion.

4 THE GROWTH OF CAPACITY

When Europeans began to visit the Middle East at the beginning of the nineteenth century, they found it poor, backward, lazy and quaint. Artists often sketched a sleeping peasant or indolent bedouin dwarfed by the ruins of a giant ancient temple. It was a sort of Middle Eastern 'old south' where all that was worthwhile had 'gone with the wind'. A great leap of imagination was required to imagine those who had built the temples and virtually created civilisation. At first few written records were available to help scholars envisage the old society, but gradually more have appeared and the picture becomes more detailed and complete. Recently, a remarkable collection of medieval Jewish papers, the Cairo Geniza documents, has been analysed to reveal the social and economic life of the eastern Mediterranean in the Middle Ages as never before. In them we can see the very reverse of the nineteenth century: the western traveller at the time of the Crusades was a poor fellow, gullible, illiterate and without polish. Coming to North Africa from a darkened Europe, he found himself in a great centre of commerce and industry. Centuries before Europe was quickened by the commercial revolutions of the Italian city states, Middle Eastern merchants were using bills of exchange, money orders, cheques and letters of credit. Some were issued by banking houses in the eastern part of what is today Iran and payable in what is today Spain. Credit and finance linked merchants deep in Africa with others thousands of miles and months of travel away in India. Rudimentary forms of insurance and limited partnerships flourished in Cairo three centuries before they were 'discovered' in Genoa and Venice.

But in the following centuries the Middle East turned its back on the sea and Europe, fracturing into tiny provinces so that few prospered as before. Sultan Saladin, known in the West as the redoubtable opponent of the Crusaders, set the fundamental economic policy of withdrawing from the sea since he could not protect his coasts from Christian pirates. His successors, poorer and weaker than he, first squeezed and then destroyed the flourishing commercial life. The dead hand of bureaucracy choked the restless spirit which had enriched it. Each retreat led to another. Poor governments impoverished their people and being poor people could not support their governments and the desperate governments further were unable to provide security so the people were forced into isolation or driven to lawlessness. Soon travel became so dangerous and expensive as to be impracticable and everyone cowered behind the town walls they could then hardly even maintain. Trade withered. Industry and agriculture dwindled. Damascus gave up damask and Toledo's steel rusted.

With the rounding of the Cape of Good Hope by the Portuguese the Middle East was no longer needed as the middleman in the spice trade: Europe bought direct at the source in the Far East. Lisbon replaced Cairo as the great market of South Asia and with Cairo fell the prosperity of Venice, Naples, Genoa, Marseilles and Barcelona. It was North Europe which quickly took up the impulses of the Renaissance. There the scale of society changed as the state replaced the city. Sheer mass and unprecedented organisational depth gave rise to new sources of industry, new possibilities of commerce, new breadth of agriculture and new effect of armies. The new scale was further multiplied by the remarkable individual drive toward worldly success that has been ascribed to the rise of Protestantism and capitalism. The English and Dutch sailors who had mastered the Atlantic soon bottled up the Islamic world in the Indian Ocean as well. The unleashing of yet a new source of energy, the nation-in-arms, came with the French Revolution. It engulfed Europe and spilled over into the Middle East where its effects were staggering — Napoleon's squares of disciplined, well armed and ordered infantry and artillery annihilated the medieval feudal cavalry of Egypt's rulers at the Battle of the Pyramids. The old order was shattered.

Among those who had witnessed this bloody demonstration of the new power was a young Albanian adventurer in the Sultan's service. After a complicated series of manoeuvres, Mehmet Ali seized the governorate of Egypt and maintained himself in power for almost half a century. A man of great sophistication and brilliance although lacking in education and almost totally uninterested in the traditions or culture of the people he ruled, Mehmet Ali began to borrow extensively from Europe. He sent dozens of missions of students and artisans to bring back the 'secrets' of European power. Upon their return, the scholars were forced to translate their school texts and the artisans were set to work in newly created industries. European experts and army officers were imported and encouraged to impart their knowledge and habits and even dress to the natives. The remnants of the old ruling caste were partly murdered, partly impoverished by confiscations and largely wasted by the military campaigns launched by the new government in Arabia, the Sudan, Greece, Syria and eventually in Turkey.

By the 1820s, Mehmet Ali had established a new order. Military in character, it was more than an army. He had shaken and recast at least the urban *élite* to staff a more state-directed, -owned, -supporting society than is imaginable today in almost any country outside the Communist world. There was one difference: the stage was the ruler himself. He was the sole merchant and landlord and Egypt was his estate. Industry was created solely to cater to state need and its principal need was to prevent the overthrow of the Pasha. So the army was the recipient and prime mover of the new organisation. It was to feed, house, equip, clothe and move the army that the modern sector of the economy was formed.

In all of this, there was no room for individual initiative. The state decided who would plough or build where, when, how long, for how much, and what would be the result of the activity. Prices were set, goods were virtually rationed. And the whim of the Pasha controlled all. This central and superior direction of the economic life of Egypt has set a pair of trends which still largely govern Middle Eastern attitudes toward the economy in most of the Arabic-speaking countries: on the one hand, the economy existed for and by the state. On the other hand, individual activity or initiative was regarded with suspicion. As the nineteenth century unfolded, this evaluation of the state and private initiative was fixed even more firmly. When the heavy hand of Mehmet Ali was removed and some relaxation was allowed in the state control of the economy, the sure and safe road to wealth was quickly staked out. It was not through investment, the creation of jobs or the introduction and development of new technologies. Rather it was through the grant of government favour. A wealthy man was one with political influence. A poor man was one without. The wealthy put money into land and even the poor dreamt almost exclusively of adding a few more square metres to their tiny domains. It would be long before these ideas would change and even today the entrepreneurs of Libya, Egypt, Syria and Iraq are few in number and, relatively speaking, passive in character. They rarely move except with the state — and that is indeed often the only way they can. Even in Saudi Arabia, where these trends were not early established or in Kuwait, where generations of commerce in the Persian Gulf and the Indian Ocean created different traditions, the role of the state is, from a Western perspective, entirely disproportionate to that of the individual. This tradition holds in the monarchies as well as in the revolutionary socialist states.

At the lower reaches of the society, the peasant farmer fervently wished and hoped only to be left alone. The appearance of a government official could only mean two things — conscription or taxation. Where they could, the villagers fled from the government and where they could not, they acquiesced in sullen defiance. The government carried out its functions (to defend the area from outside intrusion and to keep an acceptable degree of domestic public security) as well as it could, but it had few resources and found that to acquire more was an almost herculean effort. Tax collectors came with the whip in hand and escorted by armed troops. Where it could, the government subcontracted the functions of tax collection to 'farmers' who harvested the people just as the peasants themselves harvested the fields. To recruit men into the army often required elaborate ruses, ambush and kidnap. Conscripts almost always had to be taken away in chains and many mutilated themselves in the vain hope of escaping military service. The levying of conscripts or villagers provoked symbolic funerals in which 'widows' and mothers wailed to lament the effective death of their loved ones.

These experiences still today largely condition the attitude of populations toward governments and affect the capacity of government to mobilise and energise the people in the Arabic-speaking parts of the Middle East. It is the bane of today's planners just as it was probably the major factor which prevented the Middle East, despite a similar beginning, from following a road to development like Japan.

The Jewish Experience

In some ways the experience of the European Jewish community in the nineteenth century was similar but in others profoundly different. The nearly 5 million Jews who lived in Russia were, like the Egyptians, mainly villagers whose cultural and economic horizons were narrow and from which, as contemporary Yiddish writers said, they escaped only into a world of dreams. Preservation of rabbinical law was their main intellectual pursuit. But, unlike the Egyptians, they were not mired in the land. The Egyptian was wedded to the land and made comfortable by it; the Eastern European Jew, forbidden to own land, yearned for the security and status but his very yearning was a source of energy and activity. Both were backward and poor but the greater frustrations of the Jews combined as they undoubtedly were with other facts caused them, when the opportunity was thrust upon them by the pogroms of the late nineteenth century, to fall upon European culture with a voracious appetite. With no state to guide them, to protect them, or to entrap them in its embrace, large numbers of Jews made the transition in the space of a generation from the Pale of Settlement to the most sophisticated societies of that era. Evaluated by any criteria, their proportional performance in intellectual and creative matters is astonishing. Sons of pedlars advanced to the forefront of science. It was one of the aces in Chaim Weizmann's hand, as he lobbied for the Balfour Declaration, that he was an outstanding scientist, capable of contributing to the war effort.

Another point of contrast was to become increasingly important as the twentieth century unfolded: the sense of desperation. While poor, the Arabs generally lived in security. They were at home among their fellows and it was the government which was alien. The Jews, although 5 per cent of the population of Russia, were legally alien and lived amongst a population which constantly made them feel it. The Arabs could look back to a recent past of wealth and even glory; the Jews could look back too, and of course many did, but practically they knew that they could look only to themselves and their contemporaries. Often what they found among their contemporaries was a source of fear and desperation which drove them, painfully but powerfully, in a way unknown among the Arabs.

Third, whereas both Jews and Arabs traditionally found their intellectual lives in their classics and particularly in their religious literature, the experience of the Jews in the nineteenth century was, after a long period of frustration and intellectual hunger which they shared in part with other Russians, to be exposed to the hot house of European intellectual life. To capture the intensity of the experience, one need only read the great Russian novels. One can only speculate but it seems reasonable that the very classical education of the Jews had given them the powerful intellectual tools to plunge into European life. In contrast, the Arabs stayed put. Mehmet Ali started a policy which became self-perpetuating: technicians and experts and professionals came to the Middle East from Europe and performed the tasks along with but separate from the natives. They monopolised the new fields to an astonishing degree. Not only the technologies and sciences but even the more mundane modern tasks became their preserve. For the Arabs there was no sudden burst of learning, no sudden stimulus of ideas. Their world was comfortable but not invigorating, poor but not debilitating. Under the warm sun life went on, as it always had, without sudden discontinuity.

Thus is was that by the end of the nineteenth century, the experience of the Jews and Arabs came to be so markedly different and to affect differently the ways they approached nationalism, national identity, development and the evaluation of the possible. Zionism was to bring the energy, skill and resources of world Jewry to recreate the Kingdom of David; Arabism aimed to infuse and disseminate a larger sense of identity and a new vision of the possible. Much of the history of the ensuing years of this century are elaborations of this set of trends.

Jewish Land and Labour

As Herzl had told his readers in *Der Judenstaat* once sovereignty over a piece of the earth had been granted them, the Jews would do the rest themselves. In a sense, it was the *doing* itself which many thought to be the most important. Doing the job would reform, reshape, renew the Jews and strip from them the deformities and scars of the long exile in the ghettos of Europe. The early Zionists lamented being cut off from the land and from manual labour. A romantic assessment of the value of work with one's hands came to dominate the thinking of the early Zionists. *Avoda ivrit* (Hebrew labour) became a cardinal part of the Zionist philosophy. The early Zionists deplored the idea of going to a colonial area merely to exploit local labour. Thus, while large amounts of Arab labour was used in the construction of the Zionist settlements, the early Jewish settlers placed high value upon performing heavy labour themselves. Probably never before has the work ethic been so romantically and passionately adopted. The accounts of the early *kibbutzim* make them appear to have been virtually voluntary slave labour camps.

Associated with the work ethic was an assessment of the other side of the 'Jewish problem', the tyranny of land over people. In the perspective of the European experience, this was seen primarily as an aspect of Jews being excluded from the land and kept in cities and towns. Secondarily, particularly after the rise of the socialist movement, land was also seen as a tool of class oppression. Private ownership and private economic activity were thus associated with the cause of the terrible social ills of East Europe. The early, idealistic Zionist leaders did not wish to go to Palestine merely to become wealthy capitalists. They saw the task of Zionism to create communal societies wherein land would be held for the benefit of whole groups of people who would live, work and share together.

Jewish immigrants felt 'reborn' when they arrived in Palestine and many said with sad and unintended ironic comment on the later Nazi persecution that their children had become blonder and lighter of skin as they grew into the new homeland. There was an intensity that combined with skill to create by the 1930s a modern and vigorous Jewish community, one almost sealed off from the Arab community. One of the causes of the troubles of the early 1930s, according to British government studies, was precisely a result of these virtues. When the Jewish National Fund purchased land from the Arabs, Arabs were no longer allowed to work on it as they had under previous absentee land-lords. Hebrew labour, originally and in intent so liberalising and demo-cratising a concept thus came to be seen by the Arab community as apartheid.

The Zionists viewed the British administration as an anachronism, a galling form of veiled imperialism. They were annoyed at the 'colonial-ist' attitude of the administering Englishmen. While the British in no sense resembled their former Russian overlords, the Jews sensed in them an assumption of the 'white man's burden', which permeated, generally in a fairly benign fashion, the clubs as well as the govern-ment offices. What the Jews really wanted (when they had brought in enough immigrants to create a critical mass) was to get the British out of the way so they could 'get on with the job'. Almost all the British ordinances in Palestine, even those most pro-Zionist, were in some fashion restrictive. The most liberal immigration quotas were still quotas. The most favourable regulations on land transfer were still regulations. And, still in the British mind, was the phrase of the Balfour Declaration: '. . . it being clearly understood that nothing shall be done which may prejudice the civil and religious rights of the existing non-Jewish communities in Palestine . . .' At first, while the numbers were small, the Jewish community was grateful for British protection, but as it expanded from 70,000 at the end of World War I to about 400,000 in 1936, the confrontation changed. By 1936, the Jewish community of Palestine was in effect a nation if not yet wholly a state. It had its own trade unions, agricultural areas, press, schools, banks and was about to acquire its own military force. One of its first major institu-tions, the Hebrew University, was to grow in to one of the world's great educational endowments.

Yet curiously, for all their sophistication, sensitivity, energy and knowledge, the Jewish immigrants were remarkably devoid of interest in the people in whose midst they were settling. Whereas the British and the French had long been among the world's foremost students of the culture of the Middle East and even their workaday administrators enjoyed local foods, dress, mores and culture, the European Jewish immigrants seemed almost oblivious to the Arabs. It was symptomatic that the emerging leader of the Jewish community, David Ben Gurion, knew Sanskrit and Greek but never bothered to learn Arabic. Israel

Zangwill coined the widely quoted expression, 'The land without people for the people without land.' The Arabs were later to maintain that the European Jews looked upon them somewhat like the early American settlers looked upon the Red Indians: a people whose incapacities and backwardness gave them no right to the land on which they lived.

Of course there were exceptions. The writings of Martin Buber, the early policies enunciated by Arthur Ruppin and, perhaps above all, the educational mission of Yueda Magnes are monuments of the humanistic spirit. But these were standing with one foot on either side of a chasm. As the chasm opened they were bound either to fall or to choose sides. Arthur Ruppin took perhaps the only logical course: to recognise that one could not be half Zionist. Gradually during his lifetime, he gave up the idea of co-operation between the Arabs and the Jews and came to realise that however logical it might sound abstractly, assistance to the Arabs to form independent entities or nation states elsewhere had little or no bearing on the three quarters of a million Arabic-speaking inhabitants of Palestine who were as passionately attached to their lands and villages as any people anywhere. A bi-national state was even more bitterly opposed by the Jews than by the Arabs and the idea that the European Jewish community would move to the Middle East merely to be another protected minority was anathema to all Zionists. The chasm opened slowly during the gradual growth of the Jewish community in the 1920s but, with the coming of Nazism in Europe, it split wide. Ruppin, and all those who had followed him in looking for some means of accommodation with the local population, found that the imperatives of saving the European Jews were simply too urgent. The Arabs, he realised, *could not* negotiate. The troubles in Europe were not their troubles; the salvation of the Jewish community was not their struggle. Only by committing what would amount to a national suicide could they have assisted the Jews. There really was nothing on which to negotiate. One simply could not be both a Zionist and a proponent of the Arab viewpoint. Balfour's comma could not hold together a world being torn asunder. Ben Gurion put it honestly when he said that if he were an Arab he would have as completely rejected Zionism as did the Palestinian Arabs. Ironically, the very contribution to the welfare of the Arabs, the very increase of their capacity, the very diffusion of knowledge and the growth of communications, in short, the very success of the contribution of Europe to the Middle East, undermined any possible basis for compromise or conciliation.

The Growth of the Arabs

Meanwhile, these forces were transforming the Arab community. From the faint stirrings of Arab nationalism before World War I, and from the disorganisation, lack of capacity, one might almost say political illiteracy of the Arabs, in 1919, the mandate system had begun to bring about a growth of capacity. It was true that mandate was a polite subterfuge for something which a generation earlier would have been unabashedly termed imperialism. But more was changed than just the word: it was cheaper, more efficient and easier to run areas like Iraq, Transjordan, Egypt and even Palestine by employing the natives than by importing relatively expensive Europeans. Moreover, by giving the natives a semblance of feeling of control over their destiny, one converted what might have been otherwise merely a sullen, repressed population into a contributive one, which paid its own way, produced its own goods and contributed to the well-being of the imperial power. As we have seen, in Iraq, the British managed to create the façade of a national government, so skilfully exercising power behind the scenes through advisers that they were able to rule cheaply with an astonishingly small cadre of Europeans.

As the oil companies began to exploit the resources of the Middle East, they inevitably made major changes in the local economies. Although they attempted to isolate themselves and to remain unobtrusive in desolate areas far from the capital cities, they needed construction workers, servants, food, recreation, and they could make it worthwhile for local peoples and their rulers to co-operate. The royalties paid for petroleum were not much in the 1920s and 1930s, but in local terms they were significant.

In order to staff each national government, schools were opened, training missions sent abroad and bureaucracies created. The first overseas educational mission from Iraq in 1921 was comprised of only nine students. At that time, less than one half of one per cent of the population was attending government schools and the total Iraqi secondary school enrolment was 34 students. By the end of the British mandate, over 200 young men had returned from years of study abroad. But, even then, the average girl schoolchild still received only two years of schooling and of the 154 existing government schools, only 14 had as many as six grades. In 1932, Iraq had only 19 secondary schools with 129 teachers and some 2,000 students. With small variations in the numbers, this was essentially the situation in Transjordan, Libya, the Sudan and Syria. In Egypt the scale was larger. By the eve of World War I, a quarter of a million students attended school, but as late as 1931 the six public *secondary* schools enrolled only 2,500 students.

The coming of national independence, while it may have been a hollow form, gave an explosive stimulus to the growth of education and, indirectly, to the creation of national institutions. In Egypt, enrolment doubled. In the seven years of Iraqi independence before World War II, secondary school attendance increased from 2,000 to 14,000 students.

These striking figures were reinforced by the informal aspects of education. The radio, the newspaper, the introduction of the automobile, the building of rural highways, changes in styles of clothing, the spread of health services, the growth of national gendarmerie and military forces, changes in the form of land tenure, even the task of registering the land: all of these things, like the accretion of coral on the sea floor, were gradually creating structures.

Parenthetically, it should be stressed at this point that while the structures amounted to the growth of capacity for individual nation states, they also have a direct bearing on the divisions in the Arab countries. The very vocabulary associated with the new borrowings from Europe differed from Italian-oriented Libya to French-oriented Egypt to Turkish-oriented Iraq to English-oriented Jordan and Palestine. In the most trivial things — as different electrical currents, ways that forms and papers were filled out, customs of service in bureaucracies — the several Arab countries developed their independent methods and habits. In the course of these developments they naturally tended, as have the states of Black Africa for similar reasons, to look upon one another as even more alien than their European masters. There was a time during the 1930s and 1940s when it was difficult for Arab intellectuals to discuss among themselves such problems as economic development without lapsing into the European languages in which they spent their true intellectual lives. Not only were their enemies different but their teachers; often indeed the two were the same.

From these meagre resources, the independent national states acquired a reality by the end of World War II. Legally they were independent members of the new United Nations and the Arab League and however dependent they were upon their former masters they proclaimed themselves to be not only self-reliant, unified and progressive but responsible. Responsible, their leaders asserted, both for the internal well-being of their own poor and distressed people and externally for the protection of the still-leaderless, inchoate and mandated Palestinians. These assertions were to haunt the new states and their governments and dominate their politics in the 1950s and 1960s.

The Shock of Defeat

The Palestinian issue became the immediate test of capacity and responsibility. A subsequent chapter will describe the conflicts between the Arabs and Israel in some detail. Here it is appropriate to concentrate on the fact that the first clash showed how far behind the Arabs were: how disorganised and immature their leadership and how few their effective citizens. In Cairo, in 1948, public outcries, at first directed against all foreigners indiscriminately, turned quickly against the government whose incapacity and corruption, despite propaganda and censorship, were manifest. The Egyptian prime minister was assassinated. The country appeared to be on the brink of revolution and upon threats from Great Britain, both Egypt and Israel agreed to stop the war. The truce which was negotiated in the early months of 1949 put a patina of legality on the *de facto* battlefield arrangements.

No matter how they tried to disguise the fact, the defeat of the Arab states in the Palestine war of 1948 was a humiliating blow to their self-esteem. In the first test of their national independence they had utterly and miserably failed before a tiny, new nation. All over the Middle East, critics began to probe at the façade of Arab power and found how hollow it was. A wave of shock spread from capital to capital. What could have gone wrong, they asked? How was it that these nation states, the products of a mandate, the outgrowth of the Arab rebellion, peoples who had produced Islam, whose empires had spread across half the world, who kept alive the lamps of civilisation while Europe remained in the dark ages, and who proclaimed that they had a philosophy of life that transcended the shallow materialism of the West; how could these people, they asked, have lost the war to an upstart nation of moneylenders and shopkeepers, a bunch of newcomers from Europe who had no real roots in the Middle East? Excuses leapt to page. Apologists abounded: the Israelis had been saved by the West; machinations of high policy by Britain, the United States, Russia, were at work; the Western military equipment was defective. Whether they were true or not, none of the excuses satisfied even those who uttered them. The fact that each Arab government blamed the others only condemned them all. Finally, the most perceptive of the Arabs turned inward to look at their own societies and their own ethos for the answer. A leading Syrian historian, former ambassador to the United Nations and then president of the National University of Damascus, gave his harsh answers in *The Meaning of the Disaster*:

Seven Arab states declare war on Zionism in Palestine, stop impotent before it, and then turn on their heels. The representatives of the Arabs deliver fiery speeches in the highest international forums, warning what the Arab states and peoples will do if this or that decision be enacted. Declarations fall like bombs from the mouths of officials at the meetings of the Arab League, but when action becomes necessary, the fire is still and quiet, the steel and iron are rusted and twisted, quick to bend and disintegrate. The bombs are hollow and empty. They cause no damage and kill no one.

A Palestinian who had helped to found the Arab League, was equally bitter: 'In the face of the enemy the Arabs were not a state, but petty states; groups, not a nation; each fearing and anxiously watching the other and intriguing against it. What concerned them most and guided their policy was not to win the war and save Palestine from the enemy, but what would happen after the struggle, who would be predominant in Palestine, or annex it to themselves, and how they could achieve their own ambitions. Their announced aim was the salvation of Palestine, and they said that afterward its destiny should be left to its people. This was said with the tongue only. In their hearts all wished it for themselves; and most of them were hurrying to prevent their neighbours from being predominant, even though nothing remained except the offal and bones.'

The press was filled with self-critical statements calling for a complete revolution which would replace the evidently rotten political structure with something shining and new but also essentially Arab. It was these sentiments that were personified by the young group of Egyptian army officers led by Gamal Abdel Nasser who in 1952 overthrew the government of King Farouk and established a republic. As Nasser himself later wrote, it was the Palestine experience which really focused and galvanised the activities of his group. 'In Palestine I met only friends that shared the work for Egypt, but there I also discovered the thoughts that shed their light on the road ahead. I remember the days I spent in trenches pondering over our problems. Falougha was then besieged and the enemy had concentrated his guns and aircraft heavily and terribly upon it. Often have I said to myself, "here we are in these underground holes besieged. How we are cheated into a war unprepared and how our destinies have been the plaything of passions, plots and greed. Here we lay under fire unarmed." As I reached that stage in my thinking my feelings would suddenly jump across the battlefront, across frontiers to Egypt. I found myself saying, "What is happening in Palestine is that a miniature picture of what was happening in

Egypt. Our Mother-Country has been likewise besieged by difficulties as well as ravaged by an enemy. She has cheated and pushed to fight unprepared. Greed, intrigue and passion have toyed with it and left it under fire." '

First Answers

From the perspective of today, it is evident that these questions, quests and partial answers of 25 years ago were still quite superficial despite their seeming so innovative and revolutionary. As government after government in the Middle East succumbed to coups, the structures which replaced them, except for the titles on the doors, remained essentially the same. These were the troubled events of the 1950s. They constituted the drama that was reported in the press, the rise and fall of the military dictators. Unreported in the press, generally, were 'non-events' of far more significance. To these we shall now turn.

One of the things which the 1948 war made clear to all the 'existing non-Jewish communities' was their general technological backwardness. The Arab world had virtually no technically qualified professionals and its labour force was still largely employed in small-scale, almost 'cottage', industries. Even those with new skills found few opportunities. The one social institution which seemed 'objective' in its demand for skill, regardless of social origin, religion or family connections, was the army. The army alone seemed to have the capacity to mobilise force, to communicate and to ascertain whether things worked satisfactorily or at all. While the military training schools created under the mandate régimes or in the early years of independence were usually restricted to sons of the upper class, a few began to enrol competent young men of the lower middle class in the years immediately before World War II. In the first relatively open class in Egypt were all the young men who were later to play key roles in the 1952 *coup d'état*. Their social origins were not exactly 'of the people' but some were the sons of petty officials like Gamal Abdel Nasser and Anwar Sadat and had to struggle to be accepted in what had been an aristocratic preserve. The Palestine war of 1948 brought to the fore the more qualified young men and discredited the more incompetent senior officers. Middle-grade army officers began to believe the army alone had the competence to undertake the supreme national responsibility. Other groups were seen to be defective, immature or to fracture along religious, geographical or economic lines. The trade union movement never really managed to play a serious political role and even in the defence of worker rights proved largely ineffectual. A precursor of the women's liberation movement began in Egypt,

Lebanon and Iraq in the 1940s and 1950s, but its aims were extremely modest and its members lacked the cohesion and the opportunity to make a significant *entrée* into political life. Government civil servants were too ill paid, dispirited, poorly organised and divided along traditional lines to be able to become an effective political unit. Lawyers, of whom Egypt particularly produced inordinate numbers, were of little consequence as a group, although various of their members did well for themselves. The older political parties were largely discredited by the events of the Palestine war. In Egypt the Wafd party (the nationalist party of World War I) had long since lost its *élan* and legitimacy and was more apt to be blamed as the disease than regarded as the physician. Thus it was, in country after country, that the army, in default of other serious contenders and unchecked by social and political institutions — vigorous political parties, a free and critical press, an independent judiciary — intervened to topple government after government, including previously installed military governments, in a frenetic quest for the answer to the dilemma posed by the defeat in Palestine. The *coup d'état* became the practical equivalent to the election, and more than a score succeeded — many more failed — between 1952 and 1972.

Three Trends Among the Arabs

Three trends now demand our attention for their long-range impact on Middle Eastern society.

The first was the Egyptian experiment in land reform. When the young officers took over in 1952 they had virtually no ideas to solve Egypt's problems. When, almost accidently, Nasser stumbled on land reform, his clique seized the idea with gusto. The people were wretched, but were, after all, the nation. To help them uplift themselves was, by definition, a national aspiration. Moreover, to break up the economic base of the old order was a prudent political move. Land reform was thus ideal. It might even have good economic consequences by encouraging people who had felt exploited to work harder and produce more, and it would tend to create a social class allied with the ruling junta and so underpin its future. But it was hard to accomplish: there were too many people and too little land. The minimum size plot required to support a peasant family was about five acres. But in 1952, large numbers of 'the people' were actually landless and the vast majority held less than five acres. The very wealthy held large estates — the deposed king the largest of all — but their estates aggregated too little to be more than a token when divided among the land-hungry millions. Egypt tried two approaches to win more acreage. It created a new land reclamation scheme, 'Liberation Province,' which echoing the early Zionist *Kibbutzim* was to wash the land free from the desert salts and the people from the infections of poverty. 'The people' were carefully selected, were issued 'modern' dress, were trained and regrouped; their communities were planned to resemble Israeli collective farms more than delta villages. Their children were to be a new kind of Egyptian. Many forces including poverty combined to defeat these grand ideas, and while the experiment still exists, neither the land nor the people have measured up to the original intent.

Egypt also boldly resurrected a plan which had been discussed for over half a century to build a 'high dam' at Aswan. A huge project, it was to symbolise the new Egypt as the pyramids symbolised the old. Not only should it provide water for vast new areas of agriculture but power for a new industry. We will examine it in more detail later, but for now it is useful to point out that more than any other project, the high dam epitomised the new order — bold, insufficiently studied, imposed from the top and inadequately supported from below. More, in emphasising things over people, it deflected energies from where they might have made a truly revolutionary impact. In part because of the emphasis on the high dam, Egypt failed to participate in the so-called Green Revolution — which, with better seed, fertiliser, pesticide and technique pushed to the fore the individual farmer in Mexico, Pakistan and India and gave him the means to achieve a more ample way of life while providing the state with enhanced revenues.

Second, after land reform, almost all the governments in the Middle East vastly increased the numbers of students to be educated and changed the emphasis from the humanities and social sciences to the sciences and technology. In Egypt, the largest of the Arab countries, the number of enrolled students went from just short of 1 million in 1945 to approximately 7 million in 1970. Prior to 1950, almost none of these students was engaged in technical or scientific training. By 1960, enrolment in vocational training schools grew to approximately 115,000 and by 1970, 275,000. In Iraq, the corresponding figures were 7,000 and 10,000. Additionally, large numbers of trainees were employed both in state-run industries and in specialised faculties of the universities. By 1961, the Egyptians claimed that 38,000 students had graduated in the natural sciences and technology from Egyptian universities. Possibly even more significant, in the long run, was the fact that between 1957 and 1963 perhaps as many as 130,000 Egyptians passed out of the armed forces into civilian life. Weighed in the scales of modern Egyptian industry in 1961, which then employed roughly

250,000 workers, the impact of military service can be gauged to have been enormous. Soldiers coming out of the army had rudimentary technical skills, a sense of order and discipline and had been, psychologically at least, uprooted from village life. All of these accented the rise of the new industrial class.

Third, the states had to create industry. To provide the 'new men' with jobs and utilise them to create a kind of power which had not previously existed in the 'existing non-Jewish communities', was the great thrust of industrialisation in the 1950s and 1960s. Even monarchical governments adopted the idea that state control, planning and state-financed industry constituted the means to a better future.

Oil gave the impetus to the development programmes. The impact in Kuwait can be seen, dramatically, in the rise of the educational budget from $90,000 in 1942 to $33 million in 1960 to $95 million in 1972. The impact on development was most graphic in Iraq. Acting on the advice of an American mission in 1960, Iraq created a Development Board charged with planning and investing. To ensure success in its task, the Board was to receive 70 per cent of the government's revenue from petroleum. At that time the amount was about $12 million but rose rapidly over the next few years to approximately $180 million yearly. An indication of the impact of these allocations in Iraq was the fact that in 1950, when the Development Board began its work, Iraq had only five mechanical engineers. Virtually all of its planning and much of its execution had to be done by foreign firms: the Development Board generated scores of plans and studies from international consultants which swamped decision-makers, workers and consumers.

Under the impact of oil, Middle Eastern society was being totally remade: some institutions were growing while others atrophied but, as was expected, many years would have to pass before some form of internal balance would be created or some means found to digest the new wealth and learning. In those confusing times, change seemed everywhere in the air. Although few Arabs would more than guess at the direction it was going, no one questioned its utility or necessity.

The Trends in Israel

Meanwhile, in Israel, a different process was in motion. It also involved three categories of growth — the Hebraisation of European Jewish immigrants, the modernisation of the Oriental Jews and the reclamation of the land.

Hebraisation of the European Jews was, from the first, regarded by the Zionists as essential to the purpose and to the security of the homeland. Just as it was only upon Palestine as the locus of the national home that all Jews could agree, so it was only upon Hebrew that the cultural emphasis could be placed. Arthur Koestler and others have commented on the difficulty of the task before the immigrants. Hebrew was, at first, insufficient as a vehicle for modern thought or for specialised subjects. Biblical imagery was rich but lent itself no more than Koranic Arabic to physics, chemistry, economics or sociology; thus, one had not only to learn, but also constantly to *create* the language. Israel became a giant language laboratory. No one could abstain and function. Gradually modern Hebrew was codified and each successive group of immigrants found the way easier as the cultural offerings increased, as more and more people mastered Hebrew, the rewards for mastering it likewise increased. Thus, while Israel is remarkable in the broad linguistic competence of its population, Hebrew today is securely emplaced as the national tongue.

Modernisation of the Oriental Jews has been a more difficult task. Particularly the Yemeni Jewish community has proved difficult to integrate into the nation. With an historical experience much closer to that of the Arabs than to the European (Ashkanazi) or the Spanish (Sephardic) communities — between whom, of course, there were also significant differences — the Oriental communities were neither as driven by fear of the holocaust nor as invigorated by nineteenth-century nationalist thought, nor as equipped by twentieth-century technology. They had to be indoctrinated to be made to fit the mainstream of Zionism. That task was taken up especially in the schools and in the army. In Israel, one is constantly reminded of the holocaust — it is the central myth, the haunting nightmare of the modern state. Its memorial in the centre of Jerusalem is, in a sense, the innermost shrine of the Jewish people, the modern version of the Wailing Wall, and is scarcely matched by any national monument in the West. It has become the emotional centre of Zionism. The memory it symbolises links the Israeli to the foreign Zionist but had to be *taught* to the Oriental Jews from whose experience it was alien.

Almost equally alien was the effusion of ideas which swept through the European Jewish community in the closing years of the nineteenth century. Nation, for the Oriental Jew, as for the Arab, meant religion. A Jew was recognised in Ottoman society through the 'nation' of Judaism; in it he was ruled by his religious leaders under his religious law. If he was overtaxed he was as apt to be as annoyed at his leaders, who set his individual contribution, as at the government which determined only the overall amount to be paid by the community. He was not a full citizen, and that probably was annoying but compensations included avoidance of military service. Since the ideas of Locke, Paine, Jefferson and Montesquieu were unknown to him and the movements of protest growing out of Marx's ideas would have seemed outrageous or incomprehensible, he generally accepted his social position and, heresy though it may sound to modern ears, enjoyed it. When. in the aftermath of the 1948-9 war, he was uprooted and taken to Israel, he had not only to catch up intellectually but to be shocked emotionally into an essentially European world. Again his problem was that of the Arab. And, like the Arab, the Oriental Jew has not made the transition easily, fully or so rapidly as desired. Social critics in Israel still complain that the Oriental Jews remain an underprivileged, still partially alien, substratum. They charge that the state is of the Ashkanazi, by the Ashkanazi, and for the Ashkanazi.

Yet it is remarkable what Israel has accomplished to homogenise its society in a very short period. For this, the army must take much credit. Israel is an embattled state, in some ways even a garrison state, and the flow of men and women through the armed forces has been proportionally very large.

During the initial period of training basic attitudes and skills are recast with some unlearned and others learned. In Israel this process is frequently reinforced as reservists are periodically recalled for additional training. In supplementary industrial training programmes, adult education courses, and less structured civic programmes, new attitudes and skills are reinforced and supplemented with other parts of the Western technological and educational heritage while aspects of the old way of life receive what the economists term disincentives.

Lastly, Israelis pre-eminently have been involved in what is called 'nation building'. Their own planning and work has been assisted, as nowhere else in the world on a comparable scale, by vast infusions of capital from abroad. Between 1948 and 1978, the American Jewish Community raised more than $20 thousand million. Paralleling this unprecedented private initiative, the American Government assisted in two significant ways. On the one hand, it arranged that contributions to Israel would be tax exempt as though designated for domestic charities. Effectively, therefore, it may be argued that roughly half of the contributions from private sources amounted to a Federal subsidy. More significantly, Israel became the largest *per capita* recipient of American overseas aid. From 1948 to 1978, the American Government furnished Israel with $13 thousand million. Additional funds were forthcoming from Germany — about $1.5 thousand million in reparations and about

$300 million yearly in personal restitution payments. In addition, large numbers of research grants and contracts were arranged through the auspices of the American Government and through universities, foundations and businesses. While the population varied during the thirty years and the yearly amounts forthcoming fluctuated, the yearly *per capita* aid intake has now risen to about $1000 (in comparison to $50 *per capita* in Egypt).

What Israel got from abroad, it has used wisely and well. In a word, the Israelis have built a modern Western industrial society. The industry of both Europe and America finds it easy to interface with Israeli institutions. The Israelis have managed to achieve the highest living standard in the Middle East and by 1978, their Gross National Product hit $9,000 million.

These aspects of Israel are evident everywhere one turns. The streets, the houses, the dress, the diet, the cultural life, industrial production, agricultural research, the army. Israel is a modern Western industrial state and the surrounding Arab countries are still weak, poor and relatively backward. Take one statistic: the number of people who can be employed in the army. The contrast is as great as between France and the rest of Europe after the 1789 Revolution — Israel, like France, is a nation-in-arms surrounded by states in which only small percentages of citizens are fully engaged. Indeed, in crucial affairs, Israel outnumbers its Arab neighbours: it not only has more engineers, physicists, chemists, doctors and technicians but even can field larger fighting forces. In ultimate terms, it has long had the capacity to produce and control nuclear weapons. Thus, essentially, it has so outstripped the Arabs as to constitute an extraterritorial element in the Middle East, difficult to compare with its neighbours, a European country physically present in the Middle East, but intellectually apart. A source of relatively enormous strength, its very success in modernisation also constitutes a barrier to be surmounted on the road to peace.

PART TWO

5 THE COLD WAR

Once the seat of great empires, the Middle East has always been too strategic, even when poor, to be left alone. The Egyptians, most vulnerable at the junction of Africa and Asia and without great natural barriers, have been ruled since the time of Alexander the Great by Greeks, Romans, Byzantines, Persians, Arabians, Turks, Circassians, Ethiopians, Albanians, French and British. The last British troops left in the spring of 1956 only to return briefly with the French and Israelis in that autumn and today Israel is in occupation of parts of the Sinai Peninsula. For the rest of the area, to take the long view of history, war is the norm.

Whatever its own attractions — today oil, in the last century cotton, and in ancient times grain — the Middle East is a strategic crossroads. The junction of Asia, Africa and Europe, it is the road to India. Alexander inspired Napoleon's dream and the spices of the fifteenth century gave way to the diplomatic dispatches of the nineteenth. Long before the Suez Canal was dug in the 1860s, the British communicated with India by a dromedary post along the Euphrates River. Napoleon's invasion of Egypt, which he saw as the first stage of his march to the East, formulated the 'great game', the diplomatic, military and espionage encounters which Britain and Russia played throughout the nineteenth century. In the English mind of that period, armies of Cossacks were always on the verge of sweeping down upon India and at all costs had to be contained, countered or defeated before they got there. Another slightly less dramatic but even more predatory great game was played in Africa. The search for the source of the Nile by Speake, Burton, Livingstone and Stanley mesmerised a whole generation of Englishmen and was fired by more than mere geographical curiosity. In their headlong rush for African empire, Britain and France narrowly averted a war over an encounter between their venturesome agents at a tiny, remote and now forgotten Sudanese village called Fashoda. Finally, between Central Asia and Africa, the Germans and French attempted to plunge right through the Ottoman Empire with a railway to reach the Persian Gulf. *Drang nach ost* gripped all the European chancelleries; it merely sounded more impressive in German.

For much of the nineteenth century, the Middle Eastern policy of Great Britain was remarkably clear and neat — something no power has since achieved. It was to keep the northern part of the area strong as a barrier to European and particularly Russian, encroachment while keeping the south, the area with which this book is primarily concerned, weak in order to facilitate British guidance or control.

Secret Agents

In much of the political activity in and about the Middle East there has been an air of romantic unreality, but with enough substance to sustain serious concerns. The Middle Easterners saw the great desert travellers as secret agents, readying the nomadic tribes for carefully contrived wars. The British, the French, the Russians and the Germans — both the officials and the public — delighted in oriental romance. To be or know about or send a secret agent in deep (but probably obvious) disguise was a shared dream. The French Emperor Louis-Napoleon sent one of the most complex, a turncoat Jesuit priest (just to make the story more complicated he was of Jewish origin and became a Protestant) on a secret mission across central Arabia in the 1860s. The mission was so secret we still do not know its purpose. British travellers, often in disguise, wandered around the deserts of Arabia and through the mountains of Iraq making maps and taking detailed notes, to what purpose the natives could only guess. In World War I, the British had their Lawrence and the Germans their Wassmuss. (In more difficult circumstances Wilhelm Wassmuss was more effective but lacked the publicists Lawrence found in Lowell Thomas, Robert Graves, and himself.) The Jordanians and Iraqis admired but also feared the Arabic-speaking British officer, personified by Glubb Pasha (General Sir John Glubb) who seemed to be everywhere, know their country better than they, revel in their political secrets and even delight in their jokes. Perhaps the most dashing group in World War II was the long-range desert patrol of the Special Air Service which scouted behind Axis lines in Libya, blowing up airfields and almost killing Afrika Korps' Field-Marshal Erwin Rommel. In a more modern guise, President Nasser was fascinated with 'James Bond, 007'. It may someday be perceived that the James Bond image had as much influence over the more sombre African and Asian events of the 1960s as did the Lawrence legend earlier.

World War II was played out in the Middle East with scant regard for the inhabitants. Britain and Germany were the main participants with Italy and France as auxiliaries. German strategy was first to thrust across North Africa, cut the Suez Canal and so knock out British shipping in the Mediterranean, then to drive across Syria and Iran into southern Russia and force Turkey into the war on the Axis side. It failed when the Afrika Korps failed to take Egypt.

As the war ended the southern Middle East was a British preserve. In the north, however, the Russians seemed everywhere on the move. The great game seemed to begin again. First came Russian pressure on Turkey then Russia attempted to solidify the control it had acquired, with British and American approval during World War II, over northern Iran. Meanwhile, in Greece a civil war began even before the German evacuation with the two sides, thinly disguised by their Greek proxies and allies, as Russia and Great Britain.

Britain's incapacity to carry out its traditional role in the great game and fear that the resulting power vacuum would bring about a wholly new international diplomatic situation impelled President Truman, in 1947, to proclaim the Truman Doctrine. It was the same fear which created the American Central Intelligence Agency and expanded the Marshall Plan into a global development programme. The cold war in the Middle East thus had profound consequences for American domestic society and for American overseas activities. These in turn shaped events throughout the Western world for a generation.

The American Entry

In the early years of the American assumption of the British role in the Middle East, the 1950s, the Middle Easterners themselves remained essentially passive. The British-installed régime in Iraq seemed to be the most secure, conservative, pliable and intelligent of the Middle Eastern régimes and became the fulcrum of British-American policy with the Baghdad Pact its chosen instrument.

Put simply, the pact policy amounted to assisting those régimes which would and could work in concert with the United States and Britain against Russia. Once they reached that decision much followed: help on internal development programmes, assistance in increasing their capacity to defend themselves from external enemies — generally an unneeded and unsuccessful aspect of the policy — and guidance in creating or refining the internal mechanisms of public control. In the Baghdad Pact were grouped what Secretary of State John Foster Dulles called 'the nothern tier' countries, Turkey, Iraq, Iran and Pakistan. Since Turkey was a member of NATO and Pakistan a member of the SEATO, Mr Dulles could look with pride upon the creation of a political Maginot Line designed to contain Russia. This idea was reminiscent of the British diplomatic conceptions of the nineteenth century. Curiously, however, its 'goal line' remained vague. There was no 'India' to protect. Little of Africa or Asia was 'America's' to be defended or 'lost'. Moreover, the northern tier failed to take into account the reality of twentieth-century power. Power had become more than the capacity to drive a tank or fly a fighter plane across a frontier. More subtly the spread of ideas, the creation of alliances, the granting of aid or training can, and in fact did, circumvent the strongposts on the northern tier to enable Russia to penetrate deep into Africa and Asia. Although the term was never used, the Russians began to build a 'southern tier' in Egypt, the Sudan and in such far away places as Ghana, Tanzania, Indonesia.

Russia and America

It was ironic that the Russians copied the tools and techniques of the Americans and even more ironic that both, in pursuing with great determination and at considerable cost their objectives, succeeded primarily in undercutting them. When in 1958 a *coup d'état* by the American-trained and equipped Iraqi army toppled Prime Minister Nuri Said's régime, the linchpin of the Baghdad Pact, it was the Soviet-trained and equipped army of the notoriously anti-Western Gamal Abdul Nasser which seemed ready to intervene to prevent a Russian takeover. The theme was to be repeated in the ensuing years: the American-trained and equipped army of Libya produced the régime of Colonel Gaddafi the Soviet-trained and equipped army of the Sudan produced the strongly anti-communist régime of President Numeiry. America's strongest Middle Eastern ally, Turkey, has become one of the most strongly anti-American countries in the area. Ethiopia, America's showplace in Africa, has been locked in bitter hostilities with Russian trained and equipped Somalia — with both countries having swapped cold war sides. It seems, indeed, that in conception the policies associated with the cold war were to a large extent naïve and based on faulty understanding of politics. Most areas of the world, including the Middle East, are not merely stages but are peopled. The local actors may only have small parts and the drama may be focused on the imported stars who move with great acclaim across the stage. However, the bit players remain behind for the second act and the third. They are always there, amid the relics of past majesty. Napoleon was in Egypt less than two years but his Middle Eastern successor, Mehmet Ali Pasha, remained almost half a century. The German thrust into Syria was a matter of a few weeks and the German challenge in the western desert a matter of a couple of years. The British remained longer but the way they did makes the point — they allowed, encouraged and indeed built local institutions to serve as their shields and brought native politicians into the action.

In the cold war, the Russians and the Americans thought each other even more successful in getting the local players to act assigned roles. In fact neither did. Many of the bit players, having been handed the insignia of office, the costumes and the weapons, sought to play the leading roles. They even invented new roles and ad-libbed new lines. The audience took them up and they became stars in their own right.

These trends could be summed up in a kind of composite character made from the figures who moved onto the stage during the 1950s and 1960s — Nasser, Numeiry, Gaddafi, Kassem, Aref, Shishakli, Assad, Sadat. They were the most apt students of their cold war tutors, the ones who most understood how to employ the new devices and resources given them from abroad but who also, at the same time, sought to embody their own ambitions and interpretations of national purpose. Thus it was natural that each clashed most frequently and most effectively not with the unseen enemy on the other side of the cold war curtain but with the ally.

Even where the selected player did what he was told, the action often went wrong when he lost the respect of his fellows or new actors pushed him roughly aside. Unthinkingly, the foreign patron speeded the process. By forcing or encouraging allies to 'stand up and be counted' he helped to undermine them. Iraqi Prime Minister Nuri Said became increasingly unpopular in direct proportion as he became more identified with an alien power. The fact that he was encouraging his country along the lines of a major development programme which ultimately benefited the Iraqi population more than anything that anyone had ever done for them before, became politically irrelevant. In a sense he was destroyed by the very success of his programme. The greater the capacity the country developed, the more young men and women who were trained to take and exercise responsibility, the more efficient and larger the army became, the more galling it was to be prevented from taking part in the decision-making process. Nuri Said became not only a tyrant in the eyes of the Western trained technocrats, not only the puppet of a foreign power, but worse, an anachronism.

Having watched with glee the discomfiture of America in Iraq, the Russians rushed onto the scene to encourage political tendencies which those who had assumed power from the ousted régime of Nuri Said found equally abhorrent. They too had brought with them a scenario and they, like the Americans, wanted the lines spoken just so. At the high point of communist influence in Iraq, something close to a true

revolution was encouraged with a kind of proletarian militia vying with
the army for power. That was too much for those Iraqis who had
assumed power. Communist influence waned dramatically.

Positive Neutralism

President Nasser summed up common – and sensible – Middle Eastern
desires in the cold war drama in his phrase 'positive neutralism'. What
he really meant was that it would be wise for the inhabitants of the
Middle East to encourage both the Russians and the Americans to provide all they would give or could be tricked into providing – the phrase
'balanced exploitation' was coined for this aspect of the policy – so
that the Middle Easterners could take the equipment over to play out
their own scenarios. The goods were neutral: Russian or American, both
would do fine; but the policy, he suggested, should be Middle Eastern.

Viewed solely in terms of the cold war, both the United States and
the Soviet Union should have been content with positive neutralism.
Neither was. They should have been happy for entirely different reasons: the Marxists, if they believed in their projection of the long curves
of history, should have favoured anything serving or spreading the rise
of industrialisation, the dissemination of education, the creation of a
working class, etc., moves which would ultimately bring about socialism. Their conception of history should have made them delight in
America's aid and development programmes. Conversely, believing as
the Americans did, that aid stimulated economic development which
would solve many of the area's grinding social and political problems
and relieve the pressure on Israel by directing energies internally, they
should have favoured all efforts, even Russian programmes like the
High Dam, to speed development. More cynically, seeing how abhorrent were the crude techniques employed by the Russians wherever
they achieved momentary superiority, the Americans might have taken
comfort in the fact that the Russians would immunise those with whom
they dealt against Russian communism. This clearly happened in Egypt.
But personal ambition, domestic political consideration and the restless
energy of the two great powers prevented them from following their
own interests. America and Russia each thought that it must attempt to
seize the centre stage to do its act. To do less was unpatriotic, suspect,
perhaps even treasonable. Neither was able to employ any form of
subtlety. It was a mass that counted: How big was the aid programme,
how many tanks had been shipped, what was the mark number of the
latest aircraft?

The major fallacy of President Nasser's programme of balance exploitation was the tragic wastage of resources. Had the 'balanced exploitation' taken place in a different coinage — more in the tools of development and less in the weapons of war, more in the securing of markets than in the delineation of spheres of influence — the Middle East might be a much better place today. But many factors intervened to prevent this.

The first, undoubtedly, was ambition. Each of the military leaders who arose in the 1950s and 1960s had to prove himself to his own constituency, primarily the army, to stay in power (and alive) and this meant, above all, securing the latest pieces of military hardware.

Regional Cold War

Secondly, regional disputes distracted the attention and encouraged the appetites of all Middle Easterners. Egypt had its Vietnam in Yemen. Its relations with Saudi Arabia were for a time almost worse than its relations with Israel. Clashes occurred between Iraq and Syria, Syria and Jordan, Egypt and Libya, with distressing regularity. And, finally, there was the lingering background issue of the clash between Israel and the Arab countries. All the major participants, the United States, the Soviet Union, the various Arab states and the Israelis were locked into roles in a scenario over which none had sufficient control. Regardless of its pro-American stance, Israel had an independent existence in the eyes of the Russians: its leaders were Jews primarily of Russian background, associated with the Bund, a heretical version of 'orthodox' Marxism, and the Israeli intelligence service, utilising the Eastern European Jewish community, was recognised to be the most capable and skilful of the conventional intelligence penetrations of the Soviet system. It was heavily relied on, and paid for, by American Intelligence, both in the Soviet-backed area and in the Middle East. Israel, in the eyes of the Americans, was *the* Middle Eastern democracy, the only one with whom it could have a real understanding, the only country whose institutions sounded familiar and whose people easily moved in Western ways. Israeli penetration of the Soviet Union was enormously valuable, at times seemed almost vital to American security. And American anti-semites and pro-Zionists shared an interest in supporting Israel: anti-semites saw in Israel a kind of latter day Liberia, a place where unwanted American Jews could be encouraged to migrate while Zionists, perhaps slightly guilty themselves in not wishing to go to Israel, found, at least vicariously, in the Israeli experiment the culmination of the dream of generations. The Israelis feared the Russians, not only for the support the Russians gave to the Arab armies bent on destroying Israel but because the Russians still controlled and, in Israeli eyes held hostage, the largest pool of Jews outside the Western world. While Israel may some day find a way to put these facts together in its own form of 'positive neutralism', its Soviet policy is now pure cold war. In Israeli eyes, conversely, America is the final redoubt. If all else fails, America offers a refuge. But, in the meantime, America is the source of money to sustain the government and build the country, of arms to supply the army, and of lucrative contracts to build research facilities and war industries. Without American assistance, Israel could never have been created and certainly not be long sustained. These facts are repeatedly borne upon by leaders of the American Zionist community by Israeli government officials who shuttle regularly to the United States. The Israelis have built themselves the position of not only a sort of 51st state but indeed a most favoured state: in fiscal year 1978, Israeli Jews received far more *per capita* assistance from the American government (nearly $1,000) than New York City, − a total of over $2 billion − although New York City's population is four times as large, contains a larger *Jewish* population, and is, after all, a part of the United States.

The cold war is still with us, as are all the regional problems which give its particular flavour. It is unlikely to change in the near future. Sadly, it is probably also unlikely that any of the participants will learn from the past to use the energies and capacities generated by the cold war for more positive results. If, at the present time, Russia appears at a low ebb, it is unlikely to remain there. Grandiose expectations, aroused by Secretary of State Kissinger, and uncritically accepted, indeed ecstatically sought out by President Sadat, are unlikely to be satisfied. 'Openings' to the West probably will not cure the terrible scourges of poverty and peace does not seem at hand. A divided world will continue to offer choice and the restless will continue to change their minds. The equilibrium of the cold war is not one of rest but of motion.

6 HOT WARS

As practical men realised from the start, Zionism was bound to create Arab opposition and sooner or later that opposition would lead to violence. Conflict, indeed, began almost immediately upon the Arab realisation of the implications of the Zionist programme. The first clashes, before World War I, were probably merely xenophobic. By the 1920s, they had become religious and focused upon the symbolic sites of Judaism, Christianity and Islam. By the 1930s, they turned national and by the 1970s, social. The purpose of this chapter is to trace the main outlines of that development and to show its effects on the two communities.

The earliest conflicts, although bitter, were small in scale. Because the population was small, the casualties were lighter and the clashes, by the bloodier, more prolux standards of our own times, were merely 'incidents'. Translated, however, into the scale of the 1920s, they were both violent and tragic: worse, they were a school for the baser instincts that found a larger scope at a later time. The two major outbreaks of the 1920s, 1921 and 1929, were thoroughly investigated by British Government commissions. They warned of the points of conflict — essentially the points of contact — but could offer no politically acceptable way of resolving them under the terms of the Mandate. That realisation gradually dawned on the villagers and peasants of the Arab population and by 1935, with or without encouragement by its mainly religious leadership, they had become discontented with the Mandate, the British presence and, of course, Zionist settlers. In 1936, this discontent erupted into a full scale civil war.

Initially caught off guard, the British temporarily lost control of substantial portions of Palestine and were forced, like the French in Syria, to bring in large numbers of regular troops to fight the peasant irregulars. More important, the British began to train and organise a Jewish defence force, some of whose early recruits were later to become leaders of the Israeli army. As their forces built up, the British cracked down hard on the Arabs: they arrested and interned large numbers of suspects, hanged known leaders, often after drum-head courts martial and often on little evidence, and blew up houses in disputed areas. The conflict was never in doubt. The Palestinian peasant guerrillas were ill equipped, disorganised, and few in number. Moreover, as yet they had no clear political sense or structure. Gradually, their rebellion petered out on the eve of World War II. Briefly, then, anti-British feeling was manifested in Iraq, where the exiled or fugitive Arab leaders from Palestine found temporary havens. When the ambitions and emotions of the Iraqi leaders overcame their normal caution and opportunism, and when the otherwise unexceptional government of Prime Minister Rashid Ali, until then regarded as a British protégé, began to flirt with the then victorious Germans, the British quickly invaded the country (with a mainly Arab force from Trans-Jordan) and imposed the more reliable Nuri Said as Prime Minister.

Meanwhile, in Libya, an Italian 'pacification' programme was in its later stages under Marshal Graziani. Using what later in Algeria and Vietnam came to be called regroupment, Graziani had begun in 1932 to starve and bomb the bedouin who, off and on since 1912, had opposed Italian rule. By 1939, the Italians had put virtually the whole of the Libyan population behind barbed wire and Libya became as securely (and unenthusiastically) Italian as Egypt was British. Both countries became armed camps as World War II began — the Italian had a quarter of a million men in Libya against 86,000 British troops in Egypt — but the British had learned, as the Italians had not, the truth of Napoleon's remark that one could do almost anything with a bayonet but sit on it. The British found prosperity a better means of control. As in World War I they made Egypt a sanctuary — prosperous, comfortable but silent. And, at the high point of World War II, the one million troops they had stationed there were welcomed by a government they imposed upon the weak and immature king.

Meanwhile, peace came to Palestine and was gratefully accepted. The first three years of World War II were a period not only of truce but of active if separate co-operation by both Arabs and Jews with the British. Members of both communities enlisted in British military and service organisations in large numbers. At the start, those Arabs who hated the British too much to co-operate were interned or exiled and their Jewish counterparts held their fire until, after El Alamein, the Nazi tide began to ebb. Then, as the great war receded from the Eastern Mediterranean the tempo of local conflict increased. This time, it was the turn of the Jews. As they became aware of the magnitude of the holocaust in Europe, a sense of desperation seized the Palestinian Jewish community: at all costs, the remaining European Jews must be saved. No prior commitments, no pronouncements, no laws, no treaties could stand in the way. Saving the survivors was a transcendent moral obligation justifying any means and voiding all restraints and obligations.

the cause was the Nazi persecution, the barrier to positive action was the British administration. That was what the revisionist Jewish leader Vladimir Jabotinski had preached all along and after his death in 1940, his cause was rapidly and eagerly taken up by such men as Menachim Begin, but the extremists really spoke for the whole community and carried with them the more conservative leaders as well. A new war began, this time between the British and the Zionists, with the murder by Jewish terrorists in 1942 of a British Cabinet Minister, Lord Moyne, and spectacular, often bizarre, always macabre anti-British terror was to continue for the next six years. Quietly, the Zionists began to organise to bring over to Palestine the surviving European Jews. Their effort is a testament to their remarkable inventiveness and organisational capacities. One of the best kept secrets of World War II, their venture must rank as one of the most flamboyant undercover operations in a flamboyant period. They created a fictitious army brigade in Italy, complete with vehicles, uniforms, forged orders, money, weapons, everything they needed to function in the floating military community created by the war in southern Europe. Agents of the Zionist organisation located, identified, processed and turned over to this unit Jewish survivors and it conveyed them to Italian ports where they were picked up by chartered ships to be taken to Palestine. Bent on keeping the 'lid' on the Palestine issue, the British tried to intercept them and put them in neutral resting places like Cyprus. Either way, the British lost; if the Jews reached Palestine, the trouble there was bound to escalate against British policy and if they caught the poor, often sick and always miserable migrants, the British were escoriated in the world press. Yet, remarkable as it was, despite all the publicity, the mechanism of their conveyance was never revealed at the time. When one British officer tried to describe it, he was decried as an anti-semitic paranoid. Years passed before the whole story came out and then it was believed, probably, only because it was told by an English Zionist journalist as a matter of justifiable pride.

The vast underground organisation had a second purpose: to acquire the war *matériel* needed by the incipient Jewish army for the inevitable clash in the Middle East. For those who knew what they wanted, this was not so difficult as it might appear since mountains of German and Italian equipment had been abandoned in the retreat from Italy and Allied *matériel* was in dumps where it could be 'requisitioned', purchased or merely stolen. Nonetheless, the audacity and skill exhibited in this operation was far beyond the capacity of any of the Middle Eastern states then, or any of them but Israel today.

The period between the end of World War II and May 1948, when the State of Israel was proclaimed, was one of the most violent times of 'peace' ever recorded. Each month four out of each 1,000 residents became a casualty and property damage has never been calculated. The streets of Jerusalem, Acre, Jaffa, Tel Aviv, Nablus and Bethlehem resembled iron glaciers. Through the barbed wire, narrow pathways led to check-points and sentry-boxes. Sleep was fitful as the rattle of machine-gun fire and the explosion of bombs marked the hours. In the daily fighting the still-covert Jewish forces were battle tested. Made up in part of men and women already trained in the British and American armies in Europe, they included many veterans of combat against the Germans and the Italians. Thus almost before it had an army, and long before it was a state, the Jewish Agency was able to call upon specialists with skills as varied as fight pilot, commando and code breaker. By the end of the Mandate, the guerrillas and foreign recruits had merely to don uniforms to emerge as a national army.

No contrast could have been more marked than that with the Arab armies. Distrusted by the British and the French, most had lived through World War II in a sort of polite internment and only the small, British-officered Trans-Jordanian Arab Legion had limited combat experience. Few individual Arabs had gained advanced technical training in the war, and lacking significant expatriate communities, the Arab states lacked resources for recruitment abroad. The officer corps was backward and backward-looking, appointed mainly for social status and loyalty to reactionary régimes. In equipment, the armies were merely pathetic: when the Iraqi army marched out of Baghdad in 1948 most of the soldiers lacked even uniforms and few had arms. The soldiers were a rabble. The Egyptian army was lampooned as the Arabs' largest – largest, that is, in the girth of its officers. As a matter of policy, all the Arab armies were left short of ammunition and serving units were not normally issued ammunition. Maintenance was almost non-existent and Egyptian officers bitterly remarked that the equipment they were sold by their European mentors was so old and worn as to be all but useless except as a trailmarker: it broke down at such regular intervals as to form a clear trail back to base.

Thus it was that the first engagement between the Arabs and the Israelis in May 1948 was a relatively small-scale affair. The total number of troops involved and the amount of equipment engaged made it appear rather a sideshow than a major international war. It was unity of command, determination and individual initiative rather than superiority of technique, strategy or equipment which gave the Israelis their initial advantage. The fight went out of the Arabs quickly as their governments appeared more concerned to prevent one another from acquiring undue advantage than to prevent the Israelis from success.

As we have seen, it was the miserable showing in this 'first round' which was instrumental in producing a decade of *coups d'état* throughout the Arab countries.

The Israelis in 1948, of course, were under no illusions. They knew that they had won the 'first round' but when the Arabs settled back to a sullen unwillingness to accept the existence of Israel, their more perceptive leaders recognised that this round was unlikely to be the last. The weak or corrupt post-mandate governments tried to focus attention on the alien enemy. It was partly for this reason that such Israeli leaders as David Ben Gurion welcomed the 1952 *coup* that placed Gamal Abdel Nasser in power in Egypt. But their hopes were quickly disappointed: Nasser proved to be a nationalist and, above all, a nationalist schooled in the 'first round'. As a combat officer in Palestine Nasser felt personally involved in the loss of honour when that campaign failed. While it is probably true that Nasser espoused Arab nationalism only late in his career, it is also true that Egypt, as a natural leader of the Arab countries, would be drawn into the conflict almost inevitably. Consequently, the Israelis prudently set about the task of building a standing army from the heterogeneous fighters of the war of independence.

Recognising the enormous range of tasks to be done by very few people, the Israeli government adapted its organisation to conserve manpower. Ironically, the small territory of Israel proved an advantage for, while offering little room for retreat or manoeuvre, it made possible rapid transfers of men and equipment to any area from the centre and made possible the rapid call up of men from civilian life. Even so sophisticated a unit as a tank brigade could be maintained by only 200 to 300 and reach battle strength at 3,000 in a few hours. The standing army was completely 'top heavy' and almost every full-time soldier was a specialist or a commander but many of the senior officers remained partly civilian. So rapid indeed became the interchange of the army and the civilian population that virtually every civilian was for part of each year a soldier, and the army became the society in duplicate. Adapting the British wartime technique of broadcasting code words, the Israelis achieved virtually instantaneous mobilisation: by 1960, Israel found that it could maintain a standing army of no more than 50,000 and yet field a force of more than 300,000 in 48 hours.

The Israeli fascination with the army was not only for security reasons however important these were. As we have seen, a part of the Zionist drive was toward self-respect and rejection of what was seen by many Israelis as the passivity and weakness of the European Jews. The army became the pride of the nation. Moreover, it formed a school in nationhood as immigrants passed through it to learn both Hebrew and civics along with military tactics and the use of weapons. But the security aspects of the army were real enough. Inherent in the drive toward statehood was the hostility of those displaced by the Jewish immigrants and after the exodus of the Palestinian Arabs in the 1948-9 war, the displaced numbered nearly one million. Living on a meagre dole from the United Nations, in shanty towns and tent camps in the neighbouring Arab countries, the refugees were embittered, poverty-stricken, idle and eager for retaliation.

Thousands of 'incidents' occurred along the Israeli borders. Many were merely casual as farmers sought to return to lands they regarded as theirs to retrieve possessions or observe; others were commando in nature as refugees were formed into bands to harrass the Israelis. Some, on both sides, were intelligence collection forays or 'destabilising' raids. Large numbers were planned and aided by the armed forces of the Arab states. To them all the Israelis reacted sternly and effectively with massive retaliation and punitive raids. United Nations Truce Supervision officers filled volumes of reports with their investigations, and for many raids the Arabs and Israeli governments were severely condemned by the United Nations. But the raids continued and mounted in size and intensity until, in February 1955, the Israelis raided the Egyptian army headquarters in Gaza and killed 69 Egyptian soldiers.

Now thoroughly alarmed and angered, the Egyptian government, so recently welcomed by Israeli officials as the hope for a new accommodation, turned to the Soviet Union for military succour. The Gaza raid was the trigger which led to the so-called Czech arms deal. The 'deal' brought not only large quantities of late model military equipment into Arab hands but created an entirely new diplomatic situation by giving the Soviet Union a chance to leapfrog the 'northern tier' which was the very foundation of American strategy on the southern flank of the Soviet Union. In their turn angered and alarmed, the Americans sought to frighten the Egyptians away from their Soviet venture. Secretary of State Dulles failed to stop the Egyptians but was more successful in encouraging Britain, France and Israel to believe that the United States would support them in military action against Nasser. Meanwhile, in Jordan, the pro-Western government came under increasing attack and the British officers who had commanded the Jordan Arab Legion were ousted from their posts and were replaced by young nationalists. To the worried Western leaders, it seemed that, like China, the Middle East was being rapidly 'lost'.

Worsening bilateral relations with Egypt, and the feeling that Egypt was behind all the nationalist (read 'anti-Western/pro-Soviet') activity throughout the Middle East — it was Nasser's support for the Algerian revolutionaries which so infuriated the French — induced Secretary Dulles to announce on 20 July 1956 that the United States would withdraw its offer to lend Egypt $200 million towards the building of the High Dam at Aswan. Six days later, President Nasser replied by nationalising the Suez Canal and the National Bank of Egypt.

Britain could have safely ridden out this particular storm. After all, the lease on the Suez Canal had only a few more years to run and it should have mattered little what the legal position of the canal was, so long as it remained open to British shipping. It was transit, not ownership, that was ultimately of great importance to the British. However, Prime Minister Anthony Eden, himself a trained Arabist, was outraged by Egyptian behaviour. He found Nasser not to be a gentleman and spoke movingly at the time of his personal sense of hostility and anger. Personal antagonism was to play a crucial role in the judgements made by British statesmen in the coming months. Indeed, so conscious were they of the unusual nature of the decision as to overrule normal government practice so that, for example, no written records of Cabinet decisions survive.

Egyptian nationalisations set off a stream of diplomatic actions on the part of the users of the Suez Canal, led by Great Britain and the United States, to attempt to force Egypt to rescind its action. At the same time, a build-up of forces was secretly begun for a joint Anglo-French-Israeli invasion of Egypt.

In the first stages of the diplomatic crisis, the United States appeared to be willing, under easily foreseeable circumstances to turn a blind eye to the show of force. However, when it learned the full intent, the armed invasion of Egypt, the United States Government tried to dissuade Britain and France, and sternly warned Israel. Undeterred, perhaps not believing that the American position was to be taken at face value but was only face-saving, and counting on the American presidential elections, just a few days away, to sober both candidates, Israel attacked Egypt on 29 October 1956 while Britain and France, using the hostilities as an excuse and relying upon the inevitable initial confusion, issued an ultimatum ostensibly to both sides to cease military action and withdraw from the Canal (which the Israelis had not yet reached).

On 31 October the RAF bombed Egypt while the French Air Force flew defensive patrols over Israel. On 2 November despite a growing world reaction, Anglo-French forces invaded the Suez Canal and quickly captured Port Said. At that point, the United States, ominously backed by the Soviet Union (which was then engaged in suppressing its dissident satellite, Hungary) forced through a UN-backed cease-fire. Meanwhile, benefitting from the withdrawal of Egyptian forces under British and French pressure, Israeli forces occupied the whole Sinai Peninsula.

The aftermath of the war was painful to Britain and France. The government of Sir Anthony Eden fell and Anglo-American relations hit their lowest point in a generation. France, having lost a battle with Nasser, plunged even more bitterly into the unwinnable Algerian war, a war which brutalised Algeria and nearly tore apart French society. Also to pay a price were the resident British and French communities in the Middle East which have been evacuated during the fighting. Many never were able to return and none was able to recapture its former station.

Israel gained one objective — passage through Egyptian territorial waters in the Straits of Tiran to its port at Eilath on the Gulf of Aqaba. A tacit understanding was reached that no ships would be stopped from using the passage. But neither Egypt nor Israel signed the international treaty governing such waterways and no bilateral treaty sanctified the new understanding. (That was to be of fundamental importance in precipitating a new war a decade later.) In the aftermath of the 1956 war, the United Nations formed the Emergency Force (UNEF) to monitor the withdrawal of Israeli forces and subsequently to act as a buffer between Egypt and Israel, but Israel, flush with victory and feeling no need for protection, refused to allow the UN forces on its side of the frontier. (That also was to play a role in the outbreak of the 1967 war.)

Curiously, in Western eyes, the Suez war made Nasser a hero. One of its purposes was to destroy him and at the beginning of the fighting few would have given him even odds to survive. However, he did; more, he claimed with some justice a diplomatic victory within a military defeat. And even those Arab governments which detested him were forced to sing his praises. Overnight, from an aloof, cold and little known military dictator, he became a popular hero. More popular perhaps in Iraq, Jordan, Lebanon and Syria than in Egypt. He towered over the other Arab leaders and his picture dominated the covers of the magazines. His 'tough guy' stance set the style for his imitators. And, unfortunately for Egypt, he and his followers came to believe that world affairs hinge on machinations and threat, rather than upon economic strength and popular participation. The West had taught him its seamier side, and he was an apt and avid pupil.

Building on its new prestige and Nasser's popularity, Egypt attempted to intervene in the civil war which broke out in Lebanon in the spring of 1958 but was unable to score any significant successes. While given at the moment credit (or blame) for the July 1958 *coup d'état* in Baghdad, the Egyptians were as surprised as everyone else by it. After a brief period of congratulations between the 'fraternal' governments and leaders, they were increasingly at odds with its radical new dictatorship and repelled by its succession of unattractive strong men.

By 1961, it appeared that there was at least a chance that Egypt might leave aside its generally unproductive and costly foreign adventures to turn its energies toward the solution of its many overwhelming domestic social and economic problems. In this course the new American Kennedy Administration encouraged it diplomatically and with development assistance. But after promising and attempting to move in this direction, Egypt was quickly deflected by an unanticipated event, the 1962 *coup d'état* which overthrew the harsh, anachronistic government of Yemen. Had the *coup* in that remote, antique land been quick and successful, Egypt would have done little more than applaud but it was bungled and the old régime proved surprisingly resilient. Remnants of the ruling family escaped and rallied when they found a secure niche in the northern tribal area and, backed by Saudi Arabia which feared Nasser and a radical Yemen, began to counterattack. Since they appeared likely to overthrow the inept new republican government, Nasser judged it impossible for him to stand aside and watch a government proclaimed in the name of the Arab revolution, indeed virtually in his name, to go down in defeat. Each step led Egypt deeper into the rocky defiles and labyrinthine politics. Yemen became Egypt's Vietnam wrecking its development programme as surely as Vietnam was shortly to wreck President Johnson's in America.

The Yemen war was fought in difficult terrain against elusive tribal guerrillas who took a bloody toll of the conventional, cumbersome, heavy Egyptian formations. Like Vietnam, Yemen proved that little men can be crack shots. Few Egyptian villages were without their wounded and dead. But the war was a testing ground for the Egyptian army, training its soldiers in the use of armour with air power and paratroops and building its confidence as nothing had before. Indeed, the war exaggerated Egyptian confidence to the point of diminishing its capacity to analyse its own shortfalls. Having successfully undertaken large-scale combined operations there, the Egyptians were impelled forward toward a course that was to bring about the 'third round' in 1967. The steps toward that war began with a series of diplomatic moves to form alliances with the other 'confrontation' states. From bitter experience, the Arabs were learning the adage, 'those who do not hang together will hang separately'. They realised that a major cause of their failure in 1949 was their disunity. By creating a unified council of command over their several armed forces, they hoped to make better use of superior numbers to overwhelm Israeli technical and command superiority.

Both sides groped in the early stages of the crisis to perceive the other's intentions with eyes strained by years of hostility. The Israelis were convinced that the Arabs meant to 'drive them into the sea'. The Arabs were convinced that Israel, 'bastion of imperialism', working in concert with Britain, France and the United States, was determined, again to try to topple the 'progressive' régimes, and seize still more Arab territory. Alas, both were partly correct but each evaluation led to acts which justified the worst fears of the enemy. It was in this atmosphere that the Soviet and Syrian intelligence forces in May 1967 quietly passed word to the Arab leaders that Israel was on the point of launching a massive attack against Syria. American intelligence sources also confirmed that Israel was then building up its forces. The information seemed plausible since the Israeli Government had repeatedly warned the Syrian government that if guerrilla raids were mounted against Israel from Syria, Syria would be attacked.

On the other side, the Egyptians took the initiative of pressing for a united command, and raising the state of alertness of their troops. Government propaganda whipped up a storm of anti-Israeli sentiment and the general staff advised President Nasser that, fresh from battle experience in Yemen, heavily equipped with Soviet late model jet fighters and tanks, it was ready. President Nasser, who had come under increasing attacks for cowardice or backsliding from the other Arab leaders, again basked in almost universal popular acclaim. Swept forward by these enthusiasms and fears, he demanded that the United Nations remove its Emergency Force from Egyptian territory. That meant all the UN forces, the buffer between Egypt and Israel, must go since Israel had refused since 1956 to have any UN presence on its territory. Egyptian forces occupied the coastal strip at Sharm as-Shaikh on the Straits of Tiran and reasserted Egyptian sovereignty. Possibly, the Egyptians intended to stop short of hostilities with that diplomatic victory. To win but stop short of hostilities is nearly always the aim of those who precipitate crises. However, at a certain point, a crisis takes control of the men rather than the reverse. Moreover, in the fine calculation of the application of pressure and threat, politics as much as military strategy plays a part and even the most experienced leader, controlling the most intelligent government and leading the most sophisticated people, finds it difficult to react with finesse. The Egyptians were not rich in any of these attributes. Finally, even if one is a master strategist, there is the question of how the other side interprets one's actions. The Israeli interpretation was that the Arabs intended to destroy them and they decided to strike first.

Just after dawn on 5 June 1967, the Israeli Air Force struck and largely destroyed the Egyptian air force on the ground. It was Egypt's Pearl Harbor but Egypt had no vast Ocean to buffer it. So, with mastery of the air, the Israelis were able completely to overwhelm and virtually to annihilate the Egyptian army. Against the Syrians on the northern front fighting was particularly bitter with no quarter being asked or given. And, on the east, the small Jordanian force thrown into the conflict by a reluctant King Hussein (who could hardly have survived as a national leader had he stood aside after his provocative proclamations during the buildup of the crisis) was a hard fought but inevitable victory for the Israelis. The casualty figures were spectactular. The Arab forces suffered nearly 30,000 casualties and were virtually immobilised and stripped. Thousands of tanks, armoured vehicles, trucks and other pieces of equipment were either destroyed or captured. The Six Day War was an overwhelming Israeli victory and, of course, an equally overwhelming Arab defeat. Once again the Arabs were faced with a humiliating demonstration of their weakness and ineptitude.

The United States Government had tried to head off the conflict. Of this, more will be said later. But when the conflict came, the US was determined to keep more closely informed than it had been in 1956. As a result, it became briefly but painfully involved. On 8 June, in the midst of war, the USS *Liberty*, an intelligence monitoring ship (the sister ship of the better known but equally ill fated USS *Pueblo*) was attacked by Israeli jet-fighter bombers and torpedo boats in international waters off the Gaza Strip. The virtually unarmed *Liberty* managed to get off a brief 'Mayday' message that it was under attack and fighters were scrambled from the Sixth Fleet to protect it from what were assumed to be Egyptian or Russian aircraft. The Israelis then withdrew but had already hit the ship with over 800 shells and killed 34 and wounded 164 American sailors. Severely damaged, the *Liberty* limped into Malta. It subsequently was scrapped. The Israeli Government apologised and announced that its attack had been due to mistaken identity. Given the configuration and decoration of the ship — and five hours of close scrutiny by planes and boats — the excuse was, at the most charitable, lame, but it was accepted.

For allegedly intervening to aid Israel, the United States Government was denounced by the Arab states of which Egypt, Algeria, Iraq, Syria, the Sudan and Yemen severed relations.

The course of the war was predictable. By 1967, Israel had had a generation to build its power. With great intelligence, skill and foresight, and with vast foreign assistance, its economic, educational and military capacities had become those of a modern industrial state. The Israeli intelligence apparatus, incorporating large numbers of Jews from the Arab countries, could monitor and decipher the Arab radio signals and had penetrated the Arab secret services and military so that Israeli military planners had accurate and timely tactical information. Moreover, Israel was adept at the most advanced forms of electronic 'black' warfare (a fact which probably explains the attack on the *Liberty*) and was able to lead its opponents into its traps. Periodic and frequent call-ups of reserves, manoeuvres and training sessions had created what was man-for-man one of the best fighting forces in the world. Finally, profiting from the nature of its society and the small extent of its terrain, Israel was able to achieve numerical superiority in each separate engagement.

When the fighting stopped, the Israelis were in possession of the Syrian Golan Heights in the north, the entire West Bank of the Jordan to the east and the whole of the Sinai Peninsula to the banks of the Suez Canal. There is no doubt that they could have gone further in every direction had they wished for the Arab phalanx, backed by the 'progressive' powers, directed by popular leaders and armed with everything the Soviet Union could supply was smashed, twisted and burnt, and scattered over hundreds of miles of lost territory. Dispirited and disheartened, the Arabs sat back once more to try and figure out what went wrong. As in the past, they chose a scapegoat: the Commander of the Egyptian Army. He was 'guilty'. But he was not enough. His 'suicide' solved nothing. No one seemed to know what to do next.

The Israelis knew what *they* wanted from their victory with a certainty born of years of quest: they immediately tore down the barbed wire and walls and dispossessed 4,000 Arab families to consolidate Jerusalem as a Jewish city. Rapidly and effectively, they secured the conquered territories. Control was easy in Sinai, which was sparsely populated and in Golan which had been largely cleared by the fighting, but on the West Bank it set a dilemma for the Israeli Government: was the West Bank to be treated as 'occupied' or 'reclaimed'? Were its people to become Arab Israelis, like those in the rest of Israel, or Israeli-ruled Arabs? A decade later, these questions still are undecided. Outside pressure pushed the Israeli Government in one direction and internal politics in the other. But everyone agreed that effective armed opposition must be halted and the Israelis showed that they could manage that at least by their pacification of Gaza where they destroyed all Arab opposition.

The frontier along the Suez Canal became the scene of a new form of hostilities, a war of attrition, which was born of Israeli confident victory and Egyptian sullen defeat. The battles were fought at range by artillery barrages or in furtive night-time commando raids. Dug in on their side of the Canal, then blocked of course, the Israelies were said to have suffered more casualties than during the Six-Day War. Rapidly, however, they adopted new tactics. After building a modern Maginot Line, the Bar Lev Line, the Israelis covered it with mountains of sand so that it was relatively impervious to artillery shells. Against Israeli artillery, however, the Egyptians were unable to defend their cities. Thus, when the Egyptians sunk an Israeli destroyer on 21 October, the Israelis shelled and destroyed the oil refinery complex of Suez. Point by point, Israeli artillery made a wasteland of the Suez, Ismailia and Port Said, and brought about the exodus of tens of thousands of Egyptians. The war of attrition was a contest Egypt could not win.

The 'other' war, meanwhile, adopted both a new form and a new site: it moved from the Egyptian front and went underground, so to speak, as the Palestinians, now fully disenchanted with the Arab governments, took up their own cause, inspired by the Algerians *and* by the Israelis, with the traditional weapons of the weak. The terrorist attack, the commando raid, the planted bomb — tactics of ancient if disreputable lineage — replaced the tank, the jet, and the cannon. It was, inevitably, a war of deception, espionage, counter-intelligence, clandestine, lethal, and gaudy. The Arab governments, discredited and shamed, could hardly stop it although all of them were uncomfortable lest it be turned against them as it ultimately was.

What made it particularly dangerous, but also ineffective, was the Arab tendency to divide into mutually hostile groups. With everyone playing, and no one trusting the other, the Israelis rapidly penetrated each of the groups. They erected electrified barrier fences and mine fields against externally based commandos. As the French had done in Algeria, and against the 'internal' foe, they used counter-terror tactics developed in Algeria and Vietnam, including both the brutal measures (written in Palestinian law by the British in 1936) for reprisals against civilians in the area of attacks, and torture of prisoners to extract information or terrorise the would-be attackers. Sternly, they kept effective control of the occupied areas, driving those terrorists they did not kill abroad to the Arab countries and beyond. Clandestine 'hit squads' hunted down Arabs as far away as Scandinavia. When they wished to punish the Arab governments, the Israelis did so easily and at will as they demonstrated when they attacked Beirut airport and virtually wiped out the Lebanese civil air fleet on 28 December. Thus, while they were not able to stop terrorist attacks, even massive ones like the great hijackings of 1970, they made the war essentially unproductive for their enemies.

In their frustration and fury, the Palestinians turned on their Jordainian hosts and in the summer of 1970 nearly toppled the conservative and moderate government of King Hussein. The Arab-Israeli war became increasingly an Arab-Arab war and the theme once set remains to this day the *leitmotif* of the Middle Eastern struggle.

By the summer of 1970, it was clear to the Egyptians, if not yet to the Palestinians, that the long and consuming struggle was unwinnable. Eagerly the Egyptians clutched at the straw privately offered them by Israel for a ceasefire. This arrangement, known for its public manifestations as the Rogers Plan, took effect on the southern or 'formal' front in July 1970 just before the death of President Nasser.

When President Nasser died, leadership in Egypt devolved upon his colleague Anwar Sadat. Known as an amiable and unambitious man, Anwar Sadat had been the butt of many a Cairo political joke. Nasser had treated him with well-publicised scorn. Little about him gave the appearance of a great war-leader. In truth, also, he had little to lead. Egypt's foreign policy among the Arabs, seriously weakened by the catastrophe of its war in Yemen, had lost its champion with the death of Nasser. The country was nearly bankrupt and owed the Soviet Union, depending on exactly how the debt was reckoned, somewhere between $10 and $15 billion. The Egyptian public was dispirited and disaffected. In bondage to a vast and self-serving bureaucracy, it had withdrawn into inner isolation.

Ironically, as weak as Sadat was to lead a war against Israel, he was certainly too weak to bring about peace. A Nasser, with all the charisma of nationalism about him and given favourable conditions and reasonable terms, might have been able to make peace. He had, indeed, on several occasions, privately tried to work out a viable accommodation but, as we shall see in the following chapter, either the terms were never right, he was never sincere, or his adversaries made it impossible for him. Sadat would have been open to the charge of treason even to have followed some of the policies privately laid down by Nasser. Moreover, the Israeli Government in the spring of 1973 believed that it had won and it wished to force the Arabs unequivocally to admit their utter defeat. This was precisely what the Arabs could not do. Both armies thus pressed a hawkish position on their governments, the Israeli army out of a justifiable sense of pride in its capacities and the Egyptian army out of an equally justifiable sense of shame at its incapacities. The Israelis felt no need to hurry with the process of peace, secure as they were of the possession and exploitation of the Egyptian oilfields in Sinai and the welcome cheap Arab labour from Gaza and the West Bank. They had effectively destroyed the internal Arab opposition and had managed to create almost hermetically sealed borders through which virtually no commandos were able to penetrate. The Arabs, particularly the Egyptians, Jordanians and Syrians, equally but for opposite reasons were in no hurry to make peace. They recognised that the price of peace would have involved both giving up territory and, once again, publically proclaiming their incompetence. Always a dangerous admission for government in any part of the world, that admission in the Middle East had proven to be virtually a sentence of death on political leaders. If any had forgotten the assassination of King Abdullah in July 1951, they were reminded of it afresh by the murder of the visiting prime minister of Jordan in the lobby of Cairo's Sheraton hotel on 28 November 1971. To all it appeared not only prudent and praiseworthy but virtually requisite to prepare for war. Israel, Egypt, Syria and Jordan each devoted as much as 25 per cent of its gross national product to preparations for the 'next round'.

Yet who could really believe in the likelihood of that war? Competent observers found it almost ludicrous to entertain, particularly after a breakdown of Egyptian-Soviet co-operation. Relations had, for some time, been going sour. The Russians were never popular among the Egyptians and were themselves angered by the Egyptian propensity to blame the failure of their armies on Russian equipment. The Russian candidate for leadership in Egypt was Sadat's rival Ali Sabry — jailed in May 1971 — and there was a growing restiveness among the Egyptian bourgeoisie over the restrictions imposed, *à la Russe*, on their society and economy. Finally, there was the inevitable clash over conditions for the resupply of weapons and material for the Egyptian army. The Egyptians always wanted more weapons while the Russians wished to extract more than the cotton they received in return. Disagreements came to a head in the spring and summer of 1972 and finally, on 15 July, President Sadat expelled all Soviet military personnel and dependants, about 40,000 people, and ordered the Egyptian army to take over all Soviet bases and equipment.

At the time, many observers saw the Soviet expulsion as a signal to the West that Egypt was ready to perform its side of the bargain of the Rogers plan. Unfortunately, the Israelies saw it as a sign that Egypt was near collapse and that, consequently, there was even less reason to compromise with them. The Israeli leaders set the price for peace at what they knew, and admitted, to be beyond the reach of any Arab leader.

Once again, events escalated rapidly toward war. The process was recognised by outside observers by April 1973. By the end of June 1973, Presidents Sadat and Assad had formed a rough plan for an assault on Israel. Syria particularly began to receive increasing supplies of military equipment from Russia and both the Egyptian and Syrian armies began intensive training programmes and large-scale military manoeuvres. After the usual build-up of tension, war broke out, virtually simultaneously, on both the Syrian and Egyptian fronts on Saturday, 8 October 1973.

This was the first Arab offensive since 1948 and the results of the first days of fighting astonished both the Arab populace and leadership. Five Egyptian divisions managed to get across the canal after commandos had knocked out the principal Israeli defence weapon, a system of oil-bearing pipes designed to incinerate advancing Egyptian troops. Putting aside their more sophisticated Soviet weapons, the Egyptians used high-pressure water-hoses to wash away the huge sand barrier atop the Bar Lev Line and with wire-guided anti-tank missiles and the SAM-6 rocket batteries and VSU-23 anti-aircraft guns effectively neutralised the two main Israeli weapons of the past, the tank and the jet. In the north, Syrian tanks ploughed into the Israeli fortifications in even larger formations than had been launched by the Wermacht against Russia in 1941. Indeed, perhaps the most extraordinary aspect of the war as a whole was the weight of armour employed on the tiny fronts. As many as 5,000 tanks took part. To get some picture of this escalation, one must remember that during most of the great campaign of World War II in the Western Desert, the Afrika Korps and the Eighth Army each had less than 200.

The Egyptians and Syrians differed in their conceptions of the war. The Syrians began the war with a massive all-out assault and the war was fought on that front as a desperate slugging match. The carnage was immense. In contrast, the Egyptians, from the first, conceived of the fighting in largely political terms. With limited engagements but massive troop formations, they sought to create a war of sufficient proportions to force the Great Powers to intervene and solve a crisis that they alone could not hope to win. They saw the military action as a means to require effective Great Power diplomatic activity. Unlike the Syrians, the Egyptians never attempted to attack Israel proper and after the first push beyond the Bar Lev Line the Egyptian army stopped and dug into defensive positions. Failure to push forward to seize or at least block the Sinai passes which connected Israel with the front lines, while diplomatically wise, almost proved their undoing. The Egyptian front was only ten miles deep across the Canal, too little for effective manoeuvre or defence, and the situation gave the Israeli army the opportunity to regroup for a major counter-attack. This counter attack ultimately pinned the Egyptian Third Army to the southern part of the Suez Canal and opened the way for a further attack across the Canal which stopped only 60 miles — 101 kilometres — short of Cairo itself. However faulty may have been their military conception, the Egyptians were realistic in appraising the relative capacities of the two sides: the major facts which had pertained since 1948 not only had remained but had become increasingly favourable to the Israelis. Israel, the modern, industrialised, dedicated society had become relatively more so in each category while the Arabs remained relatively backward and poor. By 17 October 1973 Israel was well on its way to inflicting a stunning tactical defeat on the Egyptian forces. It was at this point that the action changed gear, from military to economic and diplomatic, and the United States and the oil-producing countries intervened to play their decisive roles.

7 AMERICAN DIPLOMACY

Throughout its turbulent history, the Middle East has rarely enjoyed what has been euphemistically termed 'the ancient and comfortable right to be left alone'. The best that can be said is that occasionally one can hear the often strident voices of diplomats above the clamour of battle and the drumming footfall of battle. But in truth it was often difficult to distinguish the one from the other for like the classical herald the diplomat often came first to warn of the arrival of the army unless his conditions were quickly met. For at least the last two millennia, most of the warriors and diplomats have come from abroad and the native peoples are accustomed to the notion that their fates should be decided at distant capitals. The pronouncements of foreign governments, not their own, actually and even rightly determine the future. Indeed, the proper, often the only feasible, role for themselves was to seek out a particular foreigner, win his favour and get him to pronounce on their behalf. In recent years, both Arabs and Israelis have followed these time-worn paths but in new ways. The Israelis have proved most adept at courting Western opinion and obtaining Western aid and alignment but the Arabs have also tried to mobilise the Third World and to play off against one another the two sides of the cold war.

Eagerly, often violently, foreign powers have asserted their presence and sought to play the roles so eagerly assigned them. But the nature and language of diplomacy have evolved even when the issues and geopolitics appear to remain much the same. Russia and America are today, in a sense, still playing the 'Great Game' of the nineteenth century — but Russia is the Soviet Union and for the Greek Orthodox Church it has substituted the Communist movement and while America has taken over Britain's role it is using the tools, goods and persuasions of an industrial society more than armies and agents. Thus, to understand current diplomacy, we must look not only at the men and the events but at the tools and techniques and then attempt to put them into the changing context of the Middle East.

The British Withdrawal

When World War II ended, the Arabs and the Jews were pressing hard to assert the symbols and even the reality of sovereignty. Britain had learned and applied deftly a policy of acquiescence on symbolism — 'let them have their flags, anthems and statues. We will keep the advisers and the airfields,' said one experienced practitioner. With grand ceremony, in 1946, the British evacuated Cairo's commanding citadel and the Kasr el-Nil barracks in the heart of Cairo and similar stations elsewhere to withdraw to less conspicuous bases. For a while, it seemed that Palestine would be the ideal base — indeed that had been a part of the original interest in Palestine — and if not Palestine then Suez. But everywhere they turned, the British found that the easy compromises of the old days were inadequate. Comfortable old relationships with the few in power were soured by unfamiliar slogans carried by strident voices. Soon, they would be emphasised by bombs and bullets and acknowledged by the more effective criticism of the foreign press and the United Nations.

First off, Britain found that the Middle East could no longer be handled as an area or issue unto itself: streaming toward it were the pitiful survivors of the Nazi holocaust. Whatever their sympathies, and they were often strong and deep, the British leaders of both parties recognised that if they allowed in the thousands of Europeans who demanded the 'right of return', they would make completely untenable their already precarious perch in the eastern Mediterranean. Why allow it? They tried not to. But they found that they were caught in an unwinnable situation: if they applied sufficient force to be effective, they were accused of being successors to the Nazis and if they did not, the policy failed and failed pathetically, shufflingly. To intercept the refugee ships was almost worse than letting them through; to catch terrorists made them national, even international heroes and brought horrifying retaliation even in England itself; to stand pat was expensive and seemed unproductive and would not long be tolerated by the public. Britain in 1945 was financially exhausted, its public tired of world power, and it depended upon the United States increasingly to help with reconstruction, to help it keep what was left and to take up such burdens as it decided to lay down. It was in this context that the United States Government made its first post-war diplomatic approaches.

The American Attitude

Those Americans who knew of the Middle East were not many. Church groups established small outposts in Jerusalem and a major Protestant mission society set up schools, hospitals and finally universities in Turkey, Lebanon, Iraq and Egypt. The Middle East was biblical, remote, almost mystical, something in a Spiritual, but not a place in the contemporary world. Jerusalem was where Jesus lived; not where Arabs and Zionists contended for sovereignty. America (unlike Britain and France) bought and sold almost nothing there; even oil then did not dominate American thinking. Texas was full of oil and besides in the populist tradition, oil was a dirty business, by nature corrupting. No one then thought of energy crises or balance of payments problems or the fall of the dollar. Besides, the issues had been decided on the battle-field. Hitler was dead and Japan defeated. No one had time for the con-fusing little issues.

But one issues was stark, horrible, almost unthinkable — the abomin-ation of the death camps. The Jewish refugee issue was something the American public cared about and understood. While few knew where Syria was, everyone knew of Belsen, Dachau and Buchenwald. Even more, Americans in their private moments, admitted to a sort of per-sonal guilt. At the most critical point in the pre-war exodus of the panic-stricken European Jews, America had closed its doors. A differ-ent policy in 1938 would have saved thousands. Blood was on Ameri-can hands too. Even more privately Americans then discriminated against Jews, more politely and more ambivalently than against Blacks, and were beginning to feel uneasy about it. Anyway, fair play de-manded that the survivors of the Nazi camps had won the right to peace and security, to a home of their own, to the certainty that never again would they be so horribly treated. That was what the war had been all about. To oppose them in these wishes was not only wrong; it was immoral. And, more practically, it was politically impossible. Yet, Americans felt, that was exactly what the British seemed to be doing. They set quotas on immigration and when they caught illegal immi-grants, often on sinking old ships, they interned the pitiful passengers on Cyprus in what looked or sounded quite like concentration camps. That also the American public could understand . . . and deplore.

The American Jewish community, strong, wealthy and politically active, realised that the time had come when it must succeed: it knew how short was the memory of wartime allies and friends, and how much shorter the memory of guilt. But most critical, the *need* was then for the emigrating refugees. Determined to get out, they might have dis-persed around the world and so begun again to rebuild lives that would, probably, again be overturned in new turmoils of anti-semitism. Yet once dispersed how many would come back to establish an Israel? Ex-perience suggested that not many would. The goal was in sight — 'to-morrow in Jerusalem' — and the momentum must not be lost. All this underlay the first major political programme of the American Jewish

Community, the so-called Biltmore Program which had demanded that '. . . the gates of Palestine be opened . . . and that Palestine be established as a Jewish Commonwealth integrated into the structure of the new democratic world.'

The point at which to apply pressure was the American Government and through it on the British Government; there, not in the Middle East was the key to the kingdom.

President Harry Truman recognised these currents and responded to them. As he liked to say, 'the buck' stopped at his desk. Acutely conscious of being overshadowed by the memory of President Roosevelt and then still barely known in his own right, Truman found the refugee issue politically attractive. At one point, indeed, Secretary of State General George Marshall threatened to resign over Truman's political use of this issue. What he did was to call for the immediate admission of 100,000 Jewish displaced persons into Palestine and encouraged the appointment of an Anglo-American Committee of Inquiry to begin its study of the Palestine problem with a visit to the Nazi death camps. The message there was clear: at all costs save the survivors. Those who visited the camps were emotionally shattered and found it difficult to tolerate those who raised other considerations. Anti-semite became almost as dangerous a charge than as Red was later to be. In both the British and American Cabinets splits developed over the issue again as though it were as new and fresh as in 1917. Passions ran high. Both Foreign Secretary Ernest Bevin and Secretary of State Marshall were swept along by the tide in which Truman pointedly remarked that he had few Arab constituents. In his public statements, Truman singled out from the report of the Anglo-American Committee only the requirement for the immediate admission of 100,000 Jews and put aside the Committee's recommendation that Palestine become a bi-national state where 'Jew shall not dominate Arab and Arab shall not dominate Jew'. These were complex issues said the President but the refugee issue was simple and immediate. It was also highly political as the Republican candidate for governor of New York – who was really already running for the presidency – called the next day for the admission 'not of 100,000 but several hundreds of thousands'.

The traditional and acceptable means of diplomacy had been overturned and the British Government felt increasingly unable to work with the American and knew that it was unable to 'go it alone'. Soon it announced that it could no longer sustain its traditional role in the eastern Mediterranean. That role, President Truman on 12 March 1947 assumed for the United States when he announced what came to be called the Truman Doctrine. For Greece and Turkey, the Doctrine meant military and economic aid; for the Palestine Mandate it meant support for the creation of new states under a United Nations arranged partition – an objective for which the United States lobbied hard in the General Assembly – and ultimately it meant the beginnings of a major extension of the Marshall Plan to cover the Middle East.

After the 1948 War

Within minutes after the proclamation of the State of Israel, the United States Government recognised it. The Soviet Union was close behind. Neither took a serious role in the ensuing Arab-Israeli war or, directly, in the efforts to bring about peace although the chief UN negotiator was an American, Dr Ralph Bunche. But, when the dust of war had settled, it became clear that one tragic result of the war was that it had given birth to a new population of refugees. Nearly one million Arab Palestinians had fled or been driven from their homes and had taken up what was assumed to be temporary residence in camps of tents in the neighbouring Arab countries. Many were unemployable women and children but even the men fell into the worst category of the under-developed Middle Eastern economies – landless agricultural labourers in an area of chronic underemployment and insufficient usable agricultural land. They were scattered throughout Lebanon (to which the bulk of the Christians had gone), Jordan, Syria and the Egyptian-administered Gaza strip. Not only were they tragic victims of the war – and however strongly one felt about Zionism or sympathised with the persecuted Jews it was undeniable that the Palestinian refugees were also victims – but they were a source of great potential danger in the context of the cold war. Whether or not the heart felt, the head pondered. What better resource for future Russian subversion than an impoverished, desperate people. So for various reasons the United States began to think in terms of a new policy initiative. It was to be the first of many attempts to 'solve' the Palestine problem.

If the United States did not really understand the complex clash of nationalism involved in the Middle Eastern problems, it did understand the problem of poverty and felt it had learned in its own depression a solution. Poor people needed jobs. Jobs were created by healthy economies. The road ahead to peace, and security from communism, was thus clear. Mr Gordon Clapp, the Chairman of the Tennessee Valley Authority (TVA), the very symbol of the New Deal, was sent to the Middle East to outline the solution. In a sense his was a solution looking for a problem. The report of his commission, published in December 1949, outlined the basis of development plans for Syria, Leban-anon, Jordan, and Iraq. The refugees, Mr Clapp believed, were merely another aspect of the surplus labour force of the Middle East. It followed that the way to solve the refugee problem was to create a labour shortage. Once the skills of the refugees were drawn into the labour pool and were productively employed, the refugees would go off the United Nations dole, fade into the economies of the countries in which they were resident and the Palestine problem would disappear.

This logic resembled very early Zionist ideas, before the Zionists got to know that there was a Palestinian Arab *community* and that the Palestinians were mainly settled farmers not nomads. The early Zionists hoped and thought that the Palestinian Arabs, to make room for the Jewish settlers, would merely 'fold their tents' and withdraw to equally or nearly as good land (which was all the same to them in any case) further inland. They did not realise or care how different the economies, ways of life or societies of settled Palestine and nomadic Jordan were. But over the years, the Zionists had become much more sophisticated about the Palestinian Arabs. The Americans in 1949 started where the Zionists had been in 1919. Without the depth of historical experience and under the circumstances that pertained in 1949, Mr Clapp may be forgiven. The fact is that then, objectively speaking, the Palestinian Arab community *had* ceased to exist; what did exist was a structureless collection of individuals, the remnants of villages squatting in ragged tents and scrap metal huts, helter skelter over the landscape of Lebanon, Syria, Jordan and Gaza. The camps were at that time appalling slums and the people in them lacked effective organisation almost more obviously than they lacked clothing or shelter. It *seemed* that whatever the outcome, over the long term, the urgent problem was to find some decent place and productive outlet for these hopeless people. Mr Clapp's programme was eminently humanitarian. It was also eminently apolitical. As the solution to the refugee problem, it was a failure. As a stimulus to the development programmes of the Arab countries, it was a considerable success and may be credited with turning their energies into directions that ultimately were of great benefit to their peoples.

The Dulles Era

Following the American election which brought President Eisenhower into office, John Foster Dulles became Secretary of State. Mr Dulles had a remarkable education for his task. Reading his speeches and writings of the 1930s, one gets the impression of a broadly humanitarian man caught up in the quest, so evident in those years, for social justice and economic prosperity. By the end of World War II, however, Mr Dulles, like many other Americans, had become terrified of the spectre of international communism and it was that spectre which shaped most of his thought on the world situation. It was natural that he should see the Middle East in terms of a communist threat and he was, as his pronouncements as Secretary made clear, shocked and dismayed to find that the responsible leaders in the Middle East did not see the world in his terms. When he took his first tour around the Middle East in 1953, he found the Arab leaders obsessed with the problem of Israel and the Israelis, conversely, with the problems of security *vis-à-vis* the Arabs. It was only in the north, he found, that his fear of Russian expansion was shared. Consequently, he put the vast majority of the efforts of the American Government into what he called the 'northern tier', Greece, Turkey, Iraq, Iran and Pakistan, which countries he linked to the defensive treaties he had helped to create in Europe and Southeast Asia.

Insofar as his attentions were turned to the south, they involved three serious attempts to get at the root of the Palestinian problem. Only one of these has been fully publicised. The first involved 'quiet diplomacy', discrete bilateral conversations — still highly classified — with the leaders of Egypt and Israel, to attempt to find what it was that really might form the basis of some kind of a deal. So discrete, so secret, so careful were these discussions that the American emissary largely misunderstood what was being said to him and the discussions came to naught.

Mr Dulles's second try, which resulted from months of study by a high level State Department committee, partially surfaced in a paper presented to the New York Council on Foreign Relations. The full study, however, has never been publicly discussed. Without going into too much detail, what it amounted to was perhaps the most complex exercise in map-making since the abortive United Nations Palestinian resolution. Put simply, Mr Dulles's plan was based on the supposition that at the heart of the Palestine problem were not the refugees, not the Palestinian people at all but 'access', the desire of the Arabs to be able to move from east to west freely and easily and the Israelis to be able to move from north to south. Mr Dulles's logical, apolitical mind sought a solution in geography: frontiers of intersecting triangles between Arab territory to the west (Egypt) and Arab territory to the east (Jordan) and northern and southern Israel. At the physical location on the ground would presumably be some sort of cloverleaf where traffic would be allowed to flow freely in all four directions. In this way, thought Mr Dulles, the major stumbling-block to peace would be removed. It is almost unbelievable, reading the deliberations of this committee, and viewing the peace plan, that no one scribbled on any of the far-fetched papers, 'but the emperor has no clothes'.

During 1953, Mr Eric Johnston, who was best known in the United States as the 'Czar' of the film industry, was made a special representative of the President to work out a third possibility by dividing the waters of the river Jordan. The underlying assumption of his mission was that if this key economic asset of Lebanon, Syria, Jordan and Israel could be satisfactorily divided among the four states, not only would a major problem be thus solved but, almost as important, the concerned countries would learn that they could safely work together to solve outstanding issues. Unfortunately, Mr Johnston and the State Department saw is mission as merely an engineering problem. His staff was to determine how much Jordan river water each of the Arab countries needed and then to assign the residue to Israel. This seemed logical, neat and straightforward. Reasonable men could surely not object to such an approach. What it did, of course, was to treat the most political issue on the frontier of the four countries as non-political. In retrospect, it seems almost inconceivable that anyone, especially a man from California, could think of water in an essentially desert area as non-political. Predictably, Mr Johnston's programme went well at 'the working level', when he was dealing with technicians, economists and engineers in the several countries, but failed completely when those charged with political responsibility became involved.

The Kennedy Administration

With the coming of the Kennedy administration in 1961 several different approaches were mooted. Secretary of State Dean Rusk, a close confidant and friend of former Secretary John Foster Dulles, continued to emphasise the 'northern tier'. For Mr Rusk, the spectre of communism was still the central issue while the problems of the Arabs and the Israelis were a nuisance preventing or making difficult actions to deal with it. President Kennedy and most of his close advisers, however, sought to encourage the Arab countries and Israel to devote their energies to internal development. It was this that lay behind the AID strategy and Public Law 480, which disposed of surplus American wheat. Egypt was a major recipient of this assistance in 1961 and 1962. Egypt was thus encouraged to devote its energies inward to come to grips with its appalling social and economic problems. As we have seen this policy was derailed by the Yemen war. America's own subsequent intervention in Vietnam also diverted American resources from essentially nation-building overseas programmes to further emphasis on military prepared-ness and the provision of arms to America's overseas allies. In the Middle East, of course, the latter meant primarily the northern tier.

The only direct diplomatic initiative at this time on the Palestine problem was a mission under the leadership of the then president of the Carnegie Endowment for International Peace, a former Member of the Policy Planning Staff, Dr Joseph Johnson. In September 1961, the American Government arranged for the United Nations to send Dr Johnson to consult with concerned governments on ways to settle the refugee problem. The idea was to put the issue before the refugees, within limited areas of choice, and under the active supervision of the United Nations, in accordance with the resolutions passed by the United Nations. Each *individual* refugee was to exercise his right to 'return' or receive compensation. The American Government believed that when actually presented with the possibility of return, each refugee would realise that there was no *Palestine* to return to and that going *to* Israel constituted a migration, an unattractive migration at that, to a new and alien country. The overwhelming majority of the refugees would pre-sumably decline 'return' and accept compensation. The crucial point was that, having been offered a choice, the refugees would lose their moral position: they would have been granted their acknowledged right to choose. Politically, they would no longer be on dead centre: they would be free to, and obviously would be encouraged to settle in Arab countries, or, perhaps, to migrate abroad.

The message which Dr Johnson took to Israel was essentially that Israel 'would have to take in some refugees she did not want, without any prior agreement on the number (which, parenthetically but most importantly, I am convinced would, under the procedures I proposed, be very small, fewer than one-tenth of the total of true refugees and their descendants)'. To the Arabs, he stressed that this was the fulfil-ment of the letter of the United Nations resolutions and might, thus, be the breaking of the log jam in Middle Eastern peace. It seemed practical and straightforward. Its only problem was that no one in the Middle East wanted to undertake it. The Israelis, reasonably, feared that either the entire Palestinian population or significant numbers would wish to 'return'. It did not want the Palestinians back. If they came back their very presence would make the continuation of the *Jewish* state incom-patible with a democratic system. The Arabs would shortly outnumber the Jewish Israelis and 80 years of Zionist labour would have been lost at the very moment of victory. There was no compelling reason why the Israelis should take such a risk. The Palestinians themselves, although not directly consulted, would probably have reacted unfavourably or even violently to what they certainly would have regarded as sharp practice on the part of the American Government. The Arab governments recognised the venture as an attempt to sweep the 'problem' under the rug by disposing of the refugees and so as antithetical to their entire policy on Palestine. Still, the Johnson mission was the major Middle Eastern diplomatic effort of the decade.

As America became increasingly involved in the build-up of the Vietnam war, the Middle East was allowed very little high level attention. Meanwhile, as a consequence of the Egyptian intervention in Yemen and the hostilities between Egypt and Saudi Arabia that intervention provoked, the United States' relations with Egypt had become hostile. Within the American Government, a number of senior officials, particularly in the CIA, put forth a notion that Egypt's President Nasser was virtually a Russian agent and that the Russians had a long range plan to stockpile sufficient arms and ammunition to enable Russian troops to be introduced virtually overnight into the area.

The 1967 War

Despite repeated warnings, the 1967 war caught the United States Government by surprise. Only two days before the war actually began, the senior responsible American official told a secret briefing of Middle Eastern specialists, that the crisis was over. Israel had given assurances to the United States that it would not move and the Egyptians had agreed to send their vice-president to the United States to negotiate.

Surprise though it was, the war was not wholly unwelcome to the American Government. Nasser was not only unpopular but was cordially disliked by the President and his senior advisers. His polices in Yemen, in which poison gas had been used, and in Saudi Arabia which had been bombed by Russian-flown aircraft, appeared even to those who knew what America was doing then in Vietnam, not merely hostile but barbaric. His pro-Soviet leanings were regarded as dangerous to American interests and he was getting his just desserts. The president apparently hoped that Nasser would himself be overthrown as a consequence of the Egyptian defeat and that a tacit but non-negotiated peace could be achieved. When Nasser was not overthrown, President Johnson announced a series of principles on which the American Government hoped that a restoration of peace would occur. Nothing very much was done about these principles, however, because diplomatic relations had been broken between the United States, which Nasser accused of intervening in the war, and virtually all of the Arab countries.

The scene of American diplomatic initiative shifted to the United Nations where in November British Minister of State for Foreign Affairs, Lord Caradon drafted Security Council resolution 242. Adopted by the Council on 22 November, 242 became the pivotal document for all subsequent peace discussions to this day. Like the Balfour Declaration with which the Palestine story began, so to speak, it is short and every word and phrase is a result of hours of consultation, compromise and debate. It reads as follows:

The Security Council,

Expressing its continuing concern with the grave situation in the Middle East,

Emphasizing the inadmissibility of the acquisition of territory by war and the need to work for a just and lasting peace in which every State in the area can live in security,

Emphazing further that all Member States in their acceptance of the Charter of the United Nations have undertaken a commitment to act in accordance with Article 2 of the Charter,

1. *Affirms* that the fulfillment of Charter principles requires the establishment of a just and lasting peace in the Middle East which should include the application of both the following principles:

(i) Withdrawal of Israeli armed forces from territories occupied in the recent conflict;

(ii) Termination of all claims or states of belligerency and respect for and acknowledgement of the sovereignty, territorial integrity and political independence of every State in the area and their right to live in peace within secure and recognized boundaries free from threats or acts of force;

2. *Affirms further* the necessity

(a) For guaranteeing freedom of navigation through international waterways in the area;

(b) For achieving a just settlement of the refugee problem;

(c) For guaranteeing the territorial inviolability and political independence of every State in the area, through measures including the establishment of demilitarized zones;

3. *Requests* the Secretary-General to designate a Special Representative to proceed to the Middle East to establish and maintain contact with the States concerned in order to promote agreement and assist efforts to achieve a peaceful and accepted settlement in accordance

with the provisions and principles in this resolution;

4. *Requests* the Secretary-General to report to the Security Council on the progress of the efforts of the Special Representative as soon as possible.

The key phrases are the assertion, in line with the charter of the United Nations, that the acquisition of territory by warfare is inadmissible that Israel should withdraw from Arab territories, and that the states should be left in peace. Left vague, however, was the designation of 'territories' — were they to be [all] *the* territories or merely [*some*] territories? The resolution allowed considerable scope for diplomatic negotiation and could only be passed in this, purposely vague, form. Moreover, the resolution concerned only the states, so the Palestinians, not a state but surely central to the problem, were left out. The resolution also required the Secretary-General to designate a representative to visit the area and act, where possible, as an arbitrator. On this resolution, the Swedish Ambassador to the Soviet Union, Mr Gunnar Jarring, became the Security Council representative and began years of fruitless consultations with government leaders throughout the Middle East.

Unreported at the time, and subsequently, was an Egyptian approach in October 1967 to the American Government to seek terms for peace. President Nasser's message to the American government was, in summary, 'we have lost the war and realise we must pay a price. Tell us what the price is and we will tell you if we can make peace.' Nasser's emissary was rebuffed. Presumably, the American Government thought Nasser could not last much longer.

Inherent in all the American diplomatic interventions from 1949 to 1970 was avoidance of politics. Issue after separate issue was sought as a key to this complex, intractable problem: economic development, division of waters, refugee compensation. When these appeared fruitless, a policy of indecision — of allowing the defeated Arabs to 'stew in their own juice' — was tried.

The Nixon Administration

When the Nixon Administration came into office in the United States, it was preoccupied with the issue which had brought down the Johnson Administration, Vietnam. At that time, the Middle East was outwardly calm and seemed unimportant: it could not compete for the time of senior officials. However, the head of the National Security Council, Henry Kissinger, wanted to find out, unofficially, if there was a possibility that the Egyptians might be interested in peace negotiations. A confidential emissary was sent to Cairo to inquire. When the answer was positive, the emissary was sent back to see if some sort of formula could be worked out. Nasser indicated his willingness and actually agreed to an unofficial rough draft of an agreement which included diplomatic recognition of Israel, demilitarisation of Sinai, and legalisation of Israeli access to Aqaba through Egyptian territorial waters. At the time, this agreement constituted a major breakthrough; however, the administration was then unwilling to take up the opportunity or even seriously to consider it.

It was not until the summer of 1970, when both Israel and Egypt found the 'war of attrition' along the Suez Canal costly and fruitless that another opportunity occurred. At that time, the United States began another much-publicised peace initiative designed to bring about a cease-fire. High-level diplomatic contacts were made by Secretary of State William Rogers, but neither the Israelis nor the Egyptians placed much confidence in American efforts. Behind the scenes, however, both Egypt and Israel wanted to end what was, for them both, unpopular meaningless and wearisome hostilities on the Canal. At that point, the Israeli Government made contact through an unofficial private emissary with President Nasser and offered a tacit ceasefire and confidential negotiations. The Egyptian Government accepted and the understanding surfaced in Nasser's last major speech before his death.*

Meanwhile, American activities in the Middle East focused mainly on Saudi Arabia and Israel. With Israel, America enjoyed an extraordinary diversity of relationships – contacts between universities, research organisations, business, labour unions, newspapers, publishing houses citizens groups and political parties – that typifies its contacts only with Great Britain and France. Some of these relationships were codified in the so-called Israel Lobby which provided a massive, sensitive and powerful political force not only in Washington but throughout the United States. The full dimensions of this activity have never been fully portrayed although a Senate Foreign Relations Committee report gives some indication of the massive scale. While normal and legal within the American system of politics, where every interest group engages in lobbying to attempt to get its programme supported and its interests protected, mentioning the fact of its existence often resulted in ugly charges of anti-semitism. What made the Israeli effort unusual in addition to its great extent and heavy funding, was that there was no

---

*While details of neither of these two initiatives are public knowledge, the author can vouch for them as he was the emissary.

opposite lobby. Put in President Truman's crass terms, there were no Arab votes. Such Arab propaganda activities as took place in the United States were clumsy, heavy-handed and often counter-productive. But leaving aside the Jewish lobby, the fact was that Israel fitted like a glove on the hand of America. Americans felt understood by the Israelis. They felt at home in Israel. There were fascinating people to talk with, interesting things to do, markets to be cultivated, researchers with ideas to be ascertained, audiences who appreciated American music, books, plays. Israel was not only a democracy but to visit it was an exciting experience. Movement back and forth between the United States and Israel, simply to take the academic community alone, was extraordinary. For such a small country as Israel, it was, indeed, unprecedented. One could hardly think of this relationship in traditional 'diplomatic' terms.

American relations with Saudi Arabia were entirely different. Despite, or even perhaps because of such films as *Lawrence of Arabia*, Americans had a vision of Arabs dressed in flowing robes, armed to the teeth, riding camels over trackless wastes. There was something in this romantic vision but it was rapidly fading. By 1970, it was almost impossible in most of Arabia to find a camel, or a camel saddle to put on it. Arabia never had many bedouin and those who remained were more likely to be seen in a truck than on a camel. The American image of Arabia was about as up-to-date as cowboys and Indians. The reality of the new Arabia was based upon the rise of the oil industry. Arabian oil was the greatest single American overseas investment and, at its height, the Arabian American Oil Company (ARAMCO) employed thousands of American administrators, technicians and labourers. But the oil industry was not alone. Dozens of major American and English companies were involved in running the national airline, building highways, providing public health, training the army, and doing the many tasks associated with the nation-building process. Relations between the United States and Saudi Arabia were difficult because of the passionate concern of King Faisal with the Palestinian issue, yet Saudi Arabia was a firm and relatively undemanding partner of the United States in the quest for regional security, conservative governmental policy and anti-communism. No one since John Foster Dulles — whom the German Chancellor Conrad Adenauer once described as the 'last of the true believers' — so passionately opposed what he believed to be the anti-religious evil of communism as King Faisal.

The 1973 War

The 1973 war brought the United States back with unprecedented vigour and publicity into the Middle Eastern area. A whole new vocabulary of diplomacy was invented to describe the ventures. 'Shuttle diplomacy' and 'step by step', were only two of the better known phrases. The winter of 1973 and the spring of 1974 were a time of frenetic activity. It was a one-man show — by Secretary of State Henry Kissinger. Kissinger like his predecessors saw the conflict as essentially between states. The Palestinians, whether or not a nation were not a state, and so were not a negotiating party. They made negotiations difficult, but they could not make peace and were not responsible participants. The participants who counted were Israel, Syria and Egypt. The diplomatic question was how to get them to negotiate. It would be difficult at best. It was the negotiating process — with its implication of recognition — that was almost the only Arab asset. Better and far easier, consequently, for the United States was evenhandedly and intelligently to act as an honest broker. To get both sides to accept American intervention was the first step. How to get them to accept? By establishing personal contact with the rulers, preventing both complete defeat and complete victory, and using American power and wealth. The circumstances were promising. Both sides of the conflict had been hurt, both sides were unhappy with the current situation, and both sides found it natural to look toward outsiders for guidance. These were the factors which Secretary Kissinger attempted to manipulate in the truce negotiations. If the Israelis had been allowed, for example, to annihilate the Egyptian Third Corps at Suez, it would have been virtually impossible for even a moderate Israeli government to negotiate peace. Israeli hawks would have pushed the government to demand conditions which no Egyptian government could satisfy and remain in power. Conversely, obviously, had the Egyptians been successful against the Israelis, as they appeared about to be in the first days of the war, there could have been no peace negotiations for the Egyptians would have won and would have destroyed the state of Israel. Consequently, the United States supplied Israel with such military assistance as would enable the Israelis to beat off the attack and stabilise the front. This was achieved through a massive airlift of American ammunition and equipment. It is extraordinary and unprecedented that the United States supplied equipment to Israel to such an extent as seriously to deplete its own reserves and landed the ammunition virtually on the battlefields so that it was immediately usable by the Israeli army. But the Israelis could not be allowed to go too far. Secretary

Kissinger wisely realised that the governments of each of the powers were themselves assets — their domestic prestige must not be allowed to be destroyed nor their rivals or domestic opponents be given grounds to make a plausible charge of treason. Each must keep intact its dignity and its aura of loyal and intelligent service to its people. The truce negotiations were thus centred essentially on minor territorial issues and, in each instance, the results were modestly generous to the defeated. Both the Egyptian and Syrian governments could be seen by their constituents to have successfully protected national interests and, indeed, to have driven rather shrewd bargains. On the other hand, nothing could be allowed to happen which seriously undermined the security of Israel, so the United States made clear that it was completely committed to the defence of Israel.

Up to this point, Secretary Kissinger's policy was brilliantly conceived and executed. He carried it out with great vigour and determination and, if he did so also with flamboyance and massive publicity, few would wish to deny him that pleasure. Another decision of his may prove more serious. Since neither the Israelis nor the Egyptians and Syrians wanted Soviet participation in the negotiations on a cease-fire, it was natural that Kissinger would not welcome them. To some extent, indeed, he exulted in their discomfort. Strategically, this may prove to have been short-sighted. Sullen and annoyed, the Soviets waited on the side-lines for new opportunities. Since the Middle East is no longer the preserve of the West, new opportunities were bound to come. It was not long before a *coup* in Afghanistan gave the Russians a diplomatic victory; then came the revolution in Iran in which the showcase of Secretary Dulles' 'northern tier' appeared to fall apart; next, disturbed by President Sadat's moves toward what appeared unilateral peace with Israel, Syria and Iraq have drawn together in a new coalition which, under the circumstances, must be close to the Soviet Union. As the lines were drawn between the 'moderates' and the 'radicals', the Soviet Union, excluded from the process of moderation, was virtually assigned the position as patron of the radicals. Thus, Kissinger's pique may prove costly indeed.

After the initial ceasefire, regardless of the policy toward the Soviet Union, the Nixon Administration's Middle Eastern policy began to go wrong in immediately discernible ways. Secretary Kissinger adopted the Israeli idea of a 'step-by-step' approach in which the rationale was to start with the easiest things first in hopes that 'momentum' would be achieved. However, the steps could quickly be seen to lead nowhere. From both the Arab and the Israeli perspectives, a step-by-step policy was one aimed at splitting the Arab camp. To give Egypt grounds for a separate peace was to put enormous pressure on Syria to cave in. Relations between Egypt and Syria have been historically, as we have seen, complicated, particularly after the abortive unification of the two states from 1958 to 1961, and Syrians have long feared isolation from the Arab cause. These fears were generated under the French Mandate and were emphasised in the wars with Israel. In 1973 and 1974, Egypt made its own cease-fire and Syria felt exposed and vulnerable; in the peace process, it seemed about to lose what protection and succour Egypt could give it.

Once more, the Palestinians were left totally out of the picture. Recognising this, and believing themselves to be on the 'endangered national species list,' the Palestinians reacted to the Sinai disengagement agreement, the logical first step after the cease-fire had been achieved on both fronts, by throwing themselves into the already simmering Lebanese civil war. They did this because the Lebanon was their last refuge and if, as they believed, both Egypt and Syria were prepared, or would be forced, to give up the struggle for their return, the Palestinians judged that they had to achieve some kind of a secure base of operations. At that point, the only possible base was Lebanon, and for their own purposes the Lebanese leftists urged the Palestinians to intervene. The Lebanese civil war as we shall see in the following chapter can arguably be directly related to the first step of Secretary Kissinger's 'step-by-step: programme.

But the major criticism of the programme is, simply, that it led nowhere. Involved was no conception of what a *solution* might be primarily because there was no conception of the problem. Thus, despite very great personal efforts on Secretary Kissinger's part, the advent of the new administration in 1977 found the Middle East problem still very much where it had been for the previous thirty years. The major differences were in the escalation of costs — many times as many people were involved, many times as much fire power was at their disposal and many times as much money was wasted on each clash than in earlier stages. The second major difference was that whether or not the Palestinians had become a state, they certainly had become a nation and it was no longer reasonable for serious, well-intentioned men to overlook this fact.

8 LEBANON AND PALESTINE

Amidst all the generation-long conflicts centring on the Palestine problem, Lebanon remained a relatively calm centre of the Middle East. As we have seen, it prospered under French nationalism. Turned toward the Mediterranean, it readily accepted Western culture and Western commerce. Its capital, Beirut, boasted two universities, one French Catholic and one American Protestant, and the relative tolerance of its government encouraged both an active intellectual life and aggressive private enterprise. Its large overseas community sent back remittances from Africa, Europe and America and periodically returned to buy land, build houses, and father children. Relatively speaking, Lebanon was prosperous. As the French allowed increasing participation, the Lebanese proved to have a talent for politics. The methods of business were translated into politics: the backroom deal was more common than street demonstrations. Where there were disputes, they were usually settled in a business-like manner. In 1942, as a culmination of many small arrangements, the leaders of the Muslim, Christian and Druze communities met to divide up the political spoils of Lebanon. It was a gentleman's agreement between politicians − in a manner Tammany Hall had often seen − and produced what came to be called the National Pact.

The Apple

The National Pact assured each of the pieces of the complex ethnic and religious mosaic of Lebanon its proper place in the state. Each community had its preserve. Each district remained under its traditional leaders and supplemented what it already had locally by a part of the growing state structure. The President, for example, was always to be a Maronite Christian, the Prime Minister a Shii Muslim, and so on down through the bureaucracy. The pork barrel was to hold no surprises − no group was to get too much but no one was to be left out. The only condition was that no one was to challenge the division: the deal once made was permanent.

The Garden of Eden parable comes to mind: politically Lebanon was a small paradise until someone tasted the apple. Lebanon's apple was the presidency. It was an office of pomp and circumstance, with honour guards, official residences − grandeur in a country with little

127

grandeur. More sordid but also attractive it offered great wealth for its holder. Once in, no one wanted to get out. The first post-war President found it impossible to give up, and in 1949 arranged to have parliament, elected for the purpose by a patently rigged election, vote to amend the constitution to allow him a second six-year term. His hand-picked delegates did as he asked but since many of them aspired to his office, they were privately furious. Paying little heed, the President sought and won re-election.

If Lebanon had been truly isolated, perhaps the system would have readjusted after his passing. However, the 1952 *coup d'etat* in Egypt put change in the air of every Arab country. The back-room deals were ventilated in the press and questions were asked about financial scandals in which the President and his relatives and friends had been involved. Finally a general strike was called and he was forced to resign.

The process began again when another (and still active) strong-man was elected to the presidency. He too found the apple irresistible and in 1957 tried to get parliament again to amend the constitution to allow him to stay in office. This time, the game got rougher and politics moved into the street, Riots broke out in the Shii Muslim and Druze areas of the south and in the capital city. Incident followed violent incident for months. The army, drawn from members and relatives of all the factions, found keeping order impossible. The President accused the Egyptians of being behind the troubles. In those days, everyone except the UN investigation mission saw agents behind every bush. Egypt did encourage the rebels, but the local issue was real. Finally, in May 1958 a general strike was proclaimed and the Muslims of Tripoli rose in armed insurrection. Then an event having nothing to do with Lebanon brought down the house.

In Baghdad on 14 July, an army brigade under the command of a than unknown Iraqi officer seized power, killed the young king and let loose a lynch mob. The British and American governments were dis tressed by the announcement that 'Baghdad' had withdrawn from the Baghdad Pact and had established full diplomatic relations with Com munist China and the Soviet Union. Iraq also withdrew from federation with Jordan. The *coup* appear to be a shattering breach in Secretary of State Dulles' diplomatic Maginot line. Some in Washington feared a general collapse of Middle Eastern 'dominoes'. The reaction was spas modic. On 15 July, at the request of the Lebanese president, several thousand American marines landed on the beach near Beirut airport For a short time, perhaps due to a misunderstanding within the Leban ese Government, the Marines and the Lebanese army appeared on the point of a hostile engagement. A firefight was narrowly avoided. Within a few days the invading American force numbered 10,000. With their presence, the Lebanese civil war gradually subsided. The President managed to survive to the end of his term but then the parliament turned to the commander of the army, General Chehab to succeed him.

Social Change

Chehab wisely did not bite the apple and in 1964 an easy transition was made to another Maronite Christian, Charles Helou, who continued to implement 'Chehabism' successfully for another six years. During those twelve years, Lebanon was ruled without disruption and with few complaints. But at a price: there was no adjustment to change. Politics, as the Lebanese understood and enjoyed it, was all but banished. Meanwhile Lebanon began to undergo fundamental social and economic changes. The very success of the imposition of law and order was to create conditions of great peril with which the Lebanon is contending today. Profiting from the relatively free and progressive economy, so markedly different from those in neighbouring countries, Lebanese businessmen attracted large amounts of capital from the new oil-rich states. Lebanon became the resort of the Arab World, and Beirut its casino. Everything that was restricted or difficult elsewhere was easy there. Lebanon began to describe itself as the Middle Eastern Switzerland, and the government bent its entire efforts on policies designed to encourage the economic boom. Property soared in value as businesses moved their headquarters from Baghdad, Cairo, Athens to get near the action.

Even more important were domestic social changes. There was a dramatic flow of villagers into Beirut which by the end of the Helou régime comprised about 40 per cent of the total population. In a sense, however, Beirut was not so much a city as a mosaic of villages: each quarter took on a religious affiliation and virtually every town and village established its block or colony. The newcomers constituted a proletariat in contrast to the older residents who had profited from the rise in land prices and their greater familiarity with urban ways. Gradually, these divisions became associated with the older religious divisions. A high correlation developed between Muslims, countrymen and the poor, while the wealthy were more apt to be urban and Christian. Added onto these terms was the already present but often unspoken old national issue: what indeed *was* Lebanon? To what degree should it be Arab, and so associated closely with the hinterland of Syria, Jordan and Iraq and identified with the pan-Arabism of Egypt? Conversely, was it right or 'national' for the French-influenced, Mediterranean-oriented Christian society to assert its Phoenician character? In short was Lebanon to be a Christian Israel?

These questions haunted Lebanese thinkers and politicians but they could hardly be asked, much less answered, without destroying the delicate balance of the National Pact. Yet, ironically, prosperity seemed to make them more urgent than had poverty. Old memories died hard even when resting on sacks of gold. The Druze still remembered that Mount Lebanon had been their state until about two centuries ago. The Sunni and Shii Muslims had been made Lebanese within living memory, and still worried about their presence in what was fundamentally a non-Muslim even if not wholly Christian state. Other religious groups were wary. The Protestants were reminded of their earlier rough treatment at the hands of the Maronites by modern restrictions on their right to work in the bureaucracy, to which the union ticket was a French (read Maronite Catholic) education. The Greek Orthodox were even less friendly to the Maronites who had usurped not only the apple but most of the rest of the fruit of this Eden. Still smaller groups watched all the larger ones with suspicion born of fear. And it was in these groups, rather than in the society as a whole or in neighbourhoods of towns or professions or classes, that membership became real. In practice, there was not a Lebanese nationality which transcended group identification. Finally and of critical importance, one out of each ten inhabitants of Lebanon by 1970 was a Palestinian refugee.

The Palestinians

Many of the Palestinians who fled to Lebanon in 1948 were Christian. They moved into shanty towns which grew first into camps and then virtually into cities under United Nations care. For years, the refugees just sat in the camps, idle, poor and sullen, living on a dole of about $20 a year each. Those who had the education made their ways back into the world, many emigrated abroad, but those without education or a profession were stuck. While all about them were profiting from the new wealth, they were exploited as a source of cheap labour and were not allowed to hold the best jobs. Gradually they became politically conscious and began to organise themselves. They had shared interests and, above all, a shared experience. From that it was a brief jump to a feeling of great injustice: why should the Lebanese (read Christians) exploit the fact that they had lost their homeland? Rapidly, their politics became radicalised and they began to find a common cause with those Lebanese who were poor, rural and mainly Muslim.

The Palestinians resembled the Lebanese in another sense: they were divided. But, homogenised by the war and the exodus and the diaspora in the camps, they no longer split neatly along religious or village lines. The old divisions reappeared in the guise of degrees of radicalisation, ideology and individual charisma. Minute doctrinal differences, disagreement over a given action, or the loyalty to a leader made unified leadership impossible.

For years, the main centre of the Palestine movement, the 'Resistance' as they called it, was in Jordan. There, after all, most of the Palestinians lived. Moreover, the Jordanian state was tolerant of the Palestinians. Most of its educated and active citizens were Palestinians and the state sought to incorporate them all. Of course, this was not only insufficient for the more active Palestinians but appeared likely to subvert their movement to recover their homeland. Particularly after the 1967 war, the Palestinians lost their faith in all the existing governments and struck out on their own. This brought them not only into conflict with the Israelis but with the Jordanian Government since each action they took against Israel from Jordan brought massive Israeli retaliation. In the manner of guerrillas, the Palestinian commandos were apt to strike and melt away, leaving the Jordanian army to bear the retaliation. And, of course, some Palestinians were more aggressive than others; so instead of a united front they resembled a spectrum. Their disunity made them vulnerable and available. For years, they were treated as political raw materials by the Arab governments: each government collected and subsidised its own band of Palestinians and used them for its own purposes. That tendency has not today been overcome nor have the Palestinians yet achieved any sort of effective unity. Indeed, their very national existence is questioned by the Israeli leadership. So an analysis of who and what they are is fundamental to the next political steps in the Middle East.

The history of all national movements tends to fall apart in the hands of the scholar: national myth is not meant to be viewed under a microscope. But clandestine, diffuse, and poor movements are even harder to chronicle or document since much of their time is spent evading contemporary adversaries and covering their trails. If the Palestinians had a model, moreover, it was the Algerian revolution which gave witness to the terrible price of indiscretion and sloppiness in security. So the details will probably ever remain in doubt. The main lines, however, begin to be visible about 1965 when the *Harakat at-Tahrir al-Falastini* (whose letters in reverse form the Arabic word *Fatah*) and the Palestine Liberation Organisation (PLO) emerged. The PLO was regarded by the radicals as an 'establishment' institution and was ridiculed for devoting itself to conferences and propaganda. Fatah, on the other hand, thought of itself as a more radical, more action-oriented, more 'Algerian' organisation. Moreover, whereas the PLO was the recognised political body, in the eyes of the other Arab governments and the Arab League, Fatah was *sui generis*. The PLO was headed by a former diplomat who had found a comfortable niche working for Saudi Arabia while the head of Fatah, Yassir Arafat, came out of the camps the hard way, winning an education as an engineer. He was as uncomfortable with the Arab leadership as was the PLO leader at home with them; the one dressed deliberately as a peasant and the other as a diplomat. It was the Arab states' failure in 1967 which put Arafat and Fatah to the fore.

Guerrilla War

In 1967, Fatah thought, the name of the game was Algeria: freedom must be won as the Algerian had won it. With the gun. But they could not win in a conventional war. The 'third round' in 1967 had proven that. The Algerians provided the model — with never more than 13,000 *millitants* they had won a war, not battles perhaps, but a war against 485,000 French troops, a million European settlers and 2 million of their own faint-hearted countrymen. That was the model Fatah took unto itself.

The model did not quite fit. Israel was not France. It was a unified society centred on the disputed territory and it managed effectively to exclude the Palestinians politically and militarily from that territory; more, it took the war to them wherever they were and used retaliation to drive a wedge between the guerrillas and their hosts. And while Europe and America were outraged by the French *colons*, they were not by the Israelis, so Israel had a freer hand against dissidents than the French. No protest marches thronged the streets of Tel Aviv as they had the streets of Paris: the Israelis were not defending a distant colony but their 'National Home'. So they were unified and effective.

What could the Palestinians do? One thing was clear: they must operate outside Israel. To some, this meant using another aspect of the Algerian arsenal, and even more widely than the Algerians: terror. So the Palestinians, or the more violent of them, particularly the radical refugee groups known as the PFLP (Popular Front for the Liberation of Palestine) under a young, American-trained Marxist doctor by the name of George Habbash, and the PDFLP (Popular Democratic Front for the Liberation of Palestine) organised hijackings and bombings against Israeli, and what they regarded as pro-Israeli, targets all over the world

Most of the PLO leaders regarded these attacks with grave misgivings, but could not bring the more violent groups to heel; moreover, they had little to substitute for the radical groups' programmes. Or, more accurately, they had one outside possibility: to take over the government of Jordan and thereby to convert Jordan as a whole into a Palestine state. That was never the announced policy but by the spring of 1970, events had more or less formed the policy for the leaders.

By that time, Yassir Arafat had managed to combine the PLO and Fatah and to become leader of both; thus he gained stature but at the cost of unity. The PLO was made up of all the guerrilla groups and so internalised all of their disagreements. Arafat found himself as a sort of prime minister of an unruly and violent parliament, commanding, in Fatah, a bare plurality, roughly a third of the votes, but the other groups kept their weapons, their codes, their organisations, and their plans.

During the spring of 1970, relations between the various Palestinian groups and the Jordan Government deteriorated into frequent small-scale clashes. At first the Jordan Government seemed to be giving in and the PFLP decided that the time had come to push harder. On 9 June, its forces seized the two main Amman hotels and took the 60 occupants hostage. Again the Jordan Government appeared to retreat. When President Nasser then announced that he was accepting a cease-fire with Israel, the radicals argued that *he too* was a traitor to the Arab cause and that they must move quickly or watch their movement die. All that was lacking was a spark. The spark was struck by the PFLP which on 7 September hijacked a gaggle of jets, a Swissair DC8, a TWA 707 and a Pan American 747; on 9 September, BOAC joined the group with a VC 10. All but the Pan American plane were flown to Jordan where the crews and passengers were held hostage while the Jordan Army watched, furious, humiliated but impotent. At the first possible moment, on 15 September, King Hussein gave the army its marching orders: to clean out the guerrillas. And the army responded with excessive zeal. Probably as many as 10,000 Palestinians were killed and it was all over in ten days. Hussein flew to Cairo to sign an armistice with Arafat.

Once more defeated and in despair, the movement collapsed upon it-self. Its base in Jordan was destroyed, many of its more active fighters were dead, and its *political* leaders were discredited. Only the terrorist remained.

Focus on Lebanon

Ever more extreme groups appeared. Increasingly, they operated from
and in Lebanon where the Lebanese Government, under an agreement
worked out in November 1969, gave them virtually a free hand in the
refugee camps and along the frontier in return for non-interference in
Lebanese politics. The terms of the deal were impossible to monitor or
to enforce and no one really wanted to do either. The Palestinians
wanted maximum local support and the Lebanese left wanted their
strong arm and numbers. It was particularly significant that at this time,
the Minister of Interior, charged with police functions, was the leftist
leader, Kamal Junblatt. And when the Lebanese failed to restrain the
Palestinians, the Israelis began to raid the south with increasing severity.
These raids in turn encouraged the Lebanese Christian right, particularly the violent Kataib Party, with discreet army backing, to attack the
Palestinians. By the spring of 1970, the lines were already drawn —
Palestinian-Lebanese Muslim left versus Israeli-Lebanese Christian right.

Unfortunately for Lebanon, it was at this moment that a weak government came to power, elected by one one vote, which, to attempt to
win broad support, discarded the security apparatus of the previous two
strong presidents. While personally known as a violent man and a strong
proponent of the Maronite position, the new President was caught in an
economic crisis over which he could exercise no control and hardly
understood. A run-away inflation further enriched and encouraged the
urban Christian propertied class and caused even greater bitterness and
distress on the rural Muslim poor and the Palestinians. It was at this
point that the understanding between the Palestinians and the Lebanese
left was clinched.

Meanwhile, finding that their frontier policy was not sufficient, the
Israelis began to strike out further afield. Following the PFLP-Japanese
attack on Lod Airport on 30 May and the 5 September murder of 11
members of the Israeli Olympic team in Munich, Israeli Prime Minister
Golda Meir authorised the Israeli Intelligence Service, Mosaad, to form
'hit' teams to hunt down and murder Palestinian activists wherever it
could find them. And, in April 1973, it escalated the scale of action by
mounting a spectacular day-long commando operation against Beirut in
which regular troops murdered three leaders of the Palestinians. Both
there and in the clandestine 'hits', innocent people often got killed. In
one of these, in Norway, murder of a non-political Arab waiter involved
a member of Mosaad in a public trial in which details of the secret war
were for the first time revealed.

At this point, one more strand must be introduced, the strand that finally precipitated the Lebanese civil war, the Sinai disengagement agreement. The disengagement agreement, a logical next step after the cease-fire, was Secretary Kissinger's master stroke. Concluded in September 1975, it brought about a pull-back of Israeli forces in Sinai and regularised the demarcation lines with the truce supervised by American technical personnel. What so worried the non-Egyptians was that it seemed to remove Egypt, in a sort of mini-peace deal, from the Arab front. To the Palestinians, it seemed further proof that the Arab governments could not be expected to take their cause seriously and that unless they could secure their base in Lebanon, they were utterly defeated. So, whatever they thought of the Lebanese, they turned virtually all their energies into Lebanese affairs.

Hardly a day passed during 1974 or 1975 without a major gun battle somewhere in Lebanon. The central government virtually ceased to exist and even the army melted away as former comrades in arms became, again, Maronite, Orthodox, Sunni, Shii, Druze, rich and poor, urban and rural. At first, the left, then aided and encouraged also by the radical Arabs including Syrian President Asaad, were only holding their own, but by the early months of 1976, it seemed clear that the Christians, then jointly encouraged, ironically by the Israelis and the Egyptians, would be defeated. It seems that only then did the consequence of a victory of the left — a reconstituted state, left-dominated and Palestine-oriented, or partition — become clear to the Syrians. Suddenly they realised that either eventuality might trigger Israeli intervention and so outflank them and cut Damascus off from its natural outlet to the sea. Dramatically and suddenly, they had to realign their policy toward the war. When restraint was unavailing on the then successful left-Palestine coalition, the Syrians joined the Israelis in secretly supplying arms to the Christian rightist groups. On land the Syrians blocked strategic areas while at sea the Israelis blockaded Sidon and Tyre.

During the spring of 1976, the Israelis stepped up the scale of their aid to the Christians and began training a new Lebanese Christian army in Israel, and arming it with American equipment. The Israeli army invaded and occupied sizable areas of south Lebanon and carried out air strikes on Palestinian targets in various parts of Lebanon. Then on 5 June, fearful of the drift of events and unable to find other means of action, the Syrian army invaded Lebanon with 450 tanks and some 20,000 soldiers. With their backing, the Christian bands were able to launch a counter attack designed to drive the Palestinians out of central Lebanon.

Under Syrian control, Lebanon was effectively partitioned on both sides of what was called 'the Green Line' with a Christian ruled north and a Druze-Muslim-Palestinian coalition under the leadership of Kamal Junblatt in the south. It was the government of the south which the Syrians attacked, fearing that if they did not, the Israelis would. Caught in the Middle, ironically, the leftists appealed to the French to intervene to save them. Older and wiser than in 1919, the French refused. But what the French could refuse, the Arab League could not. It appointed an Egyptian official, Dr Hassan Sabry El-Kholy, who had already helped to bring peace to strife-torn Jordan, as negotiator and in a marathon year, he arranged over 60 cease-fires and numerous formal and informal meetings in Damascus, Riyadh and Cairo. By the end of November 1976, it appeared — prematurely as it tragically turned out — that the war was drawing to a close under the supervision of a pan-Arab peace-keeping force which incorporated the 20,000 Syrian troops.

But the truces did not, could not, hold. Too deep and bitter were the hatred and fears generated by the current war and its evocation of deeper and older memories. Some of the events sound medieval — not that they were worse than atrocities in other recent wars but in the forms they took: Christians burned at the stake, crucified and photographed the agonies of some of those who surrendered to them from the Palestinian camp of Tel Zatar. In the ruins of Beirut, an uneasy calm intermittently held and, remarkably, new shops opened and were flooded with goods looted from the port but that peace was deceptive. Behind the commercial facade loomed the military reality, and there again the parallel was medieval: private armies, like the Italian *condottieri*, ruled every neighbourhood, filling the vacuum left by the disappearance of the national army and police. Every child seemed to have acquired a Klashnikov automatic rifle and a brace of grenades. Lebanon had become a 'people's war'.

Into this breach the Israeli armed forces stepped, in the south and frequently, from jets or naval craft, they struck at refugee camps and other targets all over Lebanon. The most spectacular events followed a Palestinian raid in March 1978 when Israel launched a full-scale invasion. About 12,000 troops took part and in a few days had seized the whole southern portion of Lebanon up to the Litani river — an area originally claimed by the Zionists in the Peace Conference in 1919. While Israel suffered less than 100 killed and wounded, they killed approximately 2,000 Arab civilians and created another quarter of a million refugees including almost the entire population of the city of

Sidon. It appeared to Israel's Arab opponents that the Zionist dream was being realised under a pretext. To some worried Israelis, it appeared likely that Israel had created its own Vietnam. As in Vietnam, it was the civilians who did the dying: the guerrillas faded away before the invading troops and the invasion left the PLO intact and more determined than ever. Fortunately, for the Lebanese and the Israelis alike, the United Nations provided yet another 'peacekeeping' force to interpose between the combatants.

But the issues remained alive and deadly. With Israeli assistance, the Christian forces prevented the UN troops from effecting their control of the south and the Syrians, reversing their position yet again, tried to blockade the Christian militias around Beirut into surrender or exodus. Then, with devastating fury, the Syrians turned their artillery on the Christian areas in what came to be called 'a sociological war', designed to separate once and for all the Christian and Muslim areas by driving out their enclaves the Christians of the south. Much of Beirut was already a waste land. An estimated $6 thousand million worth of damage had already been done and perhaps 30,000 already killed when the Syrians began their systematic destruction of the Christian quarter. No one yet knows what the human or material damage has been. But it is clear that Lebanon, as the ecumenical state of the Middle East, is dead. So strong and enduring are the enmities created by the war that national reconciliation will be impossible in this generation.

For the Palestinians, the war, however horrible as it has been, with their casualities similar to those of the Lebanese, is preferable to utter defeat: the Arab Palestinians like the Zionists of a generation ago literally have their backs to the sea. To lose is to die as a nation. And the Palestinians hover on the brink of that perdition. Small wonder that they are the outlaw of the international system for no way has yet been devised, or attempted, to make them a responsible part of it. Unless or until that happens, the often random, even meaningless hostilities continue in that tragic little country.

9 BEGIN AND SADAT

Many personalities have temporarily dominated the contemporary accounts of the Middle East. Few have left their names in our memories. Most have justified the Roman Emperor Marcus Aurelius' sombre reflection that 'This mortal life is a little thing, lived in a little corner of the earth; and little, too, is the longest fame to come — dependent as it is on a succession of fast-perishing little men who have no knowledge even of their own selves, much less of one long dead and gone.' So, up to this point, it has been possible to deal with the 'long view' of history and to discuss trends rather than personalities. Now our focus must change. One does not need to agree fully with Thomas Carlyle's dictum that the 'history of the world is but the biography of great men', to accept that the way in which the leaders *perceive* the issues exercises a great, perhaps crucial, influence on our times. So for today, at least, the saga comes to a climax with Prime Minister Menachem Begin of Israel and President Anwar Sadat of Egypt.

No figures in recent Middle Eastern history seem so unlikely as these two. Only an inexperienced writer of fiction would have invented them and surely even he would have avoided trying to put them together in one story. Yet, however unlikely their careers and their relationship, they each epitomise many of the elements of modern Zionism and Arabism; more, each has played a remarkable part in shaping the elements with which we have so far dealt into new patterns. Now let us focus on them.

Begin

Menachem Begin was born in Brest-Litovsk, the city now best remembered as the site where the Russians and Germans negotiated Russia's withdrawal from World War I, and was four years old when the Balfour Declaration was issued. Educated in Warsaw to be a lawyer, he was caught up in the power grabs which tore Poland asunder in the early days of World War II. Shortly thereafter he was imprisoned by the Russians. Begin's politics were well known to the Russians as he was an active Zionist. The Russians saw Zionism as a heresy from Marxism and as such a sinister political movement whose main effect would be to undermine the cause of revolution in Europe. Like the religiously orthodox in other times and places, the Russian Marxists more feared heresy than genuine opponents. So they imprisoned Begin along with hundreds of others, and probably he would have disappeared from this story (and from the earth), except for the accidents of war: while he was on the train to his Siberian prison, Hitler attacked the Soviet Union. It was not as a Jew but as a Pole that Begin was freed from the camps and it was as a soldier in the polish army that he found his way to Israel.

Begin, like Sadat, has told us what he wants us to know in his autobiography; it is a moving and impressive work and even in bare outline makes an almost unbelievable adventure story. This is no place to recapitulate it, but a few key facts are crucial to this story.

Before Begin was caught up in the vortex of the war, he had achieved a considerable political success as the leader of the Polish — then the largest — section of the most radical and vigorous of the Zionist youth organisations, Betar. He had found his ideal in Vladimir Jabotinsky, the most 'muscular' Zionist of his time who refused to go along with the various compromise positions offered by the British and partially accepted by such men as Weizmann in the 1920s and 1930s. Particularly strong was his denunciation of the 1936 partition scheme. Virtually alone, he questioned the right of the British — or anyone else — to lead, compromise with or even support Jewish nationalism. In a sense, his was the purist expression of the early Jewish nationalist idea of auto-emancipation. And, in those increasingly violent times, it was he who inspired the Jewish terrorist groups, Irgun Zvai Leumi and its offshoot the Stern Gang. Begin was already at one with the mentality which produced them before he left Poland — in a sense both grew out of the rejection of the defeatist attitude of the majority of European Jews — and the war gave him as it gave hundreds of others in the Palestine Mandate the capacity and the opportunity to find a new path to national salvation.

Force

The use of force has always been a painful subject among Zionists. Like the contemporary French and British imperialists, the early Zionists wished to see themselves as the bearers of civilisation to benighted natives. Unlike the British and French, they came from a background in which force was not only abhorrent but virtually precluded: it was the Jews of Europe who were the targets, not the marksmen. However, Judaism, historically, had scant regard for non-Jews. In the Bible, the penalties for sedition, rebellion and alienness were, alike, severe, indeed by modern standards of morality if not of politics, unacceptable.

Suffering from oppression themselves, for nearly two millennia, the European Jews had acquired a humanism, a culture, a sympathy which should have been the aim of more fortunate peoples. Little good it did them. What the world respected was power, and what it feared was the capacity to inflict injury. That was the bitter lesson of the pogroms. Not until they had these capacities, many felt, would the Jews be respected and safe. So Herzl himself came to realise at the time of the Dreyfus trial. What was required was a sort of 'muscular' Judaism in which Jews gained self-assurance and their rivals or enemies developed that respect and fear which alone could ensure their success. Thus modern doves and hawks had a common ancestor.

While Chaim Weizmann relied upon such leverage as he could achieve within the British Establishment (and while, as we have seen, the British thought of Zionism largely in terms of its indirect contributions to the war effort in America and Russia), Vladimir Jabotinsky marked out for himself the leadership of the 'muscular' wing of Zionism. His first aim was to assist the Allied cause, and so advance the cause of Zionism, by direct action. The aim was the creation of the nucleus of a Jewish army within the British army and eventually, in 1918, his efforts produced the Jewish Legion as a part of the Royal Fusiliers.

What Jabotinsky was proposing was, almost literally, 'in the air' among the Jewish community. The end of the war gave birth among the Jews, as among several other national groups in Europe, to an intense if vague desire to join in groups, dress in uniforms, and hold semi-mystical pageants. We tend today to remember mostly the Nazis for these traits but they were paralleled by diverse groups in Ireland, France, Italy, Poland, Russia, Greece and other lands. In their more benign forms, they were like the boy scouts and at their worst, slightly regulated mobs. What they had in common was not ideology, for some were of the right and others of the left, but the assertion of group identity and a quasi-military character. Jewish groups were formed for military exercises in Poland, Germany and Italy. Not much came of these as generally they were opposed or at least not supported by the state, whereas the better known movements were heavily subsidised and encouraged.

In the Palestine Mandate, the raw materials and even the ideology existed but the groups had not coalesced. The young men of the *kibbutzim*, were urged in a famous poem by Jabotinsky to

> Give up blood and soul
>   For the sake of the hidden duty
> To die or to conquer the mount.

The problem was, of course, that unguided and without discipline or training, all that was accomplished was a series of sporadic clashes in the hinterland and in such incidents as the Wailing Wall riots of 1929. The Jews were too few and the British were too secure. It was only as the Arabs began to mount attacks on the British (and on Jewish settlements) in the middle 1930s that the British added the ingredient so far missing from Jabotinsky's plan, military training and equipment. This was to be the contribution of Captain (later Brigadier) Orde Wingate.

Each generation sets its standards to evaluate men and events. Before Algeria and Vietnam, most Europeans and Americans found violence more exciting than abhorrent. After Algeria and during Vietnam, the modern equivalents of Wingate, Colonel Roger Trinquier from the French Army and Sir Robert Thompson, carried forward and refined Wingate's counter-guerrilla tactics, and particularly the use of terror and torture, to general acclaim among the military and civil students of war. Today, they are regarded in a different light, so here, without trying to assess the morality, let it only be said that Wingate played a significant role in emphasising the 'muscular' aspects of Zionism which subsequently led to the terrorist and more violent wings of Zionism. If any man enabled Jabotinsky to put his view of Zionism into action, it was Wingate and Wingate, of course, was a serving British officer and acting under orders. It was he who taught the uses of torture and terror, long before World War II, to the young men who would later use them against both Arab and Briton.

But, of course, in the broader sense, it was the war and particularly the horror of Nazism which devalued the coinage of civilisation. Just as Freud, reflecting upon the horror of trench warfare in World War I had commented in a letter to Einstein that men had not fallen so far in their wartime conduct since, in reality, they had not risen so high above the bestial, so in a probably unconscious parallel, Begin remarked in his autobiography *The Revolt* that

what we called 'civilised living' is not at all a necessity, is nothing more than a habit . . . No, civilisation is not essential. You shake it off quickly if you are forced to. Yet strangely enough, the less civilisation in your life, the greater your desire to live. Just to live, to live, to live. Man is a vigorous animal. Even when he is reduced to semi-bestial circumstances his will to live is elemental. He gets used to everything, except death.

'... To live, to live, to live'

For Begin, the past had been rejected before World War I but the war itself was a *rite de passage*, both a funeral and a rebirth. Behind was the old life and the old death, the Warsaw of student days and the Russia of the camps, the Poland of the passive Jews and the Europe of anti-semitism. War tore the mask of the civilised life away and revealed the ugliness of force but also the elemental vigour of life and the supremacy of the will to live. Begin was a child of these times. Whatever one may think of him or his more violent actions, one can surely understand the product of those times. There is no need to assay psycho-history, for it is all 'out front'. As Begin wrote:

> It is axiomatic that those who fight have to hate — something or somebody. And we fought. We had to hate first and foremost, the horrifying, age-old, inexcusable utter *defencelessness* of our Jewish people, wandering through millennia, through a cruel world, to the majority of whose inhabitants the defencelessness of the Jews was a standing invitation to massacre them...

When Begin arrived in Palestine with that strange nomad collection, the Polish army-in-exile, his hero Jabotinsky was dead and the local war had been eclipsed by the larger events in the Western desert and Europe. Those, or most of those, on the spot tended to look abroad where the fate of all humanity hung by the threads of convoys and the tactics of panzers; a few, like Begin, saw beyond those stirring events to the salvation of what remained of his people. Begin saw that the old ways would not suffice, and found that the war had provided both the opportunity, by distracting almost everyone else, and the model, for organised violence.

The issue, as Begin saw it upon his arrival in Palestine, was simple: in Europe Hitler was killing millions of Jews and in Palestine Britain was barring the door to the only acceptable haven for those still alive. Others were fighting Hitler; for Begin the task was in Palestine. And there, as Jabotinsky had said, history showed that force worked.

Anger against the British was almost the more intense because, in the eyes of the frustrated Zionists, their 'wickedness' was the more subtle: whereas the Nazis were obvious monsters, the British *politely* co-operated in the destruction of the Jews. Begin writes with bitterness in the first edition of his book and even a generation later he repeats and reaffirms his earlier feelings in the introduction to the second edition:

In the chapter entitled: 'We Fight, Therefore We Are', we find the following: 'One cannot say that those who shaped British Middle Eastern Policy at that time didn't want to save the Jews. It would be more correct to say that they eagerly wanted the Jews not be saved.' I wrote these harsh words on the basis of study and analysis of the facts. In the forties and fifties we had no documents to confirm our serious accusation. The day came, however, when the truth, even the most awful truth, was vindicated with the aid of historical documents.

Against this enemy, the war had to be carried forward and this enemy, unlike the Nazis, was at hand. Thus, the proper role for the Zionist, thought Begin and his fellows, was in the underground. That was the role of the Irgun.

Irgun

The principal enemy was, of course, the British administration. The Arabs were secondary, almost incidental. The thrust had gone out of their national movement in 1939 and by the time Begin arrived in Palestine it was little more than a memory. Like other Zionists, Begin hardly considered the Arabs either as a military or as a moral issue. Like Albert Camus, whose ideas were formed in that other underground, Begin brought a European, even a colonial, mentality to the issues of the Mediterranean. But the British were something else: they were worthy opponents, educated, armed, European.

Begin and his fellows were difficult for their fellow Zionists to handle; they were too violent, too embarrassing, too uncompromising. They were the fist in the Zionist glove. Their murder of a British Minister of State, Lord Moyne, in 1942 turned Churchill and others strongly against the Zionist movement at a time when they had few allies. Even when they were effective — as when they captured and flogged British prisoners and so brought an end to British flogging of terrorists — Irgun's actions were not publicly approved. It was not until after the fighting when Begin and others revealed secret accords with the regular Zionist leadership, and when the British published intercepted correspondence, that the essential unity of purpose and command of all the Zionists were revealed. Especially in carrying the war 'to the enemy', the British at home, by letter bombs or striking spectacular targets like the King David Hotel in Jerusalem, they were ahead of their times. Only now, as the former terrorists have become respected citizens and the whole world's standards have changed, have we become calloused to terror.

The Arabs

In the last days of the war against the British, which Begin and his fellows had fought with the courage, tenacity and ferocity later exhibited by the Algerians and, occasionally, by the Palestinians, the Arabs again became a significant target. When the British decided to leave, the Arab states took up the Palestinian Arab cause. But they were both ineffectual and distant. Much more significant were those Arabs resident in Palestine. While no one has ever wanted to talk about it – and the issue is still so sensitive politically in Israel 30 years later that a television programme alluding to the use of force agains the Arabs was refused permission to be broadcast – Begin and others realised that Israel could not come into being unless the Arabs could be induce to leave. If they did not, Israel might become a 'white settler' country like Rhodesia with the Jewish minority outnumbered two to one. Even with massive immigration, given the Arab birthrate, the Jews were likely to continue to be a minority. Partition would be no answer: Jabotinsky had warned of that in 1936. No, if Israel were to be born, the Arabs must not only move over; they must move out. To get them to do so was the real purpose behind the Irgun attack on the sleepy little Arab village of Deir Yassin.

Much has been written on Deir Yassin – Begin writes of it prominently in his autobiography – and in any terms it is a shocking story. It was a sort of 'surgical strike' (as the Vietnam terminology would have put it) designed both to 'take out' a potentially troublesome Arab site and to spread terror amongst the Arab population of the Mandate. The key element was that Deir Yassin was peaceful, virtually unarmed and had achieved a sort of armistice with the Zionist forces; if *it* were attacked and *its* population massacred and everyone came to know of it, panic would spread widely. That was the scenario and that is what in fact happened.

On 10 April 1948, about five weeks before the end of the Mandate at dawn, Irgun fighters attacked the village. Failing to take it they called in support from the main Jewish underground army, Hagganah. Hagganah then, apparently, for there is still some dispute over this, withdrew. Irgun then murdered the entire population, men, women and children, and called a press conference to give maximum publicity to its act. Mr Ben Gurion immediately telegraphed a message of sympathy and disclaimer to the leader of Transjordan. The French Red Cross representative, Jacques de Reynier, whose life was threatened when he tried to investigate, found only three people alive and the British Government substantiated stories of rape, mutilation and murder.

Many of the Arab bodies were charred as attempts had been made to burn them and others were thrust down water wells. About 250 bodies were subsequently buried.

Ironically, the Arabs, in charging the Zionists with the horror of Deir Yassin, helped to accomplish the Irgun purpose. Arab villagers everywhere heard of it and read it as a harbinger of things to come. By every road, like the refugees from Paris six years earlier, they poured out of their homes. As Begin laconically wrote, 'The enemy propaganda was designed to besmirch our name, in the result it helped us. Panic overwhelmed the Arabs of Eretz Israel . . . the Arabs began to flee in terror, even before they clashed with Jewish forces.' In all, as we have seen, upwards of one million people fled or were driven out of the Palestine Mandate. Deir Yassin not only saved the lives of many soldiers — being worth as Begin said 'half a dozen battalions' — but made possible, as mere recognition by the United Nations could never have done, Israel.

With the coming of independence and peace, the radical wing of the Zionist movement had become something of an embarrassment and there was, of course, no place for an underground. Begin and his movement were again moved to the fringes of politics. He and his movement were, in the eyes of those who sympathised, the 'pure' Zionists who never wavered in their quest for the complete fulfilment of the Zionist dream; the more orthodox and respectable Zionists used them as a sort of threat — the bad cop in the Mutt and Jeff act — to warn what would happen if the 'hawks' triumphed over the doves. And Begin himself, as those who knew him said, gradually settled down with his memories, accepting the fact that he would never achieve supreme power in Israel and that his day was over. Thus, it was that the shock of the victory of his transformed and renamed political party, the Likud, came in the election of May 1977 and Menachem Begin became Prime Minister of Israel.

Sadat

If there is no single Jewish experience or typical personality in Israel, still less is there one Arab. Perhaps no linguistic group is more rent with divisions than the Arab. As one of their traditional sayings puts it, 'my cousin and I against the stranger; my brother and I against the cousin'. And now added to the divisions of village, religion, tribe, way of life, nation, the Arabs are cross cut by political ideology and by experience with the wars which, one place or another, have almost continuously afflicted them since 1948. Who can speak for them is a problem only they can resolve but they have not yet done so; it is that question which haunts every assembly and each negotiation. But most of the Arabic speakers of the eastern Mediterranean are Egyptian, and Egypt has borne the brunt of the four Arab-Israel wars; Egypt plays a central role in many aspects of pan-Arab cultural and religious life; and, for better or worse, Egypt's two recent leaders, Gamal Abdul Nasser and Anwar el-Sadat, have put Egypt in the centre of Arab affairs and at the top of world headlines. It is appropriate, therefore, that the Arab opposite number to Menachem Begin should be an Egyptian, and it is statistically typical that he should be, or at least think of himself as, a villager.

Anwar el-Sadat was born on 25 December 1918 in the Egyptian delta village of Mit Abul-Kum. It is more than literary artifice, I think, that he should begin his autobiography with a phrase that evokes the sounds and smells of the village, ' "The treacle has arrived," shouts the local crier through the alleys and squares of our village. My grand-mother rushes outside, dragging me along beside her . . .' To the foreigner, the Egyptian delta village often appears a place of poverty and misery but to those who trouble to stay and observe, it gradually becomes apparent that amidst the undeniable poverty is a richness of social contact, of little pleasures and earthy delights of immense satis-faction. For the peasant, the land itself is a communion; in it he finds life, fertility, taste, smell, all of the most elemental and yet mystical qualities which made our ancestors venerate nature gods but from which we have become alienated. For all Egyptians, even the more sophisticated, human contact is a source of pleasure. Egypt has been described as a country of crowds. To the Western eye, this is appalling and each Western expert calls for birth control – and in economic terms rightly so – but to the Egyptian isolation is misery. No delight is more real to the Egyptian than children; no security more immediate than the family. The idea of loneliness hardly occurs. What to the out-sider is restraint is to him pleasure. And, if no one has very much, the little that one has becomes significant. 'The treacle has arrived' prob-ably says more than even the author realised.

But, of course, Anwar Sadat was not precisely of peasant back-ground. Like so many figures in history, he was on the fringe of his social group. Relatively wealthy in village terms, the family was what the sociologists call 'upward mobile' before Anwar was born. By owning some land and trading the family acquired enough money to get modest educations, and it was taken for granted that Anwar would go to school at a time when less than one per cent of Egyptians did. But, of course, the educational horizons of the village were narrow, and had not young Anwar moved to Cairo when he was seven, he might have remained only a prosperous villager.

Contrasts

To this point, the contrasts between the lives of Begin and Sadat could hardly be greater. It is worth pausing over them briefly. Begin begins his autobiography in a Soviet prison as he is about to be condemned to a Siberian labour camp. Sadat was to go on to prison too but the consuming bitterness was not evident – the prison itself was softer, kindlier, and it was in his own country, even if administered by foreigners. Begin was an alien in Poland and in Russia; Sadat even in prison was at home. In the larger sense, these represent feelings shared separately throughout recent history by Jews and Arabs. The intense worry about alienness has only recently afflicted one group of Arabs – the Palestinians who for a generation have lived in their diaspora; but this, among other things, has made them all but incomprehensible to the other Arabs who, whatever the shortcomings of their environment, have been at home and secure. But, of course, the intellectual horizons of the Jewish community were incomparably wider. Even in the Yiddish-speaking villages of the Russian and Polish Pale of Settlement, a sort of hothouse intellectual life was fostered. The materials were traditional   not remarkably different from those of the Islamic tradition – but an intensity of study made them a true classical syllabus. This is a difficult point to analyse but it is profoundly important in the history of the two communities: from similar materials, the Jews evolved an approach to education and an intellectual apparatus which enabled them, as we have seen, in a single generation to turn their energies to other subjects in the sciences, law, literature, and medicine, to do spectacularly well in each; Islamic studies certainly presented a similar field and the religious establishment which maintained it was not far different from the East European Talmudic scholars, yet it evoked no burning passion, no desperate quest. Knowledge, like the life of the village, was comfortable, secure, satisfying. And, as the early Zionists themselves realised, there was the final solace of the land – the Egyptian peasant does not merely farm the land: it is his bride. But the East European Jew was deliberately forced to be landless. It was as though the policy of the Tsars was to keep the Jews politically celibate and the early Zionists approached the land of Palestine, as we have seen, with an almost sexual passion.

These contrasts of environment affect not Begin and Sadat alone, but their generations, and without understanding at least their superficial effects, one cannot hope to appreciate the drama of the modern Middle East.

Into Politics

But there was a worm in Sadat's apple. In his infancy, Egypt was convulsed with anti-British feeling. Britain, as we have seen, ruled Egypt from 1882 and although it repeatedly promised to leave, did not. For the most part, the opponents of the British were members of the urban literate and relatively prosperous class, but amongst the villagers martyrs to foreign oppression were found. Sadat recounts the saga of Denshawai in which can be understood the villagers fear and hatred of the foreigner. What happened was tragic but simple: an English hunting party in 1907 shot some pet pigeons of a little village called Denshawai, and in the argument that followed a fight ensued and an Englishman was killed. Enraged, the British administration had a number of villagers flogged and several hanged. The British regarded the episode as a lesson well administered, but the Egyptians saw it in quite another light. To them it was an indication that the British did not regard them as quite human, and accounted their lives for little. What had previously seemed benign administration was revealed as tyranny and the simple peasants defending their pigeons became martyrs. In this episode nationalism was literally taken to the people as it had never been before. A ballad was composed on this theme — ballads being a sort of peasant newspaper of that time — and as a child Sadat often heard it in his village.

What Denshawai was to the villagers, the Cairo riots of 1919 were to the students. If the British did not treat the villagers as human, they refused at the end of World War I, to treat Egypt as a country. While they allowed what the Egyptians regard as 'barefoot sheep herders' from Arabia — the participants of the Revolt in the Desert — to attend the Peace Conference at Paris, they would not allow the Egyptians. It was the abortive delegation to that conference that formed the basis of Egypt's most popular political party, the *Wafd* (Arabic for delegation). Its leader, Saad Zaghlul, despite exile and intimidation, failure and ultimate corruption, remained a popular hero. What broke him, and the Egyptian national movement, was an episode parallel to the pigeon shoot at Denshawai: in the clashes in Cairo, the English officer in command of the Sudan forces, Sir Lee Stack, was murdered and the administration retaliated on Egypt as it had on the villagers. All Egypt was humiliated, beaten, dejected. That was the Cairo into which the young Sadat arrived.

A sensitive young man, Anwar Sadat was also ambitious and hard working. For a villager of his social station, the army seemed impossible as a career but it happened that just at the right moment of his life the military academy accepted a group of young men from what we would call the 'lower middle class' and through relatives and contacts, Sadat was accepted. He graduated from the Royal Military College in the spring of 1938 and, as he now remembers, immediately began to conspire with his fellows on means to get the British out of Egypt. As Sadat remembers, the conversations could hardly have been more elemental or naive. His ideal was a strong man, like Ataturk, who would lead the people. The quest for a strong man would continue long for Sadat. In each he was to be disappointed until he assumed the role himself.

At this stage in his life, Sadat's political purpose was singular: to get the British out of Egypt. Even in retrospect, he makes no attempt to coat his ideas with a veneer of socialism or civic purpose. Thus, when the German threat to England developed, Sadat naturally found it an opportunity. Westerners have tended to see this Arab fascination with the Nazis as full of social or domestic political content. It had little. It was simply fascination with those who offered a chance to get rid of the known devil even at the cost (but also with the excitement) of dealing with an unknown devil. In Egypt, however, the Germans had as little success as elsewhere since meticulously they reported by radio their activities, and the British, having broken their codes, profited more from the information they reported than did their own commanders.

As he tells his story, in his autobiography *In Search of Identity*, Sadat began to organise the Egyptian army officers in 1939 with several of those who later, under Nasser's leadership, were to carry out the *coup* in 1952. He discloses that Nasser was not among the early members. The purpose of the group, he says, was to 'seize the opportunity [afforded by the German successes against the British] and carry out an armed revolution against the British presence in Egypt ... Hitler's early victories and the British setbacks offered me the chance to act immediately'. After several naive, even foolish, attempts to stage a military demonstration, smuggle a senior officer out of Egypt and to contact General Rommel, Sadat was arrested and imprisoned. Most galling for him, he was sent to 'the aliens jail'. That was just after the battle of el-Alamein in 1942, and he spent two years in prison. Escaping in 1944, he hid nearly a year from the police until the martial law ended in 1945. Arrested again in 1946, he was charged with complicity in the murder of the minister of finance.

Again, Sadat and Begin should be read together for both record confrontations with their jailers — Begin discussing the relationship of Zionism and Communism and arguing points of law in the Soviet Constitution and Sadat charging that he had been ill treated and organising his co-defendants to refute their previous confessions. In the event, Begin got out because of the war and Sadat, after languishing in jail for a further two years, was acquitted.

The 1952 Coup

Once out of jail, Sadat missed the 1948-9 Arab-Israel war, and spent two obviously unhappy and unproductive years as an odd-job civilian. The army was his social life and his political environment; without it, he did little more than drift. Fortunately for him, almost miraculously, he was reinstated with his former rank of captain in 1950. Immediately he was back in the thick of army politics. As Sadat has pointed out, Nasser asked him not to participate in the conspiracy since the police were keeping him under observation. All Egypt was nervous after the still-unexplained riots of 'Black Friday' in January 1952 and Sadat was posted to the Gaza strip. When he received news from Nasser that the *coup* was imminent, he returned to Cairo but was, curiously and for him later embarrassingly, at the cinema when the *coup* actually took place. As he wrote ruefully:

> Was the revolution about to take place before my eyes without me? I had worked all my life for this moment; I had struggled, suffered and devoted my very existence to this glorious hour. What would be the meaning of my struggle — of the very man I call myself — if I were to be reduced to a spectator when my *raison d'être* was taking shape?

To him, however, fell the honour of announcing the *coup* over Cairo Radio at dawn of 23 July 1952.

In the period of Sadat's imprisonménts and enforced abstention from army politics, new leaders had emerged in the Free Officers' Movement. The leadership was firmly in the hands of Gamal Abdul Nasser, Sadat's Military Academy classmate, and other officers assumed the key positions around him. Although welcomed into the inner circle, Sadat was continuously overshadowed. Nasser was the most jealous of leaders and, one by one, relegated his colleagues to honorary positions without real power. In one position after another, Sadat hovered on the fringes of leadership, secretary general of the Muslim Congress, member of the governing body of the various conferences and unions and deputy speaker of the parliament. Nasser was astonishingly public in his scathing remarks about his erstwhile colleague, and Sadat suffered the humiliation of being the butt of Cairo's acid political humour. Until Nasser's death in the summer of 1970, Sadat suffered a sort of domestic exile. Then, quite unexpectedly, he was thrust into the presidency.

The Presidency

When Nasser died, two 'strong' factions emerged among his inner circle. Outside observers have thought of these as pro-Soviet and pro-American. Some justification lies behind these labels but they are more convenient than real. In any event both factions were building for a showdown and were content to allow the neutral and supposedly weak Sadat to assume the presidency until the main lines of battle were drawn. Curiously, for men accustomed to presidential politics under Nasser, they failed to realise the enormous power — almost the only power in Egypt — that automatically comes to the hand of the president. Thus, when they were ready to move, they discovered that their hands were no longer on or even near the levers of state and they were quickly rounded up, tried and sent to prison. Shortly after them went a succession of ministers and other dignitaries into retirement or private life or polite sinecures.

But, while he was president, Sadat was haunted by the ghost of 'the' president, Nasser: it was still Nasser's régime, Nasser's revolution, Nasser's Arab world. The 1973 war was what made Sadat truly the President of Egypt and a major figure in the Arab world.

The war, as we have seen, was a political triumph but nearly a military disaster. Without American intervention, it would have been an Egyptian catastrophe. Sadat has never spoken in these terms but his policies show that he realised the actuality. Coming out of the war, he determined to begin to dismantle the statist superstructure which had stifled Egypt for a generation and encourage a new form of politics and a new venture into private enterprise. Slowly the image of Nasser was allowed to tarnish — books and films were allowed or encouraged which showed the seamy side of his régime, including prison torture — and overtures were made to his enemies by redemption of sequestered property and other gestures. By 1975, Sadat had emerged both domestically and in the Arab world as a major figure in his own right and supported by a base of power which had little to do with Nasser or his legacy.

Most of Sadat's life aims had been accomplished: Egypt was truly independent, he was a major world figure, Egypt had fought a war to limited success under his control, and the Egyptian society was beginning to respond to his leadership. One major problem remained – the unresolved war with Israel. Sadat realised that the war could not be won. 1973 had shown that. But the unresolved issues dragged Egypt down at enormous, almost unbearable yearly costs, running at about 30 per cent of gross national product. The cost was not just statistical. Caught in a vicious inflation, the government subsidised the cost of foodstuffs, basic household goods, tobacco and the luxuries of the poor. All this was done with the assistance of the richer neighbours and the United States. When they and the IMF urged a more austere programme, and the Egyptian Government tried to comply, Cairo was convulsed in January 1977 with a near revolution. The army, entering domestic politics for the first time in 20 years, held firm and the government rode out the storm. But it was a sobering experience and even more sobering was the realisation that the causes of the riots were still there and growing stronger. Charges of corruption and the evident luxury of the new middle class added fuel. As the months went by, Sadat used every political trick to avoid the reckoning and to keep the concensus together behind his administration. A minor war with Libya, a stream of proclamations of economic improvement, something happened each month to divert attention but Cairo grew shabbier and public services eroded and people grew more disturbed almost by the day. Something had to be done. And with that remarkable and sincere belief in his own capacity, Sadat determined on a stunning gamble. In November 1977, he announced to the shock and consternation of his closest associates that he would make perhaps the most remarkable diplomatic foray of modern times, his mission to Jerusalem.

It was there that the improbable stories of Menachem Begin and Anwar Sadat fuse.

Jerusalem and Back

Without even informing his foreign minister (who promptly resigned), Sadat determined to fly to Jerusalem to appeal for peace. No prior commitments were asked or given. Arrangements were frantically made, primarily through the American embassies in the two capitals, and with a small group of his official family and a new foreign minister – an able and energetic former university professor of a well known Coptic Christian family with a Jewish wife – Sadat flew on 19 November to Israel. Whatever else it was, it was a media 'happening'. Hundreds of journalists descended upon Cairo and Tel Aviv to watch every move of

Sadat and Begin. Hardly a person in the Middle East missed Sadat's speech to the Knesset on 20 November and even those who disapproved, and there were and still are millions, took pride in the instant world renown and the 'end to negativism'. Nasser's 'no peace with Israel, no recognition of Israel, no negotiation with Israel' could not have been more dramatically repudiated: Sadat had done the 'undoable'. A man of great charm and charisma, he became an instant hero in Israel too.

But almost immediately things began to sour. In the eyes of the other Arabs, particularly on the 'morning after', Sadat was charged with breaking ranks with the Arab camp, with making or starting to make a separate peace, with selling out the Palestinians, and with throwing away virtually the only bargaining counter on the Arab side; recognition of Israel. His trip to Israel and speech at the Knesset were clear recognition. Within two weeks, an anti-Egyptian Arab front had taken form. Undeterred, the Egyptians commented to all who would listen that it was Egypt that had done the fighting and, if necessary, it would be Egypt alone who would make peace. On Christmas Day 1977, his birthday, Sadat entertained Begin on the Suez Canal. Then both sides got down to thinking out loud what a peace might look like.

Here the life ambitions and styles of the two leaders came to play a major role. For Begin, Israel was more than a country: it was a sacred trust above the possibilities of political deals. To give up any part of it for him and those who upheld his government was all but unthinkable. A treaty with Egypt would be welcome, as Israel, like Egypt, had huge defence expenditures and major economic problems, but the object was just that, a bilateral deal with Egypt. In Begin's eyes, the real 'Palestinians' were the Jews and, perhaps, the 15 per cent Arab minority of Israel, but the Palestinians (Arabs) were outside the issue and Israel, he repeated constantly, would never give up the 2,200 square miles of Judaea and Samaria which others called the 'West Bank' even though its population was only 0.6 per cent Jewish and 99.4 per cent Arab. Return of 'Arab' Jerusalem, Begin has repeatedly said was unthinkable. The best he could do, he said, was to allow some limited form of local-self-government for five years to the citizens of the West Bank, after which Israel would agree to review the issue.

Contrariwise, Sadat has been primarily interested in the removal of all foreign troops from the soil of Egypt. That has been his lifelong political concern from his student days as we have seen. But, interwoven in his adult life, are the politics of the Arab world. Like others of his generation he cannot escape the implications of the 1948 war even when he most detests the Palestinians. Moreover, Egypt, dependent as it is upon the largesse of the Arabs, cannot afford to 'go it alone' or become the Arab world's Vichy. So while Sadat's main attention has been on those territories occupied from Egypt — Sinai and indirectly the Gaza strip, Sadat has emphasised from his Knesset speech onward 'peace with justice' which, for him, means evacuation of conquered territories and self-determination for the Palestinians.

These have been the main issues for negotiation but the discussion has concerned timetables and form, rather than substance, for the Egyptians and for the Israelis a rather different set of issues, mainly the possibility of peace with Egypt in Sinai alone. Thus, from the beginning the talk has been at cross purposes and misunderstandings arose easily even on the same words. Naturally, as sensible, experienced men, both leaders have sought to confine the issues wherever possible to technicalities or peripheral issues — so the military committee has been heavily worked while each side took the measure of the other.

In February 1978, Sadat and Begin had hit what seemed a dead end. And Sadat in another diplomatic foray went to Washington and, in effect, turned the issue over to President Carter. In a move almost as unprecedented as his mission to Jerusalem, he asked President Carter to act as arbiter between the two sides.

To find a parallel to these remarkable delegations of authority and risk taking, one must refer to the late Middle Ages when, in theory but seldom in practice, the Pope arbitrated between Christian sovereigns. That theory was the essence of the Christian community. That it would be applied in these disorganised and contentious times is little short of astonishing. President Carter, recognising the huge responsibility, demurred and agreed to be not the arbiter but the mediator.

At that point, the United States announced what it saw as the basic conditions for peace — positions it had held uniformly for years and had reaffirmed in UN resolutions: return of Sinai minus its (in the American view) illegal settlements, and agreement that occupied territories would be freed.

Fearful that the Egyptian despair at the small pay-off for Sadat's great gamble would impell the Egyptians to make peace at any price, the Palestinians decided in March to attempt to renew the contest by striking at targets near Tel Aviv and for these Israel struck back massively and indiscriminately at refugee camps and other targets in Lebanon. More significantly, President Sadat denounced the Palestinian effort. But the Palestinians were, apparently, correct in their analysis of the negotiating process. It had all but stopped, and a visit by Begin to Washington a week later demonstrated that the American Administration thought the fault lay with Begin. His position held firm on the central issues of return of territories and the future of the Palestinians.

In June, *The Economist* cover carried the question, 'Has Begin Sunk Sadat?'

> Anwar Sadat is a president fast running out of surprises. The conseqence of that is may be that Egypt runs out of Anwar Sadat . . . Presiding over a country of ruinous poverty, in a state of ruinous war, Mr. Sadat survived as Nasser's successor, and then flourished in his own right, by a series of huge surprises. At home the intention behind those bold strokes − an intention triumphantly achieved − was to give Egyptians a sense of promise. Promise of recovered pride. Promise of better economic things to come. More housing. More jobs. Less inflation. Promise of an end to civil repression, even a start to democracy. Lastly, promise of real peace, the first, last and only precondition of everything else.
>
> All those promises are now threatened by Mr Begin's stalemate. Mr. Sadat's fortunes are running into Egypt's sand . . .

As a knowledgeable foreign observer put it in Cairo, 'Sadat has announced many new ventures but rarely cut a ribbon to open a success.' What everyone thought by the summer of 1978 was that Sadat could not stand a stalemate. And, apparently, unrest on a larger scale than any since 1952 affected the Egyptian army. It appeared that the strain was telling. Yet nothing seemed to break the deadlock. Israel was evasive and Egypt's peace plan was a repeat of the old items with merely a slightly longer timetable for compliance. A flamboyant conference of the Israeli, Egyptian and American foreign ministers at Leeds Castle in England in mid-July produced nothing. Both sides settled back to their original positions. Then on 8 August, US Secretary of State Cyrus Vance announced that President Carter would convene a meeting of Prime Minister Begin and President Sadat at the Maryland presidential retreat of Camp David.

Camp David

The meeting of the three leaders began, after weeks of frantic preparation of maps, charts and documents, briefing papers, scenarios, intelligence appreciations and all the stuff of diplomacy, in the secluded and quiet Maryland woods, on 6 September. The meeting was, in many ways, unprecedented. First, it was an incredible commitment of time by three heads of state lasting an uninterrupted 13 days, while the affairs of the three countries were delegated to others. Second, like Sadat's mission to Jerusalem, Camp David began without prior agreements or commitments whereas normally meetings of heads of state only take place after their aides have negotiated at least the main outlines of an agreement in private. Third, the leaders of the two warring countries agreed to make a third, President Carter, a full partner in their negotiations. So all three leaders had their personal prestige and political lives at stake. Each was vulnerable to failure. Yet both Sadat and Begin began the conference fully committed to positions which were, at least apparently, irreconcilable.

In the course of the 13 days and nights, the two warring leaders each threatened to leave and the meetings almost broke down on several occasions. A great deal of 'arm twisting' and, presumably (for the full details are not yet known), many promises of military and economic assistance and, perhaps, of mutual security pacts were given by President Carter. Sadat has spoken publicly and to members of his government about Carter's promise of a 'new Marshall Plan' for Egypt amounting to a score of thousand million dollars over the coming decade. (This has been repeatedly denied by the American government.) Begin believes he was promised compensation for the removal of Israeli military facilities and settlements in Sinai. And Carter thinks that Begin promised to stop building settlements in occupied West Bank for at least five years. At that point, the stories diverged and Israel has accused the United States of misunderstanding and Egypt of changing its demands; the United States accuses Israel of going back on its promises of eventual self-rule for the Palestinians and the return of Jerusalem. One clear disadvantage of the new form of diplomacy is that without adequate staff work, and during long walks in the woods, however conducive they may be to good fellowship, misunderstanding is easy among those who have lived with it all their adult lives.

What really happened at Camp David is still unclear. Most outside observers agree with *The Times* lead story on 19 September that 'The texts of the agreements between Egypt, Israel and the United States . . . show that Mr. Menachem Begin, the Israeli Prime Minister, has won a separate peace treaty with Egypt in exchange for a series of concessions which still leave his basic position unchanged.' (See Appendix for the full lead story.) As in many other international 'events' everyone declared a victory. The only immediate sour note was that Sadat lost another foreign minister who immediately (but silently) resigned.

Two documents emerged from Camp David and these were subsequently supplemented by various letters. In the first document, the personal element of the agreement is stressed,

> Muhammad Anwar al-Sadat, President of the Arab Republic of
> Egypt, and Menachem Begin, Prime Minister of Israel, met with
> Jimmy Carter, President of the United States of America, at Camp
> David from Sept 5 to Sept 17, 1978, and have agreed on the follow-
> ing framework for peace in the Middle East. They invite other parties
> to the Arab-Israeli conflict to adhere to it.

The leaders then reaffirmed UN Resolution 242 as the basis of settlement, referred to Article 2 of the UN Charter to set out a framework
for future peace negotiations, and affirmed that 'peace requires respect
for the sovereignty, territorial integrity and political independence of
every state in the area . . .' They then set out an approach to the settlement of the issue of the West Bank and Gaza in three stages: (a) a five-
year period during which the Israeli military authorities will turn over
authority to a freely-elected self-governing authority; (b) Egypt, Israel
and Jordan will 'agree on the modalities for establishing the elected self-
governing authority in the West Bank and Gaza' including a definition
of Israeli 'security locations' and the nature of joint patrols; and (c) it is
only after the self-governing authority is established that the five-year
interim period will begin, and during this period negotiations will take
place 'to determine the final status of the West Bank and Gaza and its
relationship with its neighbours and to conclude a peace treaty between
Israel and Jordan'. In the second section, bilateral Israel-Egyptian relations were specified as renouncing warfare to settle disputes and agree-
ing to negotiate a final peace treaty within three months. Both sides
agreed to full recognition, abolition of the boycott, protection of one
another's citizens, and promised to explore joint economic development, the settlement of claims and to urge UN approval of the treaty.
A separate document set up the terms of the Egyptian-Israeli deal. This
called for Israeli withdrawal from Sinai, demilitarisation of airfields and
restrictions on other military units, freedom of passage for Israel
through the Gulf of Suez and the Suez Canal, stationing of UN troops
(not to be removed unless approved by the five permanent members of
the Security Council) and a full exchange of diplomatic and other relations.

Gone from these documents was the elegance and terseness of the
Lords Balfour and Caradon. The documents clearly showed the strain of
late night drafting and trailing from them were a series of 'clarifying'
letters of which nine were released by the American Government on 22

September. In the letters, President Sadat affirmed that Arab Jerusalem is an integral part of the West Bank and Israeli measures to incorporate it should be rendered null and void. In sending this letter to Prime Minister Begin, President Carter emphasised that the United States did not recognise the Israeli annexation and that the status of Jerusalem must be decided in consultation with the Arabs.

Prime Minister Begin immediately denied that he had given promises on the West Bank beyond those in the main texts and pledged to retain captured Syrian territory; moreover, he said, Israel would continue to build up its settlements during the five-year interim period.

Almost immediately the 'framework' for peace began to show strains even on its least controversial points. But what loomed behind was the gravest point of all, the status and future of the Palestinians. On that point, President Sadat, predictably, began to show less enthusiasm and Prime Minister Begin hinted that he would have left office by the time the difficult issue of the future status of the West Bank inhabitants must be decided.

In a spectacular but also portentous ending to the year of Jerusalem to Camp David, it was announced that the Nobel Prize for Peace had been awarded jointly to Prime Minister Begin and President Sadat. The award specified that it was as much for what was hoped to be achieved as for what had already been done. That probably summed up, as honestly as one could, the real meaning of this remarkable year.

PART THREE

10 POTENTIAL FOR THE FUTURE

The Middle East is more than a set of historical memories and a catalogue of current problems: it is also a modernising, developing and growing region. For its own people, and for all the world, its resources and the uses to which they are put are of fundamental importance. So it is now time to assess what its potential is, how much has been achieved and what its prospects are for the near future. First, the physical resources.

The area discussed in this book is about 3.5 million square miles or roughly the size of the continental United States. Geographically, it can be divided into four parts: a narrow fringe of sea coast along the Mediterranean where there is substantial dew and intermittent rainfall; mountainous areas and scattered oases where rain or underground water sources sustain relatively intense agriculture; the great river valleys, particularly the Tigris-Euphrates and the Nile, which have traditionally been the scenes of large-scale, intensive agriculture and which gave rise to our earliest civilisations; and, finally, the vast steppes and the desert where little rain falls and the land can sustain only nomadic herdsmen and hunters. Generally, the whole region has long, hot and dry summers with mild wetter winters.

The contrasts in so vast an area are enormous. Parts of Lebanon, Oman, and Yemen resemble the mountain kingdoms of the Himalayas with stairsteps of terracing marching up thousands of feet of mountain face while, less than a hundred miles away, begin sandy and rocky plains which stretch virtually unpopulated and undecorated by grass or trees. While the river valley of the Nile supports a population density of almost 4,000 per square mile, the population of as much as a third of the Arabian Peninsula may be counted only in a few hundred people. Within a few miles in Lebanon, it is possible in a single day to go skiing and to swim, comfortably, in the warm blue Mediterranean. Even in a given place, the contrasts in a single day can be extraordinary. At nighttime in the desert, water will freeze and frost will cover the ground but at high noon the temperature may soar to 120 degrees or, occasionally, even higher. The desert resembles the sea in that it allows great storms to rage across hundreds of miles. In the desert, the hot, dry land heats the winds like a furnace and fills them with suffocating clouds of dust and sand. Crops are often ruined in an afternoon. Whole caravans, even armies, have been wiped out − choked and dehydrated. While the desert is not uniform except in lack of water, even in that there is substantial yearly variation. Rainfall appears to go in cycles − we are now in a wet period − but it is possible roughly to trace a line on the map where a predictable yearly rainfall of about 10 in. divides the agricultural from the nomadic areas. (See map 10.1.)

With these things in mind, it is important to evaluate any given part of the Middle East in more than its gross area: some land is critically important, densely populated or richly endowed; much is not. For example, all but 2 per cent or 3 per cent of Egypt's 386,000 square miles is economically irrelevant to the Egyptians, and about the same percentage holds for the nearly 1 million square miles of the Sudan. Even more austere is Saudi Arabia where only about 0.5 per cent of the roughly 870,000 square miles is cultivated. From this criteria, a conventional map can be seen to be misleading: Lebanon is not effectively 1 per cent of Egypt but more like 20 per cent. A more meaningful map would show the Middle Eastern areas as islands in a dry sea. That map is shown here (Map 10.2).

The Economies

Like the land, so the economies of the Middle East fall into separate categories. The area as a whole in 1978 produced $150 billion but this was not, of course, evenly divided. The economies fall into three categories − the highly developed, the oil-rich but underdeveloped and the poor. Israel is the most modern; Saudi Arabia, Kuwait, Iraq, the United Arab Emirates, Libya, Bahrain and Oman are oil rich but still underdeveloped; and Egypt, the Sudan, and Syria are the poor.

Statistically, these differences are clear: Israel has a GNP *per capita* of about $2,400 and by all developmental criteria − percentage of literacy, production of electric power, hospital beds, etc. *per capita* − is comparable to Europe or America. In the Middle East, it is uniquely the developed, modern society. Several of the thinly populated oil-producing states have higher incomes *per capita* − Saudi Arabia $7,600, Qatar $12,600, Libya $5,000 and Kuwait $13,000 − but in terms of the other determinants are obviously underdeveloped. The poor societies have low personal incomes − Egypt $370, Syria $730, Sudan $210, Yemen $250 and Jordan $760. But, particularly in Egypt, the statistics do not give a true picture since perhaps half of the population *actually* has an income per person of considerably less than $100. Moreover, in terms of education, health, capital investment per person and infrastructure, the poor societies are far behind Europe or Israel. In those

Map 10.1 Rainfall in North Africa and Arabia

Note: Shaded areas average more than 10 in. rainfall yearly and so can sustain rain-fed agriculture. Other areas require irrigation or can be cropped only spradically if at all.

Map 10.2 Cultivated Land in North Africa and Arabia

categories which equate to modern power, they are exceptionally poor, having few engineers, doctors, scientists, technicians and those they have are seldom of world class. More significantly, the societies are seldom highly organised and cohesive.

Oil

Until fairly recently, the areas where petroleum has been found were extremely sparsely populated, very poor and remote. Oil was, of course, known to exist in the Middle East from biblical times. However, its exploitation on a commercial scale is very recent. From modest beginnings in the 1930s, the oil industry has grown into the single most important economic asset of the Middle East. Iraq was the first Arab country in which an extensive search was made for petroleum. There, an international consortium, the Iraq Petroleum Company (IPC) was formed in 1925. Since both the British and the French companies in the consortium were controlled by their governments, the IPC was more than a consortium of companies: it was quasi-governmental. In addition to its principal concession in Iraq, the company also acquired concessions in areas of the Persian Gulf under strong British influence. The IPC struck oil near Kirkuk in 1927. By 1931, Iraq received almost $2 million in royalties. While this figure appears, retrospectively, almost ridiculously small, it was the beginning of a spectacular revolution of the Iraqi economy. By 1970, oil had earned Iraq $4 billion. In 1976 alone, it earned $9 billion.

The first significant entry of an American oil company came in 1928 when Standard Oil of California got oil rights for Bahrain, and five years later received a concession for Saudi Arabia. Five years later it struck oil. Meanwhile, the Gulf Oil Corporation had joined the Anglo-Iranian Oil company in a concession for Kuwait and struck oil there in 1938. World War II stopped the development of the Arabian fields. It was not until 1946 that Kuwait achieved commercial production, but by 1972, it was producing three million barrels of oil a day or slightly less than six per cent of the world's total.

Because the oil fields are both very large and often located in favourable situations — Kuwait's major field is both shallow and near the sea coast — oil production costs are generally very small in relation to world standards. The oil of Kuwait, for example, is believed to have a well-head cost of approximately 10¢ a barrel, or about one per cent of the North Sea oil of England.

During the early years of the development of the oil industry, the companies kept most of the profits. Gradually, however, the countries asserted their right to a larger share and by the 1950s the slogan '50-50' predominated.

By the 1970s a trend was established to nationalise the oil-producing companies. For the most part, nationalisation has taken place amicably and, indeed often, with profit to the producing companies. Saudi Arabia, for example, has become the largest single development centre and overseas investment of Mobil. With every conceivable cost amortised many times over, the level-headed managers of the companies recognised that what they were interested in was petroleum, not ownership. It was possible to purchase oil from nationalised companies on advantageous terms. Additionally, the producing companies could provide even nationalised companies with a variety of services for which they would be paid appropriate fees. In short, the oil companies determined not to repeat the costly and nearly fatal mistake of the Anglo-Iranian Oil Company, when nationalised by Iran in the early 1950s. They determined to ride out the nationalist storm and, indeed, to use its lusty winds to carry them further along their own profitable journeys.

The issue of oil *today* is primarily one of price. In the very early days of oil development in the Middle East, particularly in the early 1930s, the countries were paid very small royalties but the price of oil was relatively high. Shortly after the end of World War II, the price of petroleum stabilised at somewhere around $2.00 a barrel. While most other commodities increased in price, petroleum stayed level for about twenty years. Relatively speaking, energy became cheaper as each year passed. These were years of extremely wasteful use of energy, particularly of petroleum. (Our children may be sorry it was so cheap.) Then quite suddenly in the midst of the October 1973 Arab-Israeli war, the oil producers, not all of whom were Arabs or in any way interested in the Palestine problem, used that crisis to force the price of petroleum to catch up with what it would have been had it kept in trend with other world prices from 1950 onward. Almost overnight, the price of petroleum went up as much as tenfold. Some of the better grades of petroleum were sold at an auction in Iran (not an Arab country) for over $17 a barrel in early 1974. After dropping back to about $13-14 they are now set by the Organization of Petroleum Exporting Countries (OPEC) at $18-22. Saudi Arabia has taken the remarkable (and among oil-producers, unpopular) position that increases must be infrequent and moderate to prevent damage to the world financial structure and the western industrial economy upon which, the Saudis maintain, the health of the whole world economy depends. Until the spring of 1979, Saudi Arabia was able to carry OPEC with it but the

Iranian crisis undercut its position and led to a renewed increase of price. What the effects of vast new discoveries in Mexico will do is, as yet, unclear; in any case, their effects are likely to be delayed for some years. During the coming decade, it has been estimated that the United States, the major consumer, will increase its demand for imported oil ten-fold so the pressure on increased price will remain.

Boom

With the rise in the price of oil, an unprecedented boom hit the Middle East. From extreme poverty and outside neglect, the oil-producers found themselves courted as the super-rich. A few numbers will tell the story for the major producer, Saudi Arabia. In 1934 Saudi Arabia's total government revenues were about $4 million and as recently as 1946 they were only $10 million. In 1965 they were less than $7 billion but during 1978 they passed $35 billion.

Both the huge revenues and the rapidity of their growth pose the problem of accommodation of the wealth into the world capital structure. Actually, of course, accommodation is only one of three alternatives but the other two — a cut-back in production and a cut-back in consumption — appear highly unlikely. It is true that Saudi Arabia could like to cut back as Kuwait has done but there is much pressure from the West to prevent this, and Western petroleum demands are expected to grow rapidly in the decade ahead without notable alternatives. So, barring war, Saudi Arabia's oil-generated revenues will grow.

Saudi Arabia today has approximately $50 billion in overseas assets. At first it was unable to spend anything like as much as it earned. By 1978, the development programme, however, had begun to take hold and massive imports of goods and services nearly balanced revenue. With the expected rise in oil prices, however, the long-term trend is clearly one of amassing revenues.

Like the other oil-producing countries — and like domestic American oil producers — Saudi Arabia recognises that its assets are 'wasting' and, once used, cannot be renewed. When oil runs out, its planners expect no more concern for its welfare than was evident before oil. Thus, the government wisely wants to invest what it earns in those things it needs domestically, while it can afford them, and to build an economy that will be self-supporting when oil revenues fall, and to build a portfolio of overseas investments either or both to keep the value of its money until it can invest it domestically and/or to earn additional income. Let us look at these issues separately.

First, the development programme.

Saudi Arabia is an underdeveloped country with a native population of only about 5 million and a harsh, inhospitable and vast land. When it could afford to buy, it found that it needed almost everything. So, in 1970, it set up a development planning organisation. The first plan was modest but the Second Plan, 1975-80, calls for the expenditure of about $143 billion. Much of that has been spent and the total may now rise to over $200 billion. The units being undertaken are truly mind-boggling: over 300 thousand new houses, 2,000 new schools, 25,000 kilometres of new highways, 50 modern hospitals, 3 new universities, two new industrial port cities each estimated to cost over $40 billion and a system to gather the gas now flared off from the giant Arabian oil fields. The latter has been called by the *Financial Times* 'the biggest industrial project the world has ever known'. And, of course, individual Saudis are buying and living as they never before even dreamed.

All of this adds up to tremendous imports. In 1976, Saudi Arabia purchased $4 billion worth of goods and services from the United States and contracted for an additional $27 billion. It suddenly became the most important trading partner for Britain, and plays a major role in the economies of Germany and Japan. Korea, as unfamiliar to Arabians as Tibet to Englishmen, began to win road-building contracts and to fly in plane loads of workmen and engineers.

But still there was too much money.

Generously, Saudi Arabia has in the past three years given, lent or committed over $14 billion, or about 16 per cent of its GNP, to less fortunate Afro-Asian states.

The rest, now over $50 billion, is being managed by the Saudi Arabian Monetary Agency (SAMA) and is deposited with banks or invested in bonds and stocks mainly in the United States, Canada and Europe. This investment, of course, raises a touchy political problem: some Americans and Europeans are as worried about Arab takeover of their economy as are the poorer Arabs about an Israeli takeover. For this reason, SAMA has invested with the greatest caution. Its purchases of stocks, for example, are handled as discretionary trusts in which the trustee, usually a foreign bank, buys and sells at discretion for the SAMA account, merely informing SAMA of its actions, but is never allowed to purchase stocks in which the SAMA account reaches as much as 5 per cent of the outstanding shares of any company. SAMA refuses all participation in management of the companies in whose stock it invests. Most of its money, however, is not in stock but in government 'paper' so that SAMA is today the largest purchaser of US Government new obligations. Additionally, large deposits are kept in about 50 major foreign banks. Theoretically liquid, in case of need by the development programme, this money is in practice a permanent deposit.

Since Saudi Arabia accepts payment for its oil only in dollars, it has become, in effect, the major supporter of the US dollar in the world market. But its policies and the weakness of the dollar, accentuated as they are by inflation in all the Western world, puts Saudi Arabia at a considerable expense: it cannot maintain the value of its huge assets and there is a rational argument for the contention that a barrel of oil in the ground is worth more to Arabia than its current dollar equivalent invested anywhere: oil is almost certainly rising in value while the dollar is visably declining. Yet, without doing severe damage to the Western economy, in which Saudi Arabia has an obvious stake, it cannot cut back on its production to a level which would accord to its domestic needs or to a prudent economic policy. This is the dilemma with which its able Central Bank Governor must deal.

Saudi Arabia has made most of the foreseeable mistakes in its efforts to develop: it has suffered a run-away inflation, soaring at times to perhaps 50 per cent but now at about the Western European level of 10-15 per cent, with speculation in land particularly distorting its economy. Rents on houses jumped from a few hundred dollars a year to as much as $100,000 and apartments often rented for $35-50,000. Massive building programmes and subsidies have cut these figures down but they are still, in Western terms, unbelievably high. Business practices resemble those familiar in the United States in the age of the railroad barons and the early days of oil and steel so that outsiders, forgetting their own development era, are shocked by the mingling of public and private interest. Caught in the reality of fantasy, the Saudis also find themselves too few and too pampered to do much of the hard work themselves and their economy requires that virtually every worker for the new industry be imported from Yemen, Jordan, Egypt, Korea, Pakistan and Turkey. So frantic has been the pace of change that the society is obviously overtaxed and the traditional values are being undermined without replacement by a new set of values. Whether or not Arabia can stand the strain — as Iran clearly could not — remains to be seen. Recognising the danger, the government in 1978 wisely slowed the pace somewhat, but Riyadh still looks like a construction site and work in progress throughout the country is unprecedented anywhere or anytime. Even those who fear the rate of change welcome many aspects of it. Perhaps the prevailing attitude was summed up by a very able provincial governor when he said, 'Of course we are wasting much, per-

haps even most, but our people have been hungry and poor too long; it
is about time they had a feast.'

New Patterns

What is happening in Saudi Arabia today happened earlier to Iraq and
Kuwait and is beginning to happen to Oman and the United Arab
Emirates. Little by little a pattern is emerging with new forms of international organisations arising to handle the problems and to exploit the
opportunities. Kuwait led the way with the formation, under the leadership of a young, Harvard-educated Kuwaiti, of the now $3 billion
Kuwait Fund for Arab Economic Development. The Fund was patterned
on the World Bank and not only lends money but arranges for the
secondment of staff from the borrowing countries; the officers temporarily on duty with it are then put to work analysing the development
prospects of other countries so that, over the years, it has produced a
cadre – a sort of financial 'Old Boy' network – competent in develop-
mental problems of Africa and Asia. This has a potential value as great
as the Fund's capital.

Younger than the Kuwait Fund but of great promise are three new
types of organisations, the Islamic Development Bank, the Arab Investment Company and the various joint investment companies. The
Islamic Development Bank is still in the beginning stages but is wrest-
ling with the problem of mingling development investment banking
with Islamic prohibitions on usury. The Bank charter allows it to
operate anywhere in the 500 million member Islamic community and it
will ultimately grow into a financial giant. The Arab Investment Company is essentially a multinational investment bank, funded by the oil-
producing countries, to create and finance major projects approved by
the Arab governments. If current plans are followed it will grow from
its current $1.5 billion to about $5 billion by 1980. At the 'local' level,
both Kuwait and Abu Dhabi have helped to create investment companies, particularly in the Sudan and Egypt, for joint operations. These
companies are, in effect, also investment banks but are small enough,
usually about $50-200 million, to deal with more commercial pro-
jects better than can the financial giants.

This is a decade of remarkable financial experimentation. Various
sorts of consortia and joint ventures with European, Asian and American banks are now being or have been formed. Like everything else,
most of these institutions – some of which are now among the world's
largest – are very new. The Kuwait Central Bank is only a decade old.
Few of the commercial banks even in Lebanon or Egypt are twice that

age and the international ventures are much younger. The oil-producing countries are learning that money is easier to 'develop' than industry or agriculture; in the years ahead they may find themselves again where they were in the Middle Ages, experimenting on the frontiers of the international financial system. If a peaceful and profitable means can be found to help them move in that direction, the whole world will benefit today as did the Mediterranean world a thousand years ago.

The Poorer Countries

The people of the Arab Republic of Yemen have no desire to wait. They have no known oil, little industry and an underdeveloped and declining agriculture. Five years ago, they ranked toward the bottom of the World Bank's list of national economies. But their citizens were willing to work. Today one million Yemenin − virtually the whole labour force of the 6.5 million population − are sweeping the streets, pouring the concrete and carrying the bricks of Kuwait, Abu Dhabi and Saudi Arabia. Like early immigrants in America, the Yemenis live on very little, save their money and send it home. Primarily from them, the Yemen Central Bank of 1979 had accumulated foreign currency reserves of $1.6 billion with even more in private hands.

Unintentionally, the Middle East is being homogenised as the poor economies are pulled into the stream of the rich. In 1977, Egyptian workers in Libya sent more money into the Egyptian economy than the Suez Canal, and Jordan is a sort of upper grade Yemen with its better educated citizens seeking their (and Jordan's) fortune in the Gulf states. And, of course, one of the benefits to Israel of the occupation of the West Bank is the new source of labour it and Gaza have provided to the labour-short Israeli economy.

But the economic reality for most of the Middle East's inhabitants, especially for those of the poorer states, is domestic and that, above all, means agriculture. For the majority this means the Nile. Egypt, as Herodotus told us, is the 'gift of the Nile'. The yearly flood of the river for thousands of years has brought down the rain-washed soil of Ethiopia to replenish the depleted topsoils of Egypt and to build the Nile Delta. Without the Nile, Egypt would be merely another Libya, a barren stretch of sand and rock. The yearly depth of the flood was an exact measure of the crop to be expected; indeed the first example of forward economic planning took place in Egypt as, each year, the flood was measured on Nilometers. And the peasants understood what the Nile was to them: they built it into their religion and folk ways. Their aim was to get as much as possible of it on their land. They believed also that drinking the water of the Nile did for them personally what it did for the land – invigorated, restored, gave virility.

To control and regularise the river has been the aim of every intelligent government since prehistoric times. In the last century, vigorous rulers built thousands of miles of canals and constructed a number of dams and barrages to interrupt the flood and store water so that additional acres might be cultivated. By this century, Egypt's five million accessible acres were essentially fully used with many double-cropped. Theoretically, about 1.4 million additional acres could be cultivated but Egypt had run out of water. To get more water, and also to prevent destructive floods, the English engineer Sir William Willocks in 1895 sketched out a plan to build a 49 metre high dam near Aswan. The idea languished for 50 years but rise of population by 1950 had made some means to increase agricultural production a nearly vital national objective.

Shortly after the 1952 *coup*, the idea was taken up again. Agreement was reached with the World Bank and the United States to finance construction. And the dam became the symbol of the new Egypt-to-come. Like the TVA of the American Depression years, it meant rural electrification, new lands, flood control, a better standard of living and a means to ameliorate if not reverse the dreadful blight of over-population. More than a project, as vast as that would be, it became a living-legend. The High Dam is also a twentieth-century parallel to the pyramids and the Suez Canal: it has absorbed much of the money and skills and labour of a whole generation of Egyptians.

The cost of the project in money was over $1 billion and to build it naturally, Egyptians had to give up other endeavours. It made possible some new irrigation but not so much as expected, and converted existing farm lands to double or even triple cropping. While electrical output has been disappointing, it made possible rural electrification programmes and fuelled the growth of industry in the 1960s. Floods are a receding memory since the closure of the dam in 1960. And, of intangible but real value, the dam gave hope and courage when it was sorely needed to get on with national economic development.

But the side effects were disturbing: partly in mistaken hope that the dam would 'solve' the problems of Egypt, Egypt did not participate in the Green Revolution which so benefited Pakistan, India and Mexico although studies showed that Egypt might have benefited even more than they. The dam also helped to solidify the concept of state capitalism, one of the least attractive or beneficial aspects of the Nasser régime, which has been the dominant theme of Egyptian economic his tory. Strategically, the High Dam has made Egypt, as never before, a hostage to the hostile intent of neighbours. Were the dam to be breached by such natural causes as earthquakes, it could probably be repaired, but were the dam destroyed by a nuclear weapon, the whole of Egypt would be flushed into the Mediterranean Sea. Potentially, it is the greatest opening for a manmade disaster ever created.

Less dramatic but more immediate are other effects — much rich land in the Sudan and much of Nubia was destroyed by the reservoir. The dam now blocks the flow of rich new top soils and so has increased dependence upon fertilisers which, as a result of the oil price rise, are more expensive, and the now mostly stagnant waters have created new reservoirs for the snail-borne worm disease schistosomiasis biharziasis which infects more than 80 per cent of the population and may, again, lead to a scourge of malaria, which killed half a million people in the 1940s. Lesser costs are felt in the fishing industry which depended on the rich soils of the Nile floods, the brick industry which worked the silt, and new requirements for drainage brought about by excessive water use and the risen water table.

Agriculture

With the exception of Israel, where as we have seen agriculture has been favoured, agriculture is the orphan child of the Middle Eastern economy. The Arabs inherited the bedouin attitude: 'When the plough comes in the door, honour goes out of the window.' To till the land was regarded as menial, degrading, almost animal-like. Upon these older attitudes have been grafted newer notions as a consequence of the introduction of European culture. The modern world meant industry; agriculture was a thing of the past. 'The Middle East does not intend to be Europe's farm.' Finally, on an individual level, to stay 'on the farm' effectively deprived one of access to public health, a better education, clean water, and all the conveniences and excitements of the city. More, to work in the land, physically wading in the irrigation water that feeds the land, exposes one to an appalling variety of diseases. In addition to natural diseases have been imposed traditionally the twin human maladies of government oppression and poverty. Having little or no access to education and enjoying the companionship of large families, the peasants have many children. One of the consequences of this has been extreme subdivision of land as tiny inheritances had to be shared amongst many children. By the time of the 1952 revolution in Egypt, for example, 13 per cent of the land was owned in units of less than half a hectare. An additional 22 per cent was owned in units of less than two hectares, and, of course, very large numbers of the rural population were completely landless agricultural workers. Egyptian agriculture came to resemble horticulture: each tiny unit of land was intensively cultivated and, given the very small input into it, was highly productive. Everything, however, depended upon a very heavy component of manual labour and the absolute yield of the land was low. An irrigated hectare of land in Egypt today yields about one-third as much as a comparable hectare in California.

Having so little to sustain themselves and living so close to the margin of absolute ruin and starvation, the peasants have, naturally, clung tenaciously to those few things they have. Above all, they have maintained over at least the last 5,000 years an approach to land which is almost religious in character. Men have literally built themselves into the land. Possession of land is not like possession of other things: it is almost a marriage.

It is this enveloping way of life which the spread of education, the coming of television, rural electrification and sundry other improvements and innovations have disrupted. At the present time, particularly in Egypt, the disruption has not been invigorating but largely destructive. The peasants have flocked from the land into the cities in their millions, so that today well over half the population of Egypt lives in the major cities, 10 million in Cairo alone. Since virtually everything depended upon a heavy input of labour, as labour became scarce or unwilling, agricultural production has fallen.

The only real alternative to the High Dam was 'vertical expansion'. This could only come about if the Egyptian peasant could be uplifted, educated, encouraged to experiment with better seed and agricultural techniques and if a very large scale and extensive programme could be carried out to minimise the use of water and encourage drainage. All of these things were simply beyond the organisational capacity of the government and probably still beyond the cultural horizon of the peasant. The High Dam was, for all of its obvious failings, faults and expenses, a discrete project which could be accomplished and which would have a certain impact upon the agricultural economy.

Iraq and the Sudan

Agriculture in Iraq is quite different from Egypt. In the first place, in spite of the depth of Iraqi culture, there has not been the same continuity of peasant ownership. This is in large part due to the combination of the very hot climate, the destructiveness of floods of the Tigris-Euphrates complex, and the vastness of the Mesopotamian plain. As land was irrigated and farmed, it was slowly covered by a saline crust. The water from the Tigris-Euphrates complex was already fairly salty by the time it reached the Mesopotamian plain and the extreme summer temperatures left behind most of its salts while taking away most of the water. With so much land available, it was often easier for the peasant to abandon a given piece of land after five or six years, to move on to another. Iraq, particularly over the last five or six centuries, has been uniquely the home of what might be called 'nomadic irrigation agriculture'. Extremely wasteful in itself, this resulted in a minimal attachment to man to the land and consequently, to very little investment. Iraq undertakes its agricultural reforms today in the unfavourable position of having to make up for centuries of neglect by extensive drainage programmes which are of little immediate benefit. But, at the same time, without the great handicap of a conservative, hidebound peasantry it can, more easily than Egypt, introduce agricultural innovation and education.

The great hope for lateral expansion of Middle Eastern agriculture, indeed one of the three countries in the world with enormous potential for lateral agricultural expansion, is the Sudan. The Sudan is thought to have a potential arable area of approximately 30-40 million hectares, or nearly the size of France. Running the length of the Sudan is the Nile river. In the far south the White Nile creates a vast swamp, the *Sudd* of limited agricultural value to the Sudan but of tremendous ecological importance to Africa. As it goes further north, the Nile cuts into an increasingly deep valley and is surrounded by vast deserts. In the centre, the Sudan has approximately 12 million hectares in agricultural use. Eight hundred thousand hectares of this is known as the Gezira Scheme, one of the few success stories of large-scale agricultural development in Africa or Asia. Building on this experience, the Sudan now plans a considerable extension of irrigated land but is hampered by complex treaties with Egypt, governing water distribution. Tapping underground water may offer the Sudan an enormous increase of its potential. Probably by the end of this century the Sudan will have become the bread basket of Africa, as food vies with energy as the most critical product in an increasingly populous world.

The other areas of the Middle East have limited current agricultural potential. Libya, Egypt without the Nile, is largely restricted to the coastal plain unless or until large-scale desalination becomes economic. Syria is already highly developed, indeed over-developed agriculturally with too much marginal land now in use. As the Euphrates Dam project is increasingly utilised, however, Syria will be able to intensify its use of land through irrigation, and this should result in significant improvement in yields.

The current agricultural employment of the Arabian peninsula is small. However, the application of better irrigation techniques, particularly the 'centre pivot' system, combined with underground dams to hinder the flow off of rainwaters on the southwestern coastal plain, might cause a virtual agricultural revolution in Arabia and Yemen in the coming decade.

The main hope for agriculture in the Middle East is through the use of improved technology, better seed, better crop management, economics of scale and, particularly in Egypt, drainage. Theoretically, a vast increase of agricultural production is possible but the next step forward will require extensive education, changes in habits and mores, and probably significant changes in the economic and political patterns of the Arabic-speaking societies. These changes, it must be emphasised, run contrary to current trends and, coupled as they are with the low opinion of agriculture and suspicion of government, will probably require many years of efforts before practical results will be visible.

Industry

Industry is the reverse of agriculture: industry equates to modernisation and so is politically popular. A few years ago, every country wanted its own steel mill as the symbol of its commitment to the new ways of life. To enter industry, a man changed his clothing, multiplied his cash income and lost contact with the rhythm of daily life of his village or town. By definition, he became part of the city scene and benefited from what it had to offer. He also, undoubtedly, lost much of the security and pleasure of his former way of life. The rapid rise in the industrial labour force indicates how willing most people were to make this exchange.

However, and ironically, industry is also the opposite to agriculture in terms of its potential contribution: Middle Eastern markets are and will remain, small. Economies of scale are generally not spectacular, distances are large and labour relatively unproductive. Particularly where hampered by government regulation and uninvigorated by competition, industry has been unproductive and inefficient. This seems unlikely to change dramatically in the near future. Whereas, theoretically at least, agriculture could triple or quadruple within a decade, industry is unlikely to make even fractional gains.

Israel

Contrariwise, Israel has long since been a modern industrial state. Naturally, it has been gripped by many of the problems which afflict Europe and America. Its inflation rate is one of the worst in the world and this, together with frequent devaluations of its currency, has caused widespread labour unrest and population exodus. From the very early days of Zionism, there has been unease about the future. At least as many as seven, some say nine, of each ten of the early immigrants left Israel and roughly a third continued to leave during the 1920s and 1930s. Today, the emigration rate remains high but is complicated to measure, since many Israelis maintain dual citizenship. *Yordim*, as the emigrants are contemptuously called in Hebrew, are estimated at 300,000 in America and Canada and about 58 per cent of the emigrating Russian Jews elect not to go to Israel. All these figures would have probably been even less favourable to Israel, and also more significant, had not the 1948-9 and 1967 wars resulted in the exodus of over one million Arabs.

Despite the shortcomings and problems, however, there is no question that Israel is the most dynamic society in the Middle East. It is one of the fears entertained by Arabs that the same skill, determination and financial power which has accomplished so much in the unpromising land of Israel might, if peace were really achieved and the surrounding economies opened, swamp the weaker and more backward societies. Powerful economic competition is, like so many things in the Middle East, a double-edged swored – or perhaps a unique Middle Eastern artifact, both a ploughshare *and* a sword.

The arms industry is one of the major success stories of the Israeli economy. Today, arms are a major export and an Israeli fighter plane and tank are likely to come onto the world arms market soon. Israeli technology encompasses nuclear development and it has been widely known that Israel has had the potential to build a nuclear weapon since at least 1962. The Israeli atomic energy commission and the Israeli research institutes are among the best in the world, and where industry and technology are most closely allied, the Israeli economy is at its most efficient. Obviously, while these are factors of great encouragement to the Israelis, they are also factors which along with myriad social, political, cultural and military factors, make the achievement of easy relations between the relatively backward and the relatively advanced parts of the Middle East more difficult.

Accommodation

For many years, these who have thought about Middle Eastern peace

have speculated on how Israel could 'accommodate itself' to the society
to which it would have ultimately to relate. Some of the early Zionists
thought that the Arabs would be so invigorated by Jewish economic
activities that they would, themselves, become Zionists. Others thought
that the Jewish community would have to lower its standard of living
and merge, more or less imperceptibly into the Levant society. Neither
of these courses has proven feasible. For a variety of reasons, the Jewish
communities in Palestine and subsequently the state of Israel have been
set apart from the mainstream. In recent years, the Arab states, through
a complex system of boycott and non-purchase, have attempted to isolate the Israeli economy entirely from the rest of the Middle East. This
system has not always worked. The Arabs have applied the boycott
when it fitted their interest but not when it did not – for example,
they have not applied it to tourism or armaments. A certain amount of
casual trade does take place between Israel and the surrounding Arab
countries, even across apparently closed borders. Moreover, the Israelis
have found ways to enrol the surplus Arab labour of the occupied territories in the Israeli economy. But generally speaking, accommodation
has not been notable. A third course appears now open and indeed
under way: the growth of large-scale development programmes is
beginning to raise the Arabs toward a comparable wealth. 'Convergence'
may begin to affect both societies as it has elsewhere. As the Arab
economies begin to catch up, the Arabs and the Israelis will have much
more to give one another and as they come to realise it, one of the
barriers to peace will fade.

11 CONCLUSION

Three questions today begin or end all discussions on the Middle East.

- Is peace possible?
- Will the Middle East satisfy the energy needs of the West?
- Will the oil-rich Middle Eastern states play a constructive role in the world financial system?

Part of the purpose of this book is to provide the framework for answers to these questions. Answers cannot, of course, be definitive but I believe they are the following.

Peace is possible but within certain historical, strategic and psychological constraints. Briefly these are the following.

First, for the Israelis. Knowing the recurrent tragedies of Jewish history, the Israelis are unlikely voluntarily to give up Israel as a Jewish state. However desirable on philosophical and political grounds, a secular, non-racial state is not a current possibility. In Israel Arabs will remain a tolerated minority and the refugees will not be allowed back. Too many Jews have concluded that they cannot be secure in a secular state with alien neighbours. For the foreseeable future, therefore, I conclude that arguments that Israel should transform itself to achieve peace are impractical.

If that is granted, I think it unlikely that this determined, strong, rich and victorious people will give up much of what they have taken in the 1948-9 and 1967 wars. Although some Jewish voices today paraphrase the humane words of such great men as Judes Magnes, Ahad Haim and Martin Buber, these men and women are far from political authority and responsibility. Short of unlikely pressures from America or, even less likely, a major military defeat, Israel proper (that is to say within the September 1967 frontiers) must be accepted as given.

That leaves the occupied West Bank and Gaza. Many Israelis refuse to concede that these areas are not also part of Israel and despite almost universal condemnation the Israeli Government is going ahead with expropriation of Arab property and the creation of Jewish colonies in the occupied areas. Yet even in the inner circles of the ruling Likud Party, the legal status of this territory is moot. Given population ratios of over 99 to 1 in favour of the Arabs, I imagine that prudent people will ultimately concede that this area must be recognised as Arab.

How it should belong to them and precisely who 'them' — as 'administered' as a part of Jordan or as a separate state — is in dispute.

If peace is to be secured, in my opinion, the occupied areas must become a sort of Arab 'Israel'. That is to say, they must become a state and as such a symbol, an ultimate refuge, a source of identity for the 3 million Palestinians, wherever they may live, just as Israel has become for the 15 million Jews wherever they may live.

All attempts to achieve peace avoiding this central political issue have failed. Avoiding the Palestinians by direct contacts among the warring states, denying the existence of the Palestinians, dividing the waters of the Jordan, offering compensation, passing resolutions in the forums of the United Nations, and war, have all been tried. There is no logical reason to think that other alternatives, even if profoundly humane and generous, can succeed. The Palestinians, like the earlier Zionists, know that citizenship in other states, compensation, settlement in alternative areas and other devices will cause them to die as a nation.

It follows, I think, that if the Palestinians remain thwarted in this fundamental objective of statehood they will continue to fight with whatever means they can muster for as long as they can. Since they number 3 million and are now highly motivated, it is unlikely that even severe Israeli raids against their bases and refugee camps and domestic repression will break their national movement.

The more successful, indeed, the Israeli actions against them, the more desperate and dangerous they will become. Guerrilla warfare and terror are not bounded by race and geography: they have been everywhere used, and generally successfully, by the weak. Few of us, no matter how we condemn the ugly acts committed by some of them, could honestly say that we would act differently if driven by the same desperation. Until they are allowed to join the international community, the Palestinians will continue to be the outlaws of the Middle East. In this they are precisely like — and for the same reasons — the Zionists before the creation of Israel.

As I see it, the granting of statehood is the irreducible minimum. No *return* is possible; even *going to* Israel is no substitute. Compensation cannot really be offered for loss of country. Loss of job, furniture, house, yes; but how to compensate a man for the loss of his country in an era of nationalism? In any event, I think enough Palestinians will see it like that that they will not settle for less.

If this is granted, will the West Bank and Gaza suffice?

The simple answer is that short of an Arab victory in war, or revolution | in Jordan, it must. And, although this is a matter of speculation and has not been tested, I think enough Palestinians will accept that they will convince or force the others to accept.

If acceptable is it feasible? The West Bank offers only 2,200 square miles and much of that is barren; Gaza is even less economically attractive and is, geographically at least, cut off from the West Bank. Those who argue that an Arab Palestinian state makes no economic sense are right. But how much more economic sense does it make for the Middle East to spend 30 per cent of its income on arms? In the same scale Israel did not — and does not — make economic sense either. Israel could never have been born and could not continue without massive foreign remittances; is it not conceivable that similar international help could be organised for an Arab Palestine? The Palestinians are a resourceful people; given peace they will 'interface' with Israel and Jordan and those Palestinians living abroad will, undoubtedly, remit their earnings. Like the Zionists they will less *draw* succour from the new land than they will give.

Jerusalem is a separate issue. Few Christians today can understand and fewer feel the intense concern of earlier ages with the fate of Jerusalem but for Muslims and, of course, Jews, the issue is alive. The Israeli Government has said that it will never allow Jerusalem to be divided and has moved to create 'facts' which are essentially non-negotiable. Arabs have been expelled from their property and new housing built for Jews; every effort has been made to change the character of the city to make it immutably Jewish. But the Arab states and the Palestinians have not given up their claims and unless some acceptable formula is found — internationalisation and some form of guaranteed access have been suggested — Jerusalem will be the thorn in the side of any peace settlement.

The fact is that the alternatives to peace are so grim that I believe the nettle of Palestinian statehood must be grasped before a new round of violence begins.

Regarding Western energy demands, *the Middle East does not have enough oil* to keep pace with our appetite. The United States today uses over twice as much per person as the Europeans and is increasing its imports rapidly as its own resources decline.

Leaving aside the crucial arguments on whether or not it is in the interest of the producers to pump more oil or to keep the price indexed to commodities and services at more or less today's levels and whether or not income derived from the sale of oil can be protected from inflation, *oil production is near its upper limits in the Middle East*. Further increases in production will require vast and economically unattractive additional investment and will cause dangerously rapid depletion of the fields. But even if such investment were made and such rapid depletion were accepted, they *cannot* keep pace with the current rate of increase of Western demand.

The only two feasible answers are Western restraint and Western development of alternative sources of energy. The one, requiring a context which President Carter called the 'moral equivalent of war', is fundamentally unpopular in the West, will require major transformations particularly in America, and has yet to be convincingly explained or legislated in societies which have become dependent upon the automobile and electrified houses. The other answers are possibly long term (particularly in the case of solar energy), dangerous (nuclear energy), environmentally unattractive (strip coal mining), socially obsolescent (deep coal mining) and expensive (alternative sources of petroleum). The outlook is not good; but the problem cannot be pushed off to the Middle East; it is ours and must be solved here.

Even if the Middle East had the oil to meet our current needs, it is ultimately too valuable as a raw material for our industrial society as the source of plastics, fibres, medicines and other chemicals to be poured so profligately into auto tanks.

As the price of petroleum advanced, following the 1973 war, it caught up with world commodity price rises since 1945. As other prices had risen during the years from 1945 to 1973, oil actually fell in price. Arguably cheap energy was the major cause of the world economic boom of that period. By 1975 it had caught up and then began to keep pace with inflation. As shortages occur it will rise faster. And this will generate, as it has in past years, increasingly large surpluses for the producers. In some cases currency reserves are now huge. Saudi Arabia receives payment for oil in dollars (a major factor in the stability of the dollar in the world market) and now has reserves of over $50 billion. Gradually some means must be found to 'recycle' or otherwise reintegrate the capital reserves in ways more beneficial and profitable than are now being used. Can that be done? That is the third of our questions.

In the past, great wealth normally went with great power. What is unusual today is that great petroleum wealth has come to countries which, by all accepted standards, are poor and weak. In the nineteenth century, no one questioned whether or not Great Britain, France, Germany and the United States would or should use their industrial wealth to dominate the weak: they did and regarded it as their right. Today, states are more sensitive and the international order is more restrictive. Canadians fear American domination, Europeans fear *le defi americain* and Americans fear the Japanese. Protectionism is by no means dead. The mercantilists survived Adam Smith's assault and may be nearly ready for a new counterattack. This time it may be more related to finance than to production.

The question of the integration of the huge dollar holdings of the oil states will grow more, not less, acute. This is an issue which the producers cannot answer for or by themselves. In the case of Saudi Arabia, as described above on page 168, they have exercised a restraint unheard of among the wealthy of former times. But, sooner or later, the oil producers will not consent to be merely purchasers of consumer goods and probably inappropriate industrial equipment or to hold government paper but will seek to be a part of the 'action'. How will we react? On what terms will we let them buy into the game? Clearly it would be wise to begin to define the issues now before they become urgent, strident or threats to the peace.

Unasked as yet, but implicit among the questions about peace is the effect of the Egyptian separate peace with Israel on the larger issues.

As of the time of writing, it is still very attractive to Americans and to the American Government. Once again America believes it has found 'our man' and because he seems to agree with the US Government, Sadat is thought to be positive, courageous and constructive. But even the most enthusiastic must see that the policy rests on one mortal man and that man has led his country into a position of political and economic isolation from all his neighbours but one and that one is waivering. Few believe that President Numeiri can hold the Sudan to a pro-Sadat course in the face of pan-Arab opposition and the demands of his countrymen. And Israel, still, cannot take the place of the other Arabs because of its own severe economic and security problems and because so many of the issues with Egypt have not yet been resolved. As suggested above, even though the accords growing out of Camp David have, for the present, removed the main Arab military force, they have not removed the main Arab issue in the quest for peace. At best this is an unstable and temporary movement and must not deflect those who truly want peace from the main challenge – the Palestine issue – or once again they will have missed the road to peace.

I concluded an earlier book on the Middle East with words on which I cannot improve:

> In human affairs there are no crystal balls. But the future grows out of the past and is shaped by men. Knowing the past, and devoting ourselves with energy and wisdom to the present, we can create a better future.

APPENDIX A: THE CAMP DAVID AGREEMENT

Washington, Sept 18. — The following are the texts issued by the White House of the two documents agreed to at the Camp David Middle East summit meeting and signed on Sunday night, supplied by Associated Press.

The framework of peace in the Middle East

Muhammad Anwar al-Sadat, President of the Arab Republic of Egypt, and Menachem Begin, Prime Minister of Israel, met with Jimmy Carter, President of the United States of America, at Camp David from Sept 5 to Sept 17, 1978, and have agreed on the following framework for peace in the Middle East. They invite other parties to the Arab-Israeli conflict to adhere to it.

Preamble:

The search for peace in the Middle East must be guided by the following:

The agreed basis for a peaceful settlement of the conflict between Israel and its neighbours is United Nations Security Council resolution 242 in all its parts.

After four wars during 30 years, despite intensive humane efforts, the Middle East, which is the cradle of civilization and the birthplace of three great religions, does not yet enjoy the blessings of peace. The people of the Middle East yearn for peace, so that the vast human and natural resources of the region can be turned to the pursuits of peace and so that this area can become a model for coexistence and cooperation among nations.

The historic initiative by President Sadat in visiting Jerusalem and the reception accorded to him by the Parliament, Government and people of Israel, and the reciprocal visit of Prime Minister Begin to Ismaila, the peace proposals made by both leaders, as well as the warm reception of these missions by the peoples of both countries, have created an unprecedented opportunity for peace which must not be lost if this generation and future generations are to be spared the tragedies of war.

The provisions of the Charter of the United Nations and the other accepted norms of international law and legitimacy now provide accepted standards for the conduct of relations between all states.

To achieve a relationship of peace, in the spirit of article 2 of the United Nations Charter, future negotiations between Israel and any neighbour prepared to negotiate peace and security with it, are necessary for the purpose of carrying out all the provisions and principles of resolutions 242 and 338.

Peace requires respect for the sovereignty, territorial integrity and political independence of every state in the area and their right to live in peace within secure and recognized boundaries free from threats or acts of force. Progress toward that goal can accelerate movement toward a new era of reconciliation in the Middle East marked by cooperation in promoting economic development, in maintaining stability and in assuring security.

Security is enhanced by a relationship of peace and by cooperation between nations which enjoy normal relations. In addition, under the terms of peace treaties, the parties can, on the basis of reciprocity, agree to special security arrangements such as demilitarized zones, limited armaments areas, early warning stations, the presence of international forces, liaison, agreed measures for monitoring, and other arrangements that they agree are useful.

Framework

Taking these factors into account, the parties are determined to reach a just, comprehensive and durable settlement of the Middle East conflict through the conclusion of peace treaties based on Security Council resolutions 242 and 338 in all their parts. Their purpose is to achieve peace and good neighbourly relations. They recognize that, for peace to endure, it must involve all those who have been most deeply affected by the conflict. They therefore agree that this framework as appropriate is intended by them to constitute a basis for peace not only between Egypt and Israel, but also between Israel and each of its other neighbours which is prepared to negotiate peace with Israel on this basis. With that objective in mind, they have agreed to proceed as follows:

A. West Bank and Gaza:

1. Egypt, Israel, Jordan and the representatives of the Palestinian people should participate in negotiations on the resolution of the Palestinian problem in all its aspects. To achieve that objective, negotiations relating to the West Bank and Gaza should proceed in three stages.

(A) Egypt and Israel agree that, in order to ensure a peaceful and orderly transfer of authority, and taking into account the security concerns of all the parties, there should be transitional arrangements for the West Bank and Gaza for a period not exceeding five years. In order to provide full autonomy to the inhabitants, under these arrangements the Israeli military government and its civilian administration will be withdrawn as soon as a self-governing authority has been freely elected by the inhabitants of these areas to replace the existing military government.

To negotiate the details of a transitional arrangement, the Government of Jordan will be invited to join the negotiations on the basis of this framework. These new arrangements should give due consideration to both the principle of self-government by the inhabitants of these territories and to the legitimate security concerns of the parties involved.

(B) Egypt, Israel and Jordan will agree on the modalities for establishing the elected self-governing authority in the West Bank and Gaza. The delegations of Egypt and Jordan may include Palestinians from the West Bank and Gaza or other Palestinians as mutually agreed. The parties will negotiate an agreement which will define the powers and responsibilities of the self-governing authority to be exercised in the West Bank and Gaza. A withdrawal of Israeli armed forces will take place and there will be a redeployment of the remaining Israeli forces into specified security locations.

The agreement will also include arrangements for assuring internal and external security and public order. A strong local police force will be established, which may include Jordanian citizens. In addition, Israeli and Jordanian forces will participate in joint patrols and in the manning of control posts to assure the security of the borders.

(C) When the self-governing authority (administrative council) in the West Bank and Gaza is established and inaugurated, the transitional period of five years will begin. As soon as possible, but not later than the third year after the beginning of the transitional period, negotiations will take place to determine the final status of the West Bank and Gaza and its relationship with its neighbours, and to conclude a peace treaty between Israel and Jordan by the end of the transitional period. These negotiations will be conducted among Egypt, Israel, Jordan and the elected representatives of the inhabitants of the West Bank and Gaza.

Two separate but related committees will be convened, one committee, consisting of representatives of the four parties which will negotiate and agree on the final status of the West Bank and Gaza, and its relationship with its neighbours, and the second committee, consisting of representatives of Israel and representatives of Jordan to be joined by the elected representatives of the inhabitants of the West Bank and Gaza, to negotiate the peace treaty between Israel and Jordan, taking into account the agreement reached on the final status of the West Bank and Gaza.

The negotiations shall be based on all the provisions and principles of United Nations Security Council resolution 242. The negotiations will resolve, among other matters, the location of the boundaries and the nature of the security arrangements. The solution from the negotiations must also recognize the legitimate rights of the Palestinian people and their just requirements. In this way, the Palestinians will participate in the determination of their own future through:

(i) The negotiations among Egypt, Israel, Jordan and the representatives of the inhabitants of the West Bank and Gaza to agree on the final status of the West Bank and Gaza and other outstanding issues by the end of the transitional period.

(ii) Submitting their agreement to a vote by the elected representatives of the inhabitants of the West Bank and Gaza.

(iii) Providing for the elected representatives of the inhabitants of the West Bank and Gaza to decide how they shall govern themselves consistent with the provisions of their agreement.

(iv) Participating as stated above in the work of the committee negotiating to peace treaty between Israel and Jordan.

2. All necessary measures will be taken and provisions made to assure the security of Israel and its neighbours during the transitional period and beyond. To assist in providing such security, a strong local police force will be constituted by the self-governing authority. It will be composed of inhabitants of the West Bank and Gaza. The police will maintain continuing liaison on internal security matters with the designated Israeli, Jordanian and Egyptian officers.

3. During the transitional period, the representatives of Egypt, Israel, Jordan and the self-governing authority will constitute a continuing committee to decide by agreement on the modalities of admission of person displaced from the West Bank and Gaza in 1967, together with necessary measures to prevent disruption and disorder. Other matters of common concern may also be dealt with by this committee.

4. Egypt and Israel will work with each other and with other interested parties to establish agreed procedures for a prompt, just and permanent implementation of the resolution of the refugee problem.

B. Egypt-Israel

1. Egypt and Israel undertake not to resort to the threat or the use of force to settle disputes. Any disputes shall be settled by peaceful means in accordance with the provisions of article 33 of the Charter of the United Nations.

2. In order to achieve peace between them, the parties agree to negotiate in good faith with a goal of concluding within three months from the signing of this framework a peace treaty between them, while inviting the other parties in the conflict to proceed simultaneously to negotiate and conclude similar peace treaties with a view to achieving a comprehensive peace in the area. The framework for the conclusion of a peace treaty between Egypt and Israel will govern the peace negotiations between them. The parties will agree on the modalities and the timetable for the implementation of their obligations under the treaty.

Associated principles

1. Egypt and Israel state that the principles and provisions described below should apply to peace treaties between Israel and each of its neighbours — Egypt, Jordan, Syria and Lebanon.

2. Signatories shall establish among themselves relationships normal to states at peace with one another. To this end, they should undertake to abide by all the provisions of the Charter of the United Nations. Steps to be taken in this respect include:

(A) Full recognition.

(B) Abolishing economic boycotts.

(C) Guaranteeing that under their jurisdiction the citizens of the other parties shall enjoy the protection of the due process of law.

3. Signatories should explore possibilities for economic development in the context of final peace treaties, with the objective of contributing to the atmosphere of peace, cooperation, and friendship which is their common goal.

4. Claims commissions may be established for the mutual settlement of all financial claims.

5. The United States shall be invited to participate in the talks on matters related to the modalities of the implementation of the agreements and working out the timetable for the carrying out of the obligations, of the parties.

6. The United Nations Security Council shall be requested to endorse the peace treaties and ensure that their provisions shall not be violated. The permanent members of the Security Council shall be requested to underwrite the peace treaties and ensure respect for their

provisions. They shall also be requested to conform their policies and actions with the undertakings contained in this framework.

Reproduced from *The Times* by permission.

APPENDIX B: FRAMEWORK FOR AN EGYPT-ISRAEL PEACE TREATY

Framework for the conclusion of a peace treaty between Egypt and Israel:

In order to achieve peace between them, Israel and Egypt agree to negotiate in good faith with a goal of concluding within three months of the signing of this framework a peace treaty between them.

It is agreed that:

The site of the negotiations will be under a United Nations flag at a location or locations to be mutually agreed.

All of the principles of United Nations resolution 242 will apply in this resolution of the dispute between Israel and Egypt.

Unless otherwise mutually agreed, terms of the peace treaty will be implemented between two and three years after the peace treaty is signed.

The following matters are agreed between the parties:

(A) The full exercise of Egyptian sovereignty up to the internationally recognized border between Egypt and mandated Palestine;

(B) The withdrawal of Israeli armed forces from the Sinai;

(C) The use of airfields left by the Israelis near El Arish, Rafah, Ras en Naqb, and Sharm el-Sheikh for civilian purposes only, including possible commercial use by all nations;

(D) The right of free passage by ships of Israel through the Gulf of Suez and the Suez Canal on the basis of the Constantinople Convention of 1888 applying to all nations; the Strait of Tiran and the Gulf of Aqaba are international waterways to be open to all nations for unimpeded and nonsuspendable freedom of navigation and overflight;

(E) The construction of a highway between the Sinai and Jordan near Eilat with guaranteed free and peaceful passage by Egypt and Jordan; and

(F) The stationing of military forces listed below.

Stationing of forces

(A) No more than one division (mechanized or infantry) of Egyptian armed forces will be stationed within an area lying approximately 50 kilometres (30 miles) east of the Gulf of Suez and the Suez Canal.

(B) Only United Nations forces and civil police equipped with light weapons to perform normal police functions will be stationed within an area lying west of the international border and the Gulf of Aqaba, varying in width from 20 kilometres (12 miles) to 40 kilometres (25 miles).

(C) In the area within three kilometres (1.8 miles) east of the international border there will be Israeli limited military forces not to exceed four infantry battalions and United Nations observers.

(D) Border patrol units, not to exceed three battalions, will supplement the civil police in maintaining order in the area not included above.

The exact demarcation of the above areas will be as decided during the peace negotiations.

Early warning stations may exist to insure compliance with the terms of the agreement.

United Nations forces will be stationed: (a) in part of the area in the Sinai lying within about 20 kilometres of the Mediterranean Sea and adjacent to the international border, and (b) in the Sharm el-Sheikh area to ensure freedom of passage through the Strait of Tiran; and these forces will not be removed unless such removal is approved by the Security Council of the United Nations with a unanimous vote of the five permanent members.

After a peace treaty is signed, and after the interim withdrawal is complete, normal relations will be established between Egypt and Israel, including: Full recognition, including diplomatic, economic and cultural relations; termination of economic boycotts and barriers to the free movement of goods and people; and mutual protection of citizens by the due process of law.

Interim withdrawal

Between three months and nine months after the signing of the peace treaty, all Israeli forces will withdraw east of a line extending from a point east of El Arish to Ras Muhammad, the exact location of this line to be determined by mutual agreement.—AP.

Reproduced from *The Times* by permission.

APPENDIX C: TREATY OF PEACE BETWEEN THE STATE OF ISRAEL AND THE ARAB REPUBLIC OF EGYPT

The Government of the State of Israel and the Government of the Arab Republic of Egypt;

Preamble

Convinced of the urgent necessity of the establishment of a just, comprehensive and lasting peace in the Middle East in accordance with Security Council Resolutions 242 and 338;

Reaffirming their adherence to the 'Framework for Peace in the Middle East Agreed at Camp David', dated September 17, 1978;

Noting that the aforementioned Framework as appropriate is intended to constitute a basis for peace not only between Israel and Egypt but also between Israel and each of its other Arab neighbors which is prepared to negotiate peace with it on this basis;

Desiring to bring to an end the state of war between them and to establish a peace in which every state in the area can live in security;

Convinced that the conclusion of a Treaty of Peace between Israel and Egypt is an important step in the search for comprehensive peace in the area and for the attainment of the settlement of the Arab-Israeli conflict in all its aspects;

Inviting the other Arab parties to this dispute to join the peace process with Israel guided by and based on the principles of the aforementioned Framework;

Desiring as well to develop friendly relations and cooperation between themselves in accordance with the United Nations Charter and the principles of international law governing international relations in times of peace;

Agree to the following provisions in the free exercise of their sovereignty, in order to implement the 'Framework for the Conclusion of a Peace Treaty Between Israel and Egypt':

Article I

1. The state of war between the Parties will be terminated and peace will be established between them upon the exchange of instruments of ratification of this Treaty.

2. Israel will withdraw all its armed forces and civilians from the Sinai behind the international boundary between Egypt and mandated Palestine, as provided in the annexed protocol (Annex I), and Egypt will resume the exercise of its full sovereignty over the Sinai.

3. Upon completion of the interim withdrawal provided for in Annex I, the Parties will establish normal and friendly relations, in accordance with Article III (3).

Article II

The permanent boundary between Egypt and Israel is the recognized international boundary between Egypt and the former mandated territory of Palestine, as shown on the map at Annex II, without prejudice to the issue of the status of the Gaza Strip. The Parties recognize this boundary as inviolable. Each will respect the territorial integrity of the other, including their territorial waters and airspace.

Article III

1. The Parties will apply between them the provisions of the Charter of the United Nations and the principles of international law governing relations among states in times of peace. In particular:

a. They recognize and will respect each other's sovereignty, territorial integrity and political independence;

b. They recognize and will respect each other's right to live in peace within their secure and recognized boundaries;

c. They will refrain from the threat or use of force, directly or indirectly, against each other and will settle all disputes between them by peaceful means.

2. Each Party undertakes to ensure that acts or threats of belligerency, hostility, or violence do not originate from and are not committed from within its territory, or by any forces subject to its control or by any other forces stationed on its territory, against the population, citizens or property of the other Party. Each Party also undertakes to refrain from organizing, instigating, inciting, assisting or participating in acts or threats of belligerency, hostility, subversion or violence against the other Party, anywhere, and undertakes to ensure that perpetrators of such acts are brought to justice.

3. The Parties agree that the normal relationship established between them will include full recognition, diplomatic, economic and cultural relations, termination of economic boycotts and discriminatory barriers to the free movement of people and goods, and will guarantee the mutual enjoyment by citizens of the due process of law. The process by

which they undertake to achieve such a relationship parallel to the implementation of other provisions of this Treaty is set out in the annexed protocol (Annex III).

Article IV

1. In order to provide maximum security for both Parties on the basis of reciprocity, agreed security arrangements will be established including limited force zones in Egyptian and Israeli territory, and United Nations forces and observers, described in detail as to nature and timing in Annex I, and other security arrangements the Parties may agree upon.

2. The Parties agree to the stationing of United Nations personnel in areas described in Annex I. The Parties agree not to request withdrawal of the United Nations personnel and that these personnel will not be removed unless such removal is approved by the Security Council of the United Nations, with the affirmative vote of the five Permanent Members, unless the Parties otherwise agree.

3. A Joint Commission will be established to facilitate the implementation of the Treaty, as provided for in Annex I.

4. The security arrangements provided for in paragraphs 1 and 2 of this Article may at the request of either party be reviewed and amended by mutual agreement of the Parties.

Article V

1. Ships of Israel, and cargoes destined for or coming from Israel, shall enjoy the right of free passage through the Suez Canal and its approaches through the Gulf of Suez and the Mediterranean Sea on the basis of the Constantinople Convention of 1888, applying to all nations. Israeli nationals, vessels and cargoes, as well as persons, vessels and cargoes destined for or coming from Israel, shall be accorded non-discriminatory treatment in all matters connected with usage of the canal.

2. The Parties consider the Strait of Tiran and the Gulf of Aqaba to be international waterways open to all nations for unimpeded and non-suspendable freedom of navigation and overflight. The Parties will respect each other's right to navigation and overflight for access to either country through the Strait of Tiran and the Gulf of Aqaba.

Article VI

1. This Treaty does not affect and shall not be interpreted as affecting in any way the rights and obligations of the Parties under the Charter of the United Nations.

2. The Parties undertake to fulfil in good faith their obligations under this Treaty, without regard to action or inaction of any other party and independently of any instrument external to this Treaty.

3. They further undertake to take all the necessary measures for the application in their relations of the provisions of the multilateral conventions to which they are parties, including the submission of appropriate notification to the Secretary General of the United Nations and other depositaries of such conventions.

4. The Parties undertake not to enter into any obligation in conflict with this Treaty.

5. Subject to Article 103 of the United Nations Charter, in the event of a conflict between the obligations of the Parties under the present Treaty and any of their other obligations, the obligations under this Treaty will be binding and implemented.

Article VII

1. Disputes arising out of the application or interpretation of this Treaty shall be resolved by negotiations.

2. Any such disputes which cannot be settled by negotiations shall be resolved by conciliation or submitted to arbitration.

Article VIII

The Parties agree to establish a claims commission for the mutual settlement of all financial claims.

Article IX

1. This Treaty shall enter into force upon exchange of instruments of ratification.

2. This Treaty supersedes the Agreement between Egypt and Israel of September, 1975.

3. All protocols, annexes, and maps attached to this Treaty shall be regarded as an integral part hereof.

4. The Treaty shall be communicated to the Secretary General of the United Nations for registration in accordance with the provisions of Article 102 of the Charter of the United Nations.

APPENDIX D: MEMORANDUM OF AGREEMENT ON ASSURANCES SIGNED BY THE US SECRETARY OF STATE, MR CYRUS VANCE, AND THE ISRAELI FOREIGN MINISTER, MR MOSHE DAYAN, ON 26 MARCH 1979

Recognizing the significance of the conclusion of the Treaty of peace between Israel and Egypt, and considering the importance of full implementation of the Treaty of Peace to Israel's security interests and the contribution of the conclusion of the Treaty of Peace to the security and development of Israel as well as its significance to peace and stability in the region and to the maintenance of international peace and security; and:

Recognizing that the withdrawal from Sinai imposes additional heavy security, military and economic burdens on Israel;

The Governments of the United States of America and of the State of Israel, subject to their constitutional processes and applicable law, confirm as follows:

1. In the light of the role of the United States in achieving the Treaty of Peace and the parties' desire that the United States should continue its supportive efforts, the United States will take appropriate measures to promote full observance of the Treaty of Peace.

2. Should it be demonstrated to the satisfaction of the United States that there has been a violation or threat of violation of the Treaty of Peace, the United States will consult with the parties with regard to measures to halt or prevent the violation, ensure observance of the Treaty of Peace, enhance friendly and peaceful relations between the parties and promote peace in the region, and will take such remedial measures as it deems appropriate — which may include diplomatic, economic and military measures as described below.

3. The United States will provide the support it deems appropriate for proper actions taken by Israel in response to such demonstrated violations of the Treaty of Peace. In particular, if a violation of the Treaty of Peace is deemed to threaten the security of Israel, including, *inter alia*, a blockade of Israel's use of international waterways, a violation of the provisions of the Treaty of Peace concerning limitation of forces or an armed attack against Israel, the United States will be prepared to consider, on an urgent basis, such measures as the strengthening of the United States presence in the area, the providing of emer-

197

gency supplies to Israel, and the exercise of maritime rights in order to put an end to the violation.

4. The United States will support the parties' rights to navigational and overflight for access to either country through and over the Straits of Tiran and the Gulf of Aqaba pursuant to the Treaty of Peace.

5. The United States will oppose and, if necessary, vote against, any action or resolution in the United Nations which in its judgment adversely affects the Treaty of Peace.

6. Subject to Congressional authorization and appropriation, the United States will endeavor to take into account and will endeavor to be responsive to military and economic assistance requirements of Israel.

7. The United States will continue to impose restrictions on weapons supplied by it to any country which prohibit their unauthorized transfer to any third party. The United States will not supply or authorize the transfer of such weapons for use in an armed attack against Israel, and will take steps to prevent such unauthorised transfer.

8. Existing agreements and assurances between the United States and Israel are not terminated or altered by the conclusion of the Treaty of Peace, except for those contained in articles 5, 6, 7, 8, 11, 12, 15, and 16 of the Memorandum of Agreement between the government of the United States and the government of Israel (United States-Israeli assurances) of September 1, 1975.

9. This memorandum of Agreement sets forth the full understandings of the United States and Israel with regard to the subject matters covered between them hereby, and shall be carried out in accordance with its terms.

INDEX

BIOGRAPHICAL NOTE

William R. Polk read Oriental Studies at Oxford and took his doctorate in history at Harvard University where he taught until 1961. He then joined the Kennedy Administration as a Member of the Policy Planning Council responsible for the Middle East and other issues. In 1965 he resigned from the US Department of State and became Professor of History and Director of the Center for Middle Eastern Studies of the University of Chicago. In 1967 he became Director, later President, of the Adlai Stevenson Institute of International Affairs. In 1975 he retired and moved to Cairo to establish a consulting firm dealing with Europe and the Middle East. Author of over sixty articles on the Middle East, his best known books are *The United States and the Arab World* (Harvard University Press), *The Opening of South Lebanon* (Harvard), *Passing Brave* (with Willian Mares, Knopf) and *The Golden Ode* (University of Chicago Press). He is now living in Lagonisi, Greece and is at work on a history of the field of foreign affairs to be called *Neighbors and Strangers*.